First World War
and Army of Occupation
War Diary
France, Belgium and Germany

42 DIVISION
Headquarters, Branches and Services
Commander Royal Artillery
1 March 1917 - 31 March 1919

WO95/2647/2

The Naval & Military Press Ltd
www.nmarchive.com
Published in association with The National Archives

Published by

The Naval & Military Press Ltd

Unit 10 Ridgewood Industrial Park,

Uckfield, East Sussex,

TN22 5QE England

Tel: +44 (0) 1825 749494

www.naval-military-press.com

www.nmarchive.com

This diary has been reprinted in facsimile from the original. Any imperfections are inevitably reproduced and the quality may fall short of modern type and cartographic standards.

© **Crown Copyright**
Images reproduced by permission of The National Archives, London, England, 2015.

Contents

Document type	Place/Title	Date From	Date To
Heading	WO95/2647/2		
Heading	C.R.A. Mar 1917-Mar 1919		
Heading	War Diary. of H.Q. R.A. 42nd Division From 1-3-17 To 31-3-17 (Vol. III)		
Heading	War Diary Of Headquarters R.A. 42nd Division From 1.4.17 To 30.4.17 Volume IV 1917		
War Diary	At Sea and in France	01/03/1917	15/03/1917
War Diary	Caours	05/03/1917	06/04/1917
War Diary	Bois Olympe	08/04/1917	22/04/1917
War Diary	Peronne	23/04/1917	30/04/1917
Operation(al) Order(s)	42nd Divisional R.A. Order No. 1		
Miscellaneous	Preliminary Instructions For March.		
Operation(al) Order(s)	42nd Divisional Artillery Order No. 7.	21/04/1917	21/04/1917
Miscellaneous	42nd Div. Artillery.	20/04/1917	20/04/1917
Heading	Volume II War Diary Of Hd Qrs R.A. 42nd Division From 1.5.17 To 31.5.17		
War Diary	Peronne	02/05/1917	02/05/1917
War Diary	Roisel K11a 56	03/05/1917	09/05/1917
War Diary	Roisel	11/05/1917	31/05/1917
Operation(al) Order(s)	42nd Divisional Artillery Order No. 9. Appendix No 1	11/05/1917	11/05/1917
Operation(al) Order(s)	42nd Divisional Artillery Order No. 10. Appendix No 2	16/05/1917	16/05/1917
Miscellaneous	Table 'A'		
Operation(al) Order(s)	42nd Divisional Artillery Order No. 11. Appendix No 3	18/05/1917	18/05/1917
Miscellaneous	Table "A".		
Miscellaneous	March Table Table "B"		
Operation(al) Order(s)	42nd Divisional Artillery Order No. 12. Appendix No 4	26/05/1917	26/05/1917
Heading	War Diary Of Headquarters R A 42nd Division. From 1.6.17 To 30.6.17 Volume 4.		
War Diary	Ytres	01/06/1917	30/06/1917
Miscellaneous	42nd Divisional Artillery Appendix No 1	01/06/1917	01/06/1917
Miscellaneous	42nd Division. Appendix 2	04/06/1917	04/06/1917
Heading	War Diary Of Headquarters R.A. 42nd Division. From 1.7.17 To 31.7.17 Volume 3		
War Diary	Ytres	01/07/1917	31/07/1917
Miscellaneous	42nd Divisional Artillery. Disposition Report. Appendix No 1	25/06/1917	25/06/1917
Operation(al) Order(s)	42nd Division Order No. 27. Appendix No 2	03/07/1917	03/07/1917
Miscellaneous	March Table To Accompany 42nd Division Order No. 27.		
Operation(al) Order(s)	42nd Divisional Artillery Order No. 15. Appendix No 3	05/07/1917	05/07/1917
Miscellaneous	42nd D.A.C. Appendix No 4	06/07/1917	06/07/1917
Operation(al) Order(s)	58th Divisional Artillery Order No. 2 Appendix No 5	21/07/1917	21/07/1917
Heading	War Diary of H.Q. R.A. 42nd Division From 1-8-17 to 31-8-17		
War Diary	Ytres	01/08/1917	29/08/1917
Heading	War Diary of H.Q. R.A. 42nd Div. From 1-9-17 to 30-9-17		
War Diary	Ypres	01/09/1917	30/09/1917
Operation(al) Order(s)	15th Divisional Artillery Order No. 92. App 1	28/08/1917	28/08/1917

Miscellaneous	March Table To Accompany 15th Divisional Artillery Order No. 92. Appendix A.		
Miscellaneous	March Table To Accompany 15th Divisional Artillery Order No. 92 Appendix B		
Miscellaneous	42nd Divisional Artillery Warning Order No. 3. App 2	03/09/1917	03/09/1917
Miscellaneous	Programme A. Appendix A.		
Operation(al) Order(s)	42nd Div Arty Group Order No. 22. App 2	05/09/1917	05/09/1917
Miscellaneous	Programme of 4.5" How. Standing Barrages Appendix A		
Map			
Operation(al) Order(s)	Extract From 42nd Division Order No. 36 Appx 3	13/09/1917	13/09/1917
Operation(al) Order(s)	42nd Divisional Artillery Operation Order No. 38 Appx 4	29/09/1917	29/09/1917
Heading	War Diary of H.Q. R.A. 42nd Div. From 1-10-17 To 31-10-17		
War Diary		02/10/1917	31/10/1917
Operation(al) Order(s)	42nd Divisional Artillery Operation Order No. 39 Appx I	30/09/1917	30/09/1917
Miscellaneous			
Operation(al) Order(s)	42nd Divisional Artillery Operation Order No. 40	01/10/1917	01/10/1917
Miscellaneous	Addendum No. 1 to 42nd Divisional Artillery Order No. 41 Appx II	10/10/1917	10/10/1917
Operation(al) Order(s)	42nd Divisional Artillery Order No. 41	09/10/1917	09/10/1917
Miscellaneous	Table Of Reliefs		
Operation(al) Order(s)	42nd Divisional Artillery Order No. 43. Appx III	22/10/1917	22/10/1917
Miscellaneous	Table Of Reliefs.		
Miscellaneous	Right Divisional Artillery. Appx IV		
Heading	War Diary of H.Q. R.A. 42nd Div. From 1-11-17 To 30-11-17		
War Diary	Coxyde Bains	01/11/1917	26/11/1917
War Diary	Aire	30/11/1917	30/11/1917
Miscellaneous	H.Q. 42nd Division "Q" Appendix I	05/11/1917	05/11/1917
Operation(al) Order(s)	42nd Divisional Artillery Order No. 48. App. II	14/11/1917	14/11/1917
Operation(al) Order(s)	42nd Divisional Artillery Order No. 49. Appendix III	16/11/1917	16/11/1917
Miscellaneous	Addendum to 42nd Divisional Artillery Order No. 49	18/11/1917	18/11/1917
Miscellaneous	B Group.	16/11/1917	16/11/1917
Operation(al) Order(s)	42nd Divisional Artillery Order No. 51.	19/11/1917	19/11/1917
Miscellaneous	March Table for 21st Instant.		
Miscellaneous	Addendum to 42nd D.A. Order No. 51	20/11/1917	20/11/1917
Operation(al) Order(s)	42nd Divisional Artillery Order No. 52 App IV	22/11/1917	22/11/1917
Miscellaneous	March Table for 23rd Inst.		
Operation(al) Order(s)	42nd Divisional Artillery Order No. 53.	23/11/1917	23/11/1917
Miscellaneous	March Table for 24th November		
Operation(al) Order(s)	42nd Divisional Artillery Order No. 54.	24/11/1917	24/11/1917
Miscellaneous	March Table for 25th November. 1917		
Operation(al) Order(s)	42nd Divisional Artillery Order No. 55.	25/11/1917	25/11/1917
Miscellaneous	March Table for 26th November. 1917.		
Operation(al) Order(s)	42nd Divisional Artillery Order No. 56. App V	28/11/1917	28/11/1917
Miscellaneous	H.Q. 42nd D.A.C.	28/11/1917	28/11/1917
Operation(al) Order(s)	42nd Divisional Artillery Order No. 57.	29/11/1917	29/11/1917
Miscellaneous	March Table for 30th Instant.		
Miscellaneous	Table Of Reliefs to Accompany 42nd Divisional Artillery Order No.		
Miscellaneous	Table Showing allotment of Wagon Lines to 42nd Divisional Artillery		
Miscellaneous	O.C. 210th Bde. R.F.A.	30/11/1917	30/11/1917

Miscellaneous	O.C. 211th Brigade R.F.A.	30/11/1917	30/11/1917
Heading	War Diary of H.Q. R.A. 42nd Division Volume X From 1-12-17 To 31-12-17		
War Diary	Locon	01/12/1917	28/12/1917
Miscellaneous	42nd Divisional Artillery. Appendix I	04/12/1917	04/12/1917
Operation(al) Order(s)	42nd Division Order No. 53. App II	18/12/1917	18/12/1917
Operation(al) Order(s)	42nd Divisional Artillery Order No. 59. Appx III	13/12/1917	13/12/1917
Miscellaneous	Table to Accompany 42nd Div. Artillery Order No. 59.		
Miscellaneous	Addendum No. 2 to 42nd Division Order No. 52	24/12/1917	24/12/1917
Miscellaneous	42nd Divisional Artillery Location Statement Appendix IV	27/12/1917	27/12/1917
Miscellaneous	Appendix V	25/12/1917	25/12/1917
Heading	War. Diary. Of R.A. H.Q. 42nd Div. From 1st January 1918 To 31st January 1918 Volume XI		
War Diary	Locon	01/01/1918	31/01/1918
Miscellaneous	42nd Divisional Artillery. Location Statement. Appendix I	27/12/1917	27/12/1917
Miscellaneous	List Of T.M's in Position		
Miscellaneous	O.C. 210th Brigade R.F.A. Appendix II	05/01/1918	05/01/1918
Miscellaneous	First Army No. G.S. 957	27/12/1917	27/12/1917
Miscellaneous	42nd Division G.S. 120/4/46. R.A. 42nd Division No. B.M.S.1/70 Appx III		
Miscellaneous	Move.		
Miscellaneous	42nd Divisional Artillery. Appx IV	19/01/1918	19/01/1918
Miscellaneous	42nd Divisional Artillery. Appx V	17/01/1918	17/01/1918
Miscellaneous	42nd Divisional Artillery. Appx VI	24/01/1918	24/01/1918
Miscellaneous	42nd Divisional Artillery. Appx VII	31/01/1918	31/01/1918
Heading	War Diary of H.Q. R.A. 42nd Division From 1-2-18 To 28-2-18 Volume. XII		
War Diary	Locon	01/02/1918	22/02/1918
Miscellaneous	42nd Divisional Artillery Disposition Report Appx I	07/02/1918	07/02/1918
Miscellaneous	42nd Divisional Artillery Disposition Report Appx II	14/02/1918	14/02/1918
Miscellaneous	42nd Divisional Artillery Disposition Report	14/02/1918	14/02/1918
Miscellaneous	42nd Divisional Artillery. Location Of Units Appx III	17/02/1918	17/02/1918
Heading	C.R.A. 42nd Division March 1918		
Heading	War Diary Of H.Q. R.A. 42nd Division From 1/3/1918 To 31/3/18 Volume XIII		
War Diary	Hinges	03/03/1918	03/03/1918
War Diary	La Beuvriere	05/03/1918	05/03/1918
War Diary	Labeuvriere	07/03/1918	23/03/1918
War Diary	Monchy-Au-Bois	24/03/1918	25/03/1918
War Diary	Fonquevillers	26/03/1918	27/03/1918
War Diary	St Amand	28/03/1918	31/03/1918
Miscellaneous	Appendices I to VI.		
Operation(al) Order(s)	42nd Divisional Artillery Order No. 60. Appx I	01/03/1918	01/03/1918
Miscellaneous	Amendment No. 1. to 42nd D.A. Order No. 60. Appx I	02/03/1918	02/03/1918
Miscellaneous	42nd Divisional Artillery Location Statement. Appx II	03/03/1918	03/03/1918
Miscellaneous	Location Of Units Of 42nd Divisional Artillery. Appx III		
Miscellaneous	Amendment To 42nd Divisional Artillery Appx IV	21/03/1918	21/03/1918
Miscellaneous	42nd Divisional Artillery. App V	30/03/1918	30/03/1918
Miscellaneous	41st Divisional Artillery Group.	31/03/1918	31/03/1918
Heading	Headquarters, 42nd Divisional Artillery April 1918		
Heading	War. Diary. Of H.Q. R.A. 42nd Division From 1st April 1918 To 30th April 1919 Vol. XIV.		
War Diary	Henu	01/04/1918	09/04/1918

Type	Description	Start	End
War Diary	Pas	10/04/1918	10/04/1918
War Diary	Couin	16/04/1918	30/04/1918
Miscellaneous	Appendices I to VII.		
Miscellaneous	42nd Divisional Artillery. Location Statement Appx I	03/04/1918	03/04/1918
Miscellaneous	42nd Divisional Artillery. Location Statement Appx II	07/04/1918	07/04/1918
Miscellaneous	42nd Divisional Artillery. Location Statement Appx III	10/04/1918	10/04/1918
Miscellaneous	42nd Divisional Artillery. Location Statement. Appx IV	18/04/1918	18/04/1918
Miscellaneous	42nd Divisional Artillery. Location Statement. Appx V	21/04/1918	21/04/1918
Miscellaneous	42nd Divisional Artillery. Location Statement. Appx VI	24/04/1918	24/04/1918
Miscellaneous	42nd Divisional Artillery. Location Statement. Appx VII	28/04/1918	28/04/1918
Heading	War Diary of Hd. Qrs R.A. 42nd Division From 1st May 1918 To 31st May 1918 Volume XV		
War Diary		01/05/1918	31/05/1918
Miscellaneous	Approximate Front Covered	01/05/1918	01/05/1918
Miscellaneous	42nd Divisional Artillery. Location Statement. Appendix I	01/05/1918	01/05/1918
Miscellaneous	42nd Divisional Artillery. Location Statement. App II	05/05/1918	05/05/1918
Miscellaneous	42nd D.A. No. B.M. 495. App. III	31/05/1918	31/05/1918
Miscellaneous	42nd Divisional Artillery Instruction No. 1	24/05/1918	24/05/1918
Miscellaneous	Appendix "A"	24/05/1918	24/05/1918
Miscellaneous	Appendix 'B' (Issued with 42nd D.A. Instruction No. 1)	24/05/1918	24/05/1918
Miscellaneous	Appendix 'C' Issued with 42nd D.A. Instruction No. 1.	06/06/1918	06/06/1918
Miscellaneous	Appendix 'D' Issued with 42nd D.A. Instruction No. 1.	03/06/1918	03/06/1918
Miscellaneous	Appendix 'E' (Issued with 42nd D.A. Instruction No. 1		
Miscellaneous	42nd D.A. No. B.M. 404	16/05/1918	16/05/1918
Miscellaneous	42nd D.A. No. B.M. 395	14/05/1918	14/05/1918
Miscellaneous	42nd D.A. No. B.M. 374	11/05/1918	11/05/1918
Miscellaneous	Reference 41st Div. Arty. Instruction No. 6	10/05/1918	10/05/1918
Heading	War Diary of H.Q. R.A. 42nd Div. From 1st June 1918 To 30th June 1918 Vol. XVI		
War Diary	Pas-En Artois	01/06/1918	06/06/1918
War Diary	Bus-En-Artois	07/06/1918	30/06/1918
Miscellaneous	42nd Divisional Artillery Location List App I	09/06/1918	09/06/1918
Miscellaneous	42nd Divisional Artillery Location List App II	13/06/1918	13/06/1918
Miscellaneous	42nd D.A. No. B.M. 1/21 Appendix III Appendix III	11/06/1918	11/06/1918
Miscellaneous	42nd Divisional Artillery-Location List. App IV	16/06/1918	16/06/1918
Miscellaneous	42nd Divisional Artillery-Location List. App V	19/06/1918	19/06/1918
Miscellaneous	42nd Divisional Artillery-Location List. App VI	23/06/1918	23/06/1918
Miscellaneous	42nd Divisional Artillery-Location List. AppVII	26/06/1918	26/06/1918
Operation(al) Order(s)	42nd Divisional Artillery Order No. 10. App VIII	28/06/1918	28/06/1918
Miscellaneous	42nd Divisional Artillery-Location List. App IX	30/06/1918	30/06/1918
Heading	HQ RA 42 D Vol 18		
Miscellaneous	DAG Base		
War Diary	Bus	01/07/1918	07/07/1918
War Diary	123 Central	10/07/1918	15/07/1918
War Diary	Authie	16/07/1918	31/07/1918
Operation(al) Order(s)	42nd Divisional Artillery Order No. 15. App 'A'	01/07/1918	01/07/1918
Miscellaneous	Amendment No: 1 To 42nd Divisional Artillery Order No: 15.	01/07/1918	01/07/1918
Miscellaneous	42nd Divisional Artillery-Location List. App 'B'	03/07/1918	03/07/1918
Operation(al) Order(s)	42nd Divisional Artillery Order No. 13. App 'C'	29/06/1918	29/06/1918
Miscellaneous	42nd D.A. No. B.M. 5/59 App. 'D'	06/07/1918	06/07/1918
Miscellaneous	Addendum No 1 to 42nd Divisional Artillery Order No 13.	01/07/1918	01/07/1918
Miscellaneous	Position to cover Colincamps Switch & Purple Line.		

Miscellaneous	Positions To Cover		
Miscellaneous	42nd Divisional Artillery-Location List. App 'E'	07/07/1918	07/07/1918
Miscellaneous	42nd Divisional Artillery-Location List. App 'F'	10/07/1918	10/07/1918
Miscellaneous	42nd Divisional Artillery-Location List. App 'G'	14/07/1918	14/07/1918
Operation(al) Order(s)	42nd Divisional Artillery Order No. 18. App 'H'	15/07/1918	15/07/1918
Miscellaneous	Table Of Tasks-Issued With 42nd Div. Arty. Order No. 18	15/07/1918	15/07/1918
Miscellaneous		16/07/1918	16/07/1918
Operation(al) Order(s)	42nd Divisional Artillery Order No. 16. App I	04/07/1918	04/07/1918
Miscellaneous	To Accompany 42nd D.A. Order No. 16 "Appendix A".		
Operation(al) Order(s)	42nd Divisional Artillery Order 19. App. 'J'	15/07/1918	15/07/1918
Miscellaneous	Addendum No. 2 to 42nd D.A. Order No. 19.	17/07/1918	17/07/1918
Miscellaneous	42nd Divisional Artillery-Location List. App 'K'	17/07/1918	17/07/1918
Operation(al) Order(s)	42nd Divisional Artillery Order No. 21. App 'L'	18/07/1918	18/07/1918
Miscellaneous	Table Of Tasks to Accompany 42nd Divisional Artillery Order No. 21.	18/07/1918	18/07/1918
Miscellaneous	42nd D.A. No. B.M. 9/35 App M	19/07/1918	19/07/1918
Operation(al) Order(s)	42nd Divisional Artillery Order No. 20.	16/07/1918	16/07/1918
Miscellaneous	Addendum To 42nd Divisional Artillery Order No. 20		
Miscellaneous	42nd Divisional Artillery-Location List. App 'O'	21/07/1918	21/07/1918
Operation(al) Order(s)	42nd Divisional Artillery Order No. 22. App 'P'		
Miscellaneous	Table to Accompany 42nd Div. Arty. Order No. 22.	21/05/1918	21/05/1918
Miscellaneous	42nd Divisional Artillery-Location List. App 'Q'	24/07/1918	24/07/1918
Operation(al) Order(s)	42nd Divisional Artillery Order No. 25. App 'R'		
Miscellaneous	Addendum No. 1. to 42nd Divisional Artillery Order No. 23.	23/07/1918	23/07/1918
Miscellaneous	42nd Divisional Artillery-Location List. App 'S'	28/07/1918	28/07/1918
Operation(al) Order(s)	42nd Divisional Artillery Order No. 24. App 'T'	28/07/1918	28/07/1918
Miscellaneous	Addendum No. 1. to 42nd Divisional Artillery Order No 24		
Operation(al) Order(s)	42nd Divisional Artillery Order No. 25. App 'U'	27/07/1918	27/07/1918
Miscellaneous	42nd Divisional Artillery-Location List. App 'V'	31/07/1918	31/07/1918
Heading	War Diary Of Headquarters Royal Artillery, 42nd Division from 1st August 1918 to 31st August 1918		
War Diary	Authie	06/08/1918	15/08/1918
War Diary	Bus	18/08/1918	24/08/1918
War Diary	Bucquoy	27/08/1918	29/08/1918
War Diary	Grevillers	30/08/1918	30/08/1918
Miscellaneous	42nd D.A. No. B.M. 1/283 App I	06/08/1918	06/08/1918
Operation(al) Order(s)	42nd Divisional Artillery Order No. 27. App II	09/08/1918	09/08/1918
Miscellaneous	42nd Divisional Artillery-Location List. App III	18/08/1918	18/08/1918
Miscellaneous	Right Sector-IV Corps. App IV	21/08/1918	21/08/1918
Miscellaneous	42nd Divisional Artillery No. B.M. 107 App V	20/08/1918	20/08/1918
Miscellaneous	Artillery Notes For Mobiles Warfare. App VI	03/09/1918	03/09/1918
Heading	War Diary of HQ RA. 42nd Divn. From 1/9/18 To 30/9/18 Vol XIX		
War Diary	Grevillers	01/09/1918	04/09/1918
War Diary	Riencourt	05/09/1918	21/09/1918
War Diary	Velu	22/09/1918	29/09/1918
Miscellaneous	42nd Divisional Artillery-Location Statement. Appendix I	18/09/1918	18/09/1918
Miscellaneous	42nd D.A. No. B.M. 1/44.	26/09/1918	26/09/1918
Miscellaneous	Amendment No. 1 to 42nd D.A. Instructions No. 1	24/09/1918	24/09/1918
Miscellaneous	42nd D.A. Instruction No. 1 (Preliminary) App II		
Miscellaneous	42nd Divisional Artillery-Location Statement. App III	25/09/1918	25/09/1918

Operation(al) Order(s)	42nd Divisional Artillery Order No. 36. App IV	27/09/1918	27/09/1918
Miscellaneous Map	Addendum No. 1 to 42nd D.A. Order No. 30	28/09/1918	28/09/1918
Miscellaneous Map	42nd D.A. No. B.M. 1/47 App V	27/09/1918	27/09/1918
Heading	War Diary of H Q. R.A. 42nd Division From 1/10/18 To 31/10/18 Vol. XX		
War Diary	Velu	01/10/1918	08/10/1918
War Diary	Trescault	09/10/1918	09/10/1918
War Diary	Esnes	12/10/1918	12/10/1918
War Diary	Beauvois	12/10/1918	31/10/1918
Miscellaneous	42nd Divisional Artillery-Location Statement App B	11/10/1918	11/10/1918
Miscellaneous	R.F.A. Group. 42nd Division. App A	14/10/1918	14/10/1918
Miscellaneous	Amendment No. 1 to 42nd D.A. Order No. 38 App 'C'	19/10/1918	19/10/1918
Operation(al) Order(s)	42nd D.A. Order No. 38.		
Miscellaneous	42nd D.A. No. B.M. 13/4 App 'D'	19/10/1918	19/10/1918
Miscellaneous	42nd D.A. No. B.M. 1/115 App 'E'	21/10/1918	21/10/1918
Operation(al) Order(s)	42nd Divisional Artillery Order No. 39. App F	22/10/1918	22/10/1918
Miscellaneous	Amendment No. 1 to 42nd D.A. Order No. 39.	22/10/1918	22/10/1918
Heading	War Diary of 42nd D.A. H.Q. From Nov. 1st 1918 To Nov. 30th 1918 Vol XXI		
War Diary	Beauvois	01/11/1918	05/11/1918
War Diary	Potelle	08/11/1918	08/11/1918
War Diary	La Haute	09/11/1918	09/11/1918
War Diary	Rue Hautmont	11/11/1918	30/11/1918
Heading	War Diary of HQ. RA. 42nd Division from 1/12/1918 To 31/12/1918 vol. XXII		
War Diary	Hautmont	01/12/1918	14/12/1918
War Diary	Jeumont	15/12/1918	15/12/1918
War Diary	Thuin	16/12/1918	18/12/1918
War Diary	Montignies	19/12/1918	31/12/1918
Heading	War Diary. Of Head Quarters. 42nd Div. Artillery. From 1st January 1919. To 31st January 191		
War Diary Miscellaneous	Montignies S/Sambre	01/01/1919	31/01/1919
Heading	War Diary. Of Headquarters, 42nd Div. Artillery. From 1st February 1919. To 28th February 1919. Volume XXV		
War Diary	Montignies	01/02/1918	28/02/1918
Heading	War Diary of Head Quarters, 42nd Div. Arty. From 1st March 1919 To 31st March 1919. Volume XXVI.		
War Diary	Montignies Sur Sambre	01/03/1919	31/03/1919

505/24/7 (2)

050/24/7 (2) am

42ND DIVISION

C. R. A.

MAR 1917-FEB 1919
MAR 1919

CONFIDENTIAL

WAR DIARY,

of

H.Q. R.A. 42nd DIVISION.

From - 1-3-17
To.   31-3-17.

(VOL. III)

CONFIDENTIAL

Vol 3

WAR DIARY

OF

HEADQUARTERS R.A. 42nd DIVISION

FROM 1.4.17 TO 30.4.17.

VOLUME IV. 1917.

Army Form C. 2118.

WAR DIARY
INTELLIGENCE SUMMARY

(Erase heading not required.)

H.Q. R.A.
42nd DIVISION
SHEET. 1.

Place	Date	Hour	Summary of Events and Information	Remarks and references to Appendices
AT SEA and in FRANCE	1-3-17 to 16-3-17		Ref. ce Map 1/100,000 ABBEVILLE, SHEET 14. 42nd Divisional R.A. in process of arriving in FRANCE – Port of disembarkation MARSEILLES – Area of concentration CAOURS (Ref. Map 1/100,000, ABBEVILLE)	P.R.M.
CAOURS	5-3-17		H.Q.R.A. arrives CAOURS.	P.R.M.
"	9-3-17		B.M.R.A. returns to H.Q.R.A. 42 Div. after attachment to 1st Div. Arty.	P.R.M.
"	13-3-17		MAJOR GENERAL B.R. MITFORD C.B., D.S.O., G.O.C. 42nd Div., inspected Divisional R.A. seeing each Battery in its own area.	P.R.M.
"	16-3-17		All 42nd Div. R.A. have arrived in CAOURS area and are billeted as follows:–	P.R.M.
			H.Q.R.A. ..... CAOURS	
			H.Q. 210 Bde ..... CAOURS	
			A. 210 "	
			B. 210 " ..... ST NICHOLAS DES ESSART.	
			C. 210 " ..... L'HEURE	
			D. 210 "	
			H.Q. 211 Bde	
			A " " ..... GRAND LAVIER	
			B " "	
			C " "	
			D 211 Bde ..... PONT LE GRAND	
			H.Q. D.A.C. ..... DRUCAT	
			No.1 X 3 Section D.A.C. ..... DRUCAT	
			No. 2 Section ..... LE PLESSIEL	
			1 Heavy Trench Mortar Battery & 3 Medium T.M. Batteries are being formed and trained by the 4th Army at the Trench Mortar School, VAUX, for the 42nd Div. R.A. The B 2 of R.F.A. & the D.A.C. proceed with Training & Equipping as Part III War ESTABLISHMENTS	P.R.M.

Army Form C. 2118.

WAR DIARY
INTELLIGENCE SUMMARY

H.Q.R.A. 42nd Div'n.

SHEET. 2.

(Erase heading not required.)

Instructions regarding War Diaries and Intelligence Summaries are contained in F. S. Regs., Part II. and the Staff Manual respectively. Title Pages will be prepared in manuscript.

Place	Date	Hour	Summary of Events and Information	Remarks and references to Appendices
			Ref to MAP TOQOUS ABBEVILLE. SHEET.14.	
CAOURS	17-3-17		The Advance Party of 10 officers & 16 N.C.O'n R.A., who had been attached to 1st Div. R.A., return to their units.	P.R.M.
"	20-3-17		16 officers & 256 O.R. (1 Section per Battery, less drivers) proceed to MEAULTE for attachment to 1st Div. R.A.	P.R.M.
"	24-3-17		Maj. B.R. DOBSON R.F.A. assumes Company command of the D.A.C. subject to confirmation by G.H.Q.	P.R.M.
"	24-3-17		The Advance Party of 16 Off. & 256 O.R. return to their batteries from 1st D.A. less 4 officers & 4 N.C.O."s who proceed for instructional attachment to 48th D.A.	P.R.M.
"	25-3-17		(575 Riders & 45 L.D. horses drawn from Remount depot, ABBEVILLE. 269 O.R. from R.F.A. depot join the D.A.C.	P.R.M.
"	26-3-17		B.M.R.A., 8 Off. & 8 N.C.O."s proceeded to the 4th Army Arty. School, VAUX, for a Course. Personnel of Divl. R.A. Trench Mortar Batteries (1 Heavy & 3 Medium) arrive from T.M. School and are Billeted at Le PLESSIEL, 7 Officers & 133 O.R. also 12 - 2" mortars. Temp Capt. LEVITT joins as D.T.M.O.	P.R.M.
"	28-3-17		⟨ 30 vehicles & 134 animals drawn by D.A.C. from A.H.T.D.	P.R.M.
"	29-3-17		Lt Col. JOLIFFE R.F.A. arrives to take over Command of D.A.C. together with 8 officers & 320 O.R. These are surplus to establishment, presumably sent in error.	P.R.M.
"	30-3-17		34 vehicles, & 268 animals drawn by D.A.C. from A.H.T.D. to complete establishment.	P.R.M.

P.R. Mitchell
Maj.
B.M.R.A. 42 Div.

1-4-17

Army Form C. 2118.

WAR DIARY
INTELLIGENCE SUMMARY
(Erase heading not required.)

HD. Qrs R.A. 42nd Division

SHEET 1

Place	Date	Hour	Summary of Events and Information	Remarks and references to Appendices
CAOURS	1.4.17		MAP 1/100,000 ABBEVILLE. DISTRIBUTION OF 42nd DIV. R.A. HQ R.A. — CAOURS HQ 210th Bde. — CAOURS A 210 — ST NICOLAS DES ESSART B 210 — L'HEURE C 210 D 210 HQ 211th Bde. — GRAND LAVIER A 211 B 211 — PONT LE GRAND C 211 — DRUCAT D 211 — DRUCAT HQ 42nd D.A.C. — LE PLESSIEL No 1 Sect — DRUCAT " 2 Sect " 3 Sect 42nd Div TM. B's 3 LE PLESSIEL 1 Heavy & 3 Medium Formation and equipment of 42nd Div Amm Column completed.	m. to Corps
	3.4.17			
	4.4.17 to 6.4.17		42nd Div Arty moved by march route to BOIS OLYMPE halting for nights at ST SAVEUR and FOUILLOY 42nd Div Amm Col to FROISSY. (1/100,000 AMIENS 17.I.2.) See 42nd Div R.A. Order A21 (3.4.17) attached.	App. No 1 m. to Corps
BOIS OLYMPE	8.4.17 9.4.17		211th Bde R.F.A. with (under section of R.I Sect D.A.C. moved by march route to VILLERS FAVON halting for night at DOIGNT. HQ and major lines at TEMPLEUX LA FOSSE. Batteries moved to positions. Being attached to 148th Div Artillery. A & B 211th Bde R.F.A. (48th Div). (1/40,000 62C) R.F.A attached 241st Bde R.F.A. (45 Div). (1/40,000 62C). HQ R.A. moved from BOIS OLYMPE to PERONNE. Moves of 210th Bde R.F.A. and 42nd D.A.C. carried out in accordance with R.A Order 207 d. 21.4.17 attached	m. to Corps App No 2 m. to Corps
	18.4.17 22.4.17			

WAR DIARY
INTELLIGENCE SUMMARY

Army Form C. 2118.
SHEET 2

Place	Date	Hour	Summary of Events and Information	Remarks and references to Appendices
PERONNE	23.4.17		Bn "A" "B" & "D" Batteries 210th Bde R.F.A. occupied positions on 59th Divn Front and are under orders of C.R.A. 59th Divn. Hq'rs 210th Bde R.F.A. at ROISEL. Wagon Lines BOUSSY and HAMELET	w. p. to Capt.
	28.4.17		MAJOR P.R.MITCHELL R.G.A. Brigade Major R.A. to Bn admitted to hospital	
	29.4.17		Orders for relief of 48th Divn Artillery by 42nd Divn Artillery issued. B.G.R.A. and S.C.R.A. proceeded to 48th Divn Artillery Hqrs (K.11.a.96) to arrange reliefs and taking over following reliefs effected during night 29/30th:-	w. p. to Capt.
			1 Section A 210 relieved 1 Sect A 211 at F.29.a.52.	
			1 Section B 210 " B 211 " F.27.a.16.	
			1 Section C 210 moved from LEMIESNIK BIVOUAC and relieved 1 Sect A 240 (48" Divn) at F.29.C.9.5.	
			1 Section A 211 (on relief by A 210) relieved 1 Section C 241 (48th Divn) at F.8.C.52.	
			1 Section B 211 (on relief by B 210) " R 241 (48th Divn) at W.30.C.81	
	30.4.17		Hq 210th Bde R.F.A. moved to ST EMILIE.	w. p. to Capt.
			During night 30th/1st May following further moves for relief of 48" Divn Arty were carried out:-	
			1 Section A 210 relieved section A 211 as above.	
			1 Section B 210 " B 211 "	
			1 Section C 210 " A 240 "	w. p. to Capt.
			1 Sect D 210 " D 240 at F.14.d.96	
			1 Sect A 211 " C 241 as above	
			1 Sect B 211 " B 241 as above	

W. P. Wright Capt.
for Brigade Transport R.A.
to Brunie

2449 Wt. W14957/M90 750,000 1/16 J.B.C. & A. Forms/C.2118/12.

SECRET.   Copy No: 5

42nd DIVISIONAL R.A. ORDER NO: 1

Reference MAPS 1/100000 ABBEVILLE Sheet 14
                1/100000 AMIENS   Sheet 17
                1/250000 Sheets 3 & 4
                1/40000 Sheets 62C & 62D
                                                          3.4.17

(1) 42nd Divisional Artillery will march to Camp in square R.3 and BOIS OLYMPE as follows:-
    4th inst ABBEVILLE &xSTxNAMEN AREA to ST.SAUVEUR
    5th inst ST.SAUVEUR   to   POUILLOY
    6th inst POUILLOY   to   BOIS OLYMPE AREA
    The Trench Mortar Batteries will proceed direct to BOIS OLYMPE on 4/4/17 by Motor Lorry.

(2) Transport for Brigades R.F.A. & for D.A.C. will be as detailed in this office No:16 dated 2/4/17

(3) The unexpended portion of the Forage and Supplies for the 4th together with rations for 2 days will be taken on the march, as will Forage for the 5th. Forage for the 6th will be drawn at ST.SAUVEUR.

(4) Starting Point for 4th Junction of roads in AILLY-LE-HAUT-CLOCHER. UNITS WILL PASS THE STARTING POINT as follows:-
        R.A.H.Q.   11.5 a.m.
        210th Bde.R.F.A.   11.10 a.m.
        No:1 Sect.D.A.C.   11.35 a.m.
        H.Q.,D.A.C. &)
        No:3 Sect.D.A.C.   11.50 a.m.
        211th Bde.R.F.A.   12.5 p.m.
        No:2 Sect.D.A.C.   12.30 p.m.
    This allows of the usual 10 minutes halt at 12.0 noon
    Nos.1 and 3 Sections D.A.C. will be attached to 210th Bde.R.F.A. during the 3 days march. No:2 Section to 211th Bde.R.F.A.

(5) Representatives from Units, as detailed in Preliminary Order, will meet S.C.R.A. at the cross-roads La CHAUSSEE at 12.0 noon to be allotted Billeting Areas.

(6) A rear party composed as follows:-
        1 Officer & 6 men   210th Bde.R.F.A.
        1 Officer & 6 men   211th Bde.R.F.A.
        1 Q.M.S. & 6 men   42nd D.A.C.
    will be left behind to square up billets and adjust any claims. The party detailed from the D.A.C. will also be responsible for the billets and claims of the T.M.Batteries at LE PLESSIEL. These parties will rejoin their Units at ST.SAUVEUR in the evening

(7) 6 Motor Lorries for the transport of T.M.Batteries will report to the D.T.M.O. on the evening of the 3rd inst.
    The D.T.M.O. will make all arrangements to load up and leave LE PLESSIEL at 9.0 a.m. having previously personally inspected all billets and adjusted all claims.
    On arrival at BOIS OLYMPE he will arrange for the billeting of his men.

(8) An advance billeting party composed as follows:-
        210th Bde.R.F.A.   9 other ranks
        211th Bde.R.F.A.   9 other ranks
        42nd D.A.C.   4 other ranks

                                                    continued.

continued:-

under 2/Lieut. WILSON will proceed by motor lorry direct to
BOIS OLYMPE leaving 210th Bde Headquarters at 9.0 a.m.
The D.A.C. party will report at 210th Bde.Headquarters before
that hour.
The party from 211th Brigade will meet the lorry in Cathedral
Square ABBEVILLE at 9.30 a.m.

(9) At 1.0 p.m. there will be a halt of 40 minutes to feed (and
water if possible)

(10) As soon as the head of the Column arrives at ST.SAUVEUR each
Brigade and the D.A.C. will send 2 orderlies to report to
Lieutenant HASTINGS R.E. who will be with R.A.H.Q.
This will be done on each day's march.

(sgd) B.T. Mitchell

Major,

B.M.R.A. 42nd Division.

Issued at.........
By...Orderly....
As under.
Copy No: 1 to O.C.210th Bde R.F.A.
  "   " 2 to O.C.211th Bde R.F.A.
  "   " 3 to O.C.42nd D.A.C.
  "   " 4 to 42nd D.T.M.C.
  "   " 5   War Diary,
  "   " 6   File.

Copy No 5.

PRELIMINARY INSTRUCTIONS FOR MARCH.

ADVANCED & REAR PARTIES

(1) 1 Officer & 4 men from the leading Brigade will march half a mile ahead of the Column and will warn all Control Posts of the advance of the Column.
A Rear party of 1 officer & 4 men will be detailed by the Rear Brigade to march 800 yds. in rear to prevent straggling.
The above will be found by each Brigade until such time as the Brigades join up on the road S.E. of ABBEVILLE.

(2) POLICING

1 Officer per Brigade & 1 N.C.O. per Battery & Section D.A.C. will be told off to act as police on the line of march.
They will see that correct distances are maintained and that the Traffic Orders laid down in Fourth Army S.O. para 221 are strictly adhered to.
This does not absolve Unit Commanders from responsibility in the above matter.

(3) HALTS

All watches will be synchronized in Brigades.
Battery Commanders & Section Commanders (D.A.C.) will halt their own Units exactly at every clock hour, when sub-sections will dismount without orders at once.
The march will be continued at exactly 10 minutes past the hour.
Halts however will never be made in towns & cross-roads will never be blocked.

(4) ORDER OF MARCH

Complete Sections (1 & 2) of D.A.C. will march behind the Brigade to which they are attached. They will not be split up with the Batteries.
Forage & Supply wagons will march with the Batteries to which they are attached.
Headquarters 42nd D.A.C. & the remainder of No:3 Section will march in rear of the 210th Brigade.
The strictest march discipline will be maintained by all.

(5) TRENCH MORTAR BATTERIES

T.M.Batteries will proceed independently in Motor lurries.

(6) BILLETING PARTY:

The B.C.R.A. will precede the Column in a lorry. He will be accompanied by the following party:- All Adjutants & Interpreter and 1 representative (either officer or senior N.C.O.) from each Battery or Section D.A.C.
Instructions as to picking up this party will be issued later.
The D.T.M.O. will make his own arrangements for billeting the T.M.personnel.

(7) TELEPHONE CABLE

Os.C.Brigades will make arrangements to leave behind on the 4/4/1 a sufficient party to reel in all Brigade & Battery cable, with instructions to join their Units at the first nights halt.

(8) DISTANCES

The following distances will be observed on the march:-
A clear distance of 50 yards between Batteries
"   "   "   " 25   "   "   Sections of each Battery

Issued at.....
By. ....
As follows:-
Copy No:1 to O.C.210th Bde R.F.A.
 "   " 2 " O.C.211th Bde R.F.A.
 "   " 3 " O.C.42nd D.A.C.
 "   " 4 " 42nd D.T.M.O.
 "   " 5 " WAR DIARY
 "   " 6   FILE

P.R.Mitchell
Major,
B.M.R.A. 42nd Division

SECRET.   II   Copy No. 6

42nd DIVISIONAL ARTILLERY ORDER NO:7.

21-4-17.

Reference Map 1/40,000, Sheet 62.C.

1. Following moves will take place tomorrow, 22nd inst.

    (a) A/210 and B/210 to BOUCLY.
    (b) D/210 to HAMELET. (K.20.b.)

    route HERBECOURT - BIACHES - PERONNE - DOINGT - TINCOURT.

    (c) No.2 Section D.A.C. (less S.A.A. Subsection) to BOUCLY.
    route CARTIGNY - BRUSLE.

    (d) H.Q. & No.3 Section and S.A.A. Subsection of No.I Section, D.A.C. & C/210 to LE MESNIL BRUNTEL.

    route HERBECOURT - BIACHES - PERONNE - DOINGT.-

    (e) H.Q. 210th Bde R.F.A. to ROISEL.

    On completion of moves Units in (a),(b) & (c) will come under orders of 59th Divnl R.A.
    They will reinforce 59th D.A. in the line on the 23rd.
    O.C. D.A.C. will arrange to send back horses on the 23rd to fetch up those vehicles he is unable to transport on the 22nd and to bring them up to LE MESNIL BRUNTEL on the 24th.
    A suitable escort must be left at FROISSY for these vehicles.

2. 210th Bde. R.F.A. and No.3 Section D.A.C. will start from their respective areas at 9.30 a.m.
    No.2 Section D.A.C.(less S.A.A. Subsection) will arrange their own time of starting.

3. The unexpended portion of the day's supplies only need be carried. Rations for consumption on 23rd will be drawn by supply wagons at LE MESNIL BRUNTEL on completion of the march.
    This does not apply to No.2 Section D.A.C. who will draw supplies for 23rd before they march.

                                            cont./-

4. 210th Bde R.F.A. will arrange to draw 2-18pdr. guns from I.O.M. PERONNE as they march through. The remaining 2-18pdrs will be left with I.O.M. till completed (about Tuesday 24th.) when O.C. 210th Bde R.F.A. will arrange to draw them.

5. Os. C. 210th Bde R.F.A. & D.A.C. will arrange to send suitable parties on ahead to arrange billets.

6. A rear party must be left in every case to clean up billets and horse-lines. They will rejoin their units on the march.

P.R. Mitchell
Major.
Brigade Major. R.A.
42nd Division.

Issued at... 1830.
By... D.R.L.S.

Copies to:-

No. 1 to H.Q. 42nd Division.
    2 " 210th Brigade R.F.A.
    3 " 42nd D.A.C.
    4 " O.C. No.2 Section, D.A.C.
    5 " 59th Divnl. Artillery.
    6. " File.

SECRET.

~~295th Brigade R.F.A.~~
~~178th Infantry Bde.~~
~~59th Division.~~
42nd Div. Artillery.
~~3rd Corps Artillery.~~

59th Div. Arty.
No.G/185.

1. Relief and reinforcement of 295th Brigade R.F.A., 59th Division, by 210th Brigade R.F.A., 42nd Division will be carried out in accordance with following programme.

2. 21/4/17   Advance Parties arrive.   ) O.C., 295th Bde R.F.A.
) will select by 6 p.m.

3. 22/4/17   Batteries arrive at Wagon) 22nd, positions
                       Lines.   ) for B & D Batteries.

             H.Q. - ROISEL.   )
             A & B Batteries - BOUCLY   )
             D Battery - HAMELET.   ))
             1 Section D.A.C. - BOUCLY.

4. 23/4/17   One Section of A Battery, 210th Bde will relieve one section of A Battery, 295th Bde.
                 The relieved section of A Battery, 295th Bde will proceed to a Wagon line at BOUVINCOURT.
                 B & D Batteries, 210th Bde, will prepare positions.

5. 24/4/17   4 Guns of A Battery, 295th Bde will be relieved by 4 Guns of A Battery, 210th Brigade & will proceed to BOUVINCOURT.
                 B & D Batteries 210th Brigade will occupy their positions.

6. The Batteries of 210th Brigade will be for tactical purposes under the Command of O.C., 295th Brigade R.F.A. and will form part of Left Group.

                                       V. D. Heather
                                                       Major, R. A.,
                     Brigade Major, R. A., 59th Division.,

20/4/17.

Vol 4

CONFIDENTIAL.

VOLUME II

WAR DIARY

___ OF ___

HD QRS R.A. 42ND DIVISION.

FROM   1 . 5 . 17
TO   31 . 5 . 17.

Army Form C. 2118.

HD QRS R.A
42nd DIVISION
SHEET I

WAR DIARY
or
INTELLIGENCE SUMMARY
(Erase heading not required.)

Place	Date	Hour	Summary of Events and Information	Remarks and references to Appendices
PERONNE	2.5.17		H.Q.R.A moved to K.H.A.86 (MAP FRANCE 1/40.000 Sheet 62.c.) by march route from PERONNE. B.G.R.A assumed command of Artillery covering the Left Division of III Corps Front. The artillery of 42nd Division with addition of two 18pdr Batteries of 45th Divn Artillery divided into two groups:— RIGHT GROUP consisting of 210th Brigade R.F.A. and "B" and "D" Batteries 240th Bde R.F.A (45th Divn) under command of Lt Col A. BIRTWISTLE C.M.G (210th Bde R.F.A) LEFT GROUP consisting of 211th Brigade R.F.A. under command of Lt Col C.E WALKER T.D. (211th Bde R.F.A) 45th Divn A.R.P taken over by 42nd Divn Arty.	m. 2.70 cwpt. m. 2.76 cwpt.
ROISEL KHA 56 FARMS	3.5.17		Inter arrangements with 59th Divn. RIGHT GROUP cooperated in operations at COLOGNE and MALAKOFF FARMS. (1/20000 62 B.N.W) MAP REFS 1/20.000 62 C N E and 62 B N W	m. 2. M Corps
	4.5.17		CAPT A. R. RONEY-DOUGAL M.C. R.A Brigade Major R.A. 1st Divn attached a/o a/B.M.R.A. 42 Divn vice MAJOR P. R. MITCHELL in hospital.	m. 2. 76 Corps
	8.5.17		RIGHT GROUP R.A cooperated with 59th Divn in operations on 59th Divn Front assisting in Barrage at following selected points.. (a) L.6.a.55 & F.30.027 (b) F.30.c.32.2 to F.30.277 (c) F30.375.32 G.730.367. "A" & "D" Batteries 240th Bde R.F.A (45th Divn) joined RIGHT GROUP and moved into selected positions. MAJOR D.K TWEEDIE R.A (32nd Divn) attached. CAPT A. R. RONEY-DOUGAL M.C R.A rejoined 1st Divn Arty. as a/ Bde Major R.A.	m. 2. M Corps
	9.5.17		MAJOR P. R. MITCHELL rejoined from hospital	

WAR DIARY

INTELLIGENCE SUMMARY

(Erase heading not required.)

HQRS R.A
42ND DIVISION.
SHEET 2

Army Form C. 2118.

Place	Date	Hour	Summary of Events and Information	Remarks and references to Appendices
ROISEL	11.5.17		Batteries 42d Div Arty attached RIGHT GROUP withdrawn from line and return to wagon lines in accordance with 42nd Div Arty Order No 9 (copy attached)	Appendix No 1
			X/42 T.M.B. (medium) proceeded complete to VAUX-EN-AMIENOIS to attend course at 4th Army School of Mortars.	" " " copy
	12.5.17		MAJOR P.R. MITCHELL proceeded on leave to ENGLAND.	
	17.5.17		42nd Division to be relieved by 2nd & 3rd Cavalry Divisions. Infantry reliefs commenced. Artillery reliefs to be carried out in accordance with 42nd Div Arty Order No 10 (copy attached)	Appendix No 2
				" " " copy
	19.5.17	9 p.m.	Artillery reliefs commenced in accordance with programme. 1 Section 73 210, 1 Section C.210 and 1 Gun A.210 withdrawn to wagon lines in relief by R.H.A Batteries of 2nd Cavalry Division	" " " "
	20.5.17	3 a.m. 6 a.m. 3.35 a.m.	Enemy heavily bombarded GUILLEMONT FARM and subsequently attacked. S.O.S signal sent up & 210th Bde R.F.A with assistance from 211th Bde R.F.A put down barrage in defence. Enemy attacked three times but failed in main objective.	" " " copy
		9 p.m.	Relief of 210th Bde R.F.A (less D 210) completed. One section of each Battery 211th Bde R.F.G relieved by section R.H.A Battery of 2nd Cavalry Division and returned to wagon lines	" " " "
			Also Y 42 T.M.B. (medium) attached to 2nd Cavalry Division & moved to MARQUAIX.	" " " "
			to D 210 Bde R.F.A	
	21.5.17		210th Bde R.F.A (less D Battery) and No 1 Section 42nd Div Amm. Col / proceeded (less 4 horses spare with teams & personnel) by march route	" " " "

Army Form C. 2118.

WAR DIARY or **INTELLIGENCE SUMMARY**
(Erase heading not required.)

HDQRS R A
42nd Division

SHEET No 3

Place	Date	Hour	Summary of Events and Information	Remarks and references to Appendices
	21/5/17		To new area XI Corps in accordance with march table attached to Appendix 2. and come under orders of B.G.R.A. 20th Division	" " "
	22/5/17		Relief of 211th Bde R.F.A. completed. 42nd Div A.R.P. handed over to 2nd Cavalry Division R.B.R.A. handed over command to C.R.A. 2nd Cavalry Division HQRA, 211th Bde R.F.A. and 42nd B.C.C. (less No 1 Section) moved by march route to new area in accordance with table attached to Appendix 2 Relief of 20th Div Arty by 210th Bde R.F.A. commenced in accordance with 42nd Div Artillery Order No 11 (copy attached)	Appendix No 3. " " "
	23/5/17		B.G.R.A. assumed command taking over from B.G. R.A. 20th Divn 20th Div A.R.P. at NEUVILLE handed over to 42nd Div Arty. (MAP 1/20,000 57 C SE) Artillery reliefs as in Appendix 3 continued	" " "
	24/5/17		Artillery reliefs completed. 42nd Div Artillery now divided into three groups for tactical purposes RIGHT GROUP consisting of C 210 C 211 and Section D 211 under command of MAJOR J.C. BROWNING D.S.O. CENTRE " " A 211 B 211 and 1 Section D 211 " " LT COL C.E. WALKER T.D D.S.O. LEFT " " A 210 + B 210 " " LT COL A BIRTWISTLE C.M.G	" " "

Army Form C. 2118.

WAR DIARY
INTELLIGENCE SUMMARY

(Erase heading not required.)

Place: HD Qrs R.A. 42nd Divn
SHEET No. 4

Date	Hour	Summary of Events and Information	Remarks and references to Appendices
24.8.17		Major P. R. MITCHELL returned from leave. X.42 T.M Battery returned from course at VAUX-EN-AMIENOIS.	M. o W. insts
26.8.17		Y.42, X.42 and Z.42 T.M Batteries moved from PERONNE to new Divisional area, being billetted at BERTINCOURT.	M. o W. insts
26.8.17		Right Group R.A. relieved by 157th Bde R.F.A. (35th Divn) in accordance with 42nd Divn Artillery Order No. 12 (copy attached) Batteries forming this Group rejoining their own Brigades.	Appendice No. 24
30.8.17			M. o W. insts
31.8.17.		18 pdr Subsection of No. 2 Sect D.A.C. moved to CLAY QUARRY. (37 c y 3 c.d.) to join 5gth D.A.C.	

M. o Mitchell Cupht
Acting/Cmpt. R. a.
for Brig. Champion R.A.
42 Divn

APPENDIX No 1.

SECRET.   Copy No. ......5......

42nd DIVISIONAL ARTILLERY ORDER NO:9.

                                                11th May 1917.

1. (a) The Batteries of 48th Divisional Arty
   at present attached to 42nd Divnl Artillery
   will be withdrawn to their Wagon Lines
   to-night, May 11th, with the exception of
   1 Section of B/240 which will be withdrawn
   on the night of 12th inst.
   O.C.210th Bde R.F.A. will issue the necessary
   orders.

   (b) The remainder of the 48th D.A.C. at
   present attached to 42nd D.A. will be
   withdrawn to BUIRE tonight.
   O.C. 42nd D.A.C. will issue the necessary
   orders.

2. Above Units will march with Echelons full.

3. O.C. 210th Bde R.F.A. will arrange for a
   guard to be put on any ammunition left
   dumped at the vacated battery positions and
   will inform the B.C.R.A. as to how many of
   these rounds he is taking over and how many
   are required to be withdrawn to A.R.P.

4. ACKNOWLEDGE.

                                        P.R.Mitchell
                                            Major.
                                        Brigade Major, R.A.
                                        42nd Division.

Issued at... 4-20 PM.
By............ Orderly......

Copy No.1. to 210th Brigade R.F.A.
  "   2. " 42nd Div. Amm. Column.
  "   3. " 48th Divisional Artillery.
  "   4. " 42nd Division.
  "   5. " FILE.

SECRET.

APPENDIX No 2

BM 16.

22

S E C R E T   Copy No.........

42nd DIVISIONAL ARTILLERY ORDER No.10.

Reference map 1/40,000,
Sheets 57c. and 62c.   16-5-17.

1. The 2nd Cavalry Division (less Artillery) will relieve the 42nd Division (less Artillery) on the nights May 16th/17th to 18th/19th.
   G.O.C., 2nd Cavalry Division will take over command of the line at 9 a.m. on 19th instant at which hour 42nd D.H.Q. will close at K.11.a.7.9. and re-open at FLAMICOURT (PERONNE).

2. 42nd Divisional Artillery will be relieved by the R.H.A. of 2nd and 3rd Cavalry Divisions and 296th Brigade R.F.A. of 59th Division on the nights of May 19th/20th to 21st/22nd in accordance with Table 'A'. 42nd Divisional Artillery will relieve the 20th Divisional Artillery on May 22nd/23rd to 24th/25th.
   The C.R.A. 2nd and 3rd Cavalry Division will take over from the C.R.A., 42nd Division at 10 a.m. May 22nd at which hour the Divisional Artillery H.Q. will close at K.11.a.8.6. and re-open at LITTLE WOOD YTRES.

3. D/210th Battery R.F.A. will remain and be attached to the 2nd Cavalry Division.
   4 wagons of the howitzer sub-section of No.1 Section D.A.C. will remain and be attached to D/210 for ammunition supply.
   The wagon lines of D/210 will be moved on 21st May to the position vacated by A/210 in order to be nearer the battery.

4. On relief the 42nd Divisional Artillery will march by Brigades according to Table 'A' attached.
   19th Mobile Veterinary Section will accompany the 210th Brigade, R.F.A.
   No.1 Section D.A.C. will march with 210th Brigade R.F.A., and be under orders of O.C., 210th Brigade, R.F.A.
   When on the march distances of 400 yards will be kept between batteries.

5. 210th Brigade, R.F.A. less D/210 will fill their Echelons from the ammunition at their present gun positions. Any ammunition left behind will be collected in one dump at each battery position. It will be handed over to relieving R.H.A. Batteries and subsequently collected by the 296th Brigade, R.F.A. Receipts will be taken.
A statement showing the quantity and nature of ammunition left, giving map references, will be forwarded to this office by 9 a.m. on 21st instant together with the daily statement showing the amount and nature of ammunition remaining on charge of Units.

The 211th

- 2 -

The 211th Brigade R.F.A. will leave all ammunition in present gun positions and hand over to relieving batteries. They will fill their Echelons from the A.R.P. by the morning of May 22nd receipts will be taken for ammunition handed over and details of amount and nature of ammunition handed over will be forwarded to this office by 9 a.m. on 22nd inst., together with the statement of amount and nature of ammunition remaining on charge of Units.

The D.A.C. will move with Echelons full drawing any ammunition required to complete from the A.R.P. before moving. Statement of amounts and nature of ammunition on charge of D.A.C. will reach this office by 9 a.m. on the 22nd instant.

6. Telephone lines, battery map boards, maps and papers referring to the present front will be handed over to the incoming Brigades and batteries.

7. Units will go out with full establishment of wire.

8. Brigade Commanders and Battery Commanders will hand over Command ~~at 12 noon on the day after their 1st Sections have been relieved,~~ when relief is complete.

9. The 59th Divisional Artillery will take over the 18 pounder and 4.5" howitzer ammunition at the 42nd Division A.R.P. at noon 21st instant. Statement of ammunition handed over will be sent to this office immediately on completion.

The 2nd Cavalry Division will take over the S.A.A., grenades etc., at the A.R.P. at a date to be notified later.

Instructions as to taking over 20th Division A.R.P. will be issued later.

10. Tents and shelters will be removed to the new area. Trench stores, area stores and huts will be handed over to relieving Units

Transport arrangements will be notified later. A dump for the Division will be formed in an Adrian hut at VILLERS FAUCON. All stores surplus to what can be carried and for which additional transport cannot be immediately provided will be stored there.

42nd D.A.C. will detail an officer and each battery or Section, D.A.C. one storeman only to remain in charge.

All ranks of this party will be provided with 7 days rations.

11. Supply refilling points will be notified later.

12. ACKNOWLEDGE.

Major, R.A.
a/B.M., R.A., 42nd Division.

Issued at...............

Issued at... 9 am
On... 16/5/17
By... D.R.L.S.

```
Copy No. 1 to 5.  to 210th Brigade, R.F.A.
         6 to 10.  "  211th Brigade, R.F.A.
        11 to 14.  "  42nd D.A.C.
        15.        "  42nd D.T.M.O.
        16.        "  Staff Captain, R.A., 42nd Division.
        17.        "  IIIrd Corps R.A.
        18.        "  42nd Division.
        19.        "  59th Divisional Artillery.
        20.        "  20th Divisional Artillery.
        21.        "  S.S.O., 42nd Division.
        22.        "  War Diary.
        23.        "  FILE.
        24         "  R.H.A. 2nd + 3rd Cavalry Divn.
```

TABLE 'A'.

Date of relief.	Units relieved.	Relieving Units.	Place to which Units withdrew. on relief.	Date of moving to 20th Division area	Date of going into action in 20th Division area.
Nights of:-					
19th/20th May	1 Section of each 18 pdr Bty of 210th Bde R.F.A.	R.H.A. of 2nd & 3rd Cavalry Divisions	Present wagon lines		To YTRES on 21st, Route LIERAMONT-NURLU-ETRICOURT. NOT to enter LIERAMONT before 12 noon.	May 22nd/23rd
20th/21st May	Remainder of 210th Bde R.F.A. less D/210.	- do -	- do -		) To YTRES on 22nd Route LIERAMONT-NURLU-ETRICOURT.	May 23rd/24th
20th/21st May	1 Section of each Bty of 211th Bde,R.F.A.	296th Brigade, R.F.A.	- do -		)	May 23rd/24th
21st/22nd May	Remainder of 211th Bde R.F.A.	- do -	- do -		)	May 24th/25th
22 20th/21st	1st Sect D.A.C.	None			) To BUS on 21st with 210th Bde RFA.	
21st May 20th/21st	2nd Sect D.A.C.	59th D.A.C.			To BUS on 22nd.	
	Hqrs & 'B' Echelon D.A.C.	None			To YTRES on 22nd Route as above.	
	T.M. Personnel at present at PERONNE.	None			To YTRES on 21st.	

※ March orders follow

APPENDIX No 3

SECRET.

Copy No...........

ORDER
42nd DIVISIONAL ARTILLERY/No.11.

Reference 1/40,000, Sheet 57c and 62c.

18-5-1917.

----

1. 42nd Division will relieve the 20th Division now holding the front HAVRINCOURT WOOD - VILLERS PLUICH, starting on the night 19th/20th and completing on the night 24th/25th inst.

   The 20th Division front is held by three brigades in the line, each Brigade with three battalions in the line and one Brigade in reserve.

   One Field Company is allotted to each Brigade front.

   The Artillery is divided into three groups, one covering each Brigade front.

   There are two Field Ambs. in the line, each serving approximately one half of the Divisional front; the third Field Amb. is in Corps employ.

2. (i) Inf. Brigades will relieve as follows :-

42nd Division.		20th Division.		Date	Trench
Bdes relieving	Field Coy.	Bde	Field Coy.		Sector.
				May.	
127th	427th	61st	84th	19/20.	Left.
126th	428th	59th	96th	21/22.	Centre.
125th	429th	60th	83rd	22/23.	Right.

   (ii) Advanced dressing stations will be at :-

   RUYAULCOURT., NEUVILLE., METZ. (Q.20.d.2.2.)

3. (i) 20th Divisional Artillery is distributed into three groups, these will be relieved by the Artillery Brigades of the 42nd Division according to Table "A".
   (ii) C.R.A., 42nd Division will take over Command of the Artillery covering the Division at 10 a.m. May 23rd.
   (iii) The 20th Divisional Artillery will come under the orders of G.O.C., 42nd Division until relieved.

4. (i) No movements are to take place East of the BROWN Line of defence, running through RUYAULCOURT - NEUVILLE - METZ and Q.29.a. before 9 p.m.
   (ii) Any local Brigade orders regarding intervals between units will be complied with.
   (iii) The progress of reliefs (including that of Artillery) will be reported daily to D.H.Q.

5. All telephone wires, battery map boards, maps and papers x connected with the front will be handed over, also trench stores.

6. Pending the issue of a defence scheme by this Division Brigades will act in accordance with the orders contained in 20th Divisional Defence Scheme and 20th Division Orders Nos. 171 and 174, copies of which should be taken over from Brigades when relieving.

7. The G.O.C., 42nd Division will take over Command of the line from the G.O.C., 20th Division at 10 a.m. May 23rd at which hour 42nd D.H.Q. will close at FLAMICOURT (PERONNE) and open at LITTLE WOOD South of YTRES (P.28.b.5.0).

8. Divisional Artillery Reliefs will be carried out in accordance with Table "A" attached.

9. ACKNOWLEDGE.

Major, R.A.
a/B.M., R.A., 42nd Division.

Issued at ....
On............................
By............................

Copy No.1 to 5. to 210th Brigade R.F.A.
   6 to 10. 211th Brigade R.F.A.
   11 to 14. 42nd D.A.C.
   15. to 42nd D.T.M.O.
   16   Staff Captain, R.A., 42nd Division.
   17   IIIrd Corps R.A.
   18   42nd Division.
   19   20th Divisional Artillery.
   20   S.S.O., 42nd Division.
   21   War Diary.
   22   File.

TABLE. "A".

Unit of (20th D.Art.)	Position	Group	To be relieved by unit of 42nd D.Art.	Night of.

91st Brigade, R.F.A.

A/91 Battery	Q.20.d.3.5.	Centre	A/211	∅ 23/24 & 24/25th
B/91 Battery	Q.13.b.7.3.	Centre	B/211	∅ 23/24 & 24/25th.
C/91 Battery	Q.22.c.7.7.	Right	C/211	∅ 23/24 & 24/25th.
D/91 Battery 1 Scetion	Q.8.d.8.6.	Centre	D/211 1 Section	23/24th.

92nd Brigade, R.F.A.

A/92 Battery	Q.7.a.2.3.	Left.	A/210	∅ 22/23 & 23/24th.
B/92 Battery	Q.1.a.2.3.	Left.	B/210	∅ 22/23 & 23/24th.
C/92 Battery	Q.22.d.4.4.	Right.	C/210	∅ 22/23 & 23/24th.
D/92 Battery 1,Section.	Q.28.b.7.2.	Right.	D/211 1 Section.	23/24th.

NOTE:-
∅ Where two dates are given, one section will be relieved on the first night, and the remaining two sections on the second night.

RIGHT GROUP H.Q. is at Q.27.c.4.3.

CENTRE GROUP H.Q., is at P.18.c.7.6.

LEFT GROUP H.Q., is at P.10.a.2.7.

MARCH TABLE   TABLE "B".

Date.	Unit.	Destination.	Starting point & time of passing it.	Route	Remarks.
21st	210th Bde R.F.A. (less D/Battery)	VALLULART WOOD. V.33.	Cross Roads E.22.d.7.6. 11-30 a.m.	VILLERS FAUCON - LIERAMONT - NURLU - ETRICOURT	O.C.210 Bde will arrange time for 1st Section D.A.C. to start.
	1st Section D.A.C.	BUS		As for 210th Bde to P.32.d.38. thence via LECHELLE.	
	B/210 march by LONGAVESNES to LIERAMONT where it joins 210th Bde				
22nd	211th Bde R.F.A.	VALLULART WOOD. V.33.	Corner of Wood E.28.b.8.8. 11-30 am.	AIZECOURT LE BAS - LIERAMONT - NURLU - ETRICOURT.	
	2nd Section D.A.C.	BUS.	Cross roads E.22.d.7.6. 12-30 p.m.	As for 210th Bde to P.32.d.38. thence via LECHELLE.	
	H.Q., & 'B' Echelon. D.A.C.	YTRES.		Via LONGAVESNES to LIERAMONT where it joins 2nd Section D.A.C.	'B' Echelon will be for the present at ROCQUIGNY with the advanced section at YTRES.

Advanced parties to be sent on in the morning under Brigade and D.A.C. arrangements.

No Unit to enter LIERAMONT before 12 noon.

400 yards distance between Batteries and Sections of D.A.C.

APPENDIX No 4

SECRET.   C O P Y NO:........ 23

42nd DIVISIONAL ARTILLERY ORDER NO:12.

Reference Map 1/40,000 SHEET 57c.   26-5-17.

1. The Right Group, 42nd D.A. will

   (a) be relieved in their present positions by the 157th Bde R.F.A., 35th D.A. on the nights of May 28th/29th and May 29th/30th as follows:-

   May 28th/29th

   One Section C/210 relieved by One Section A/157th.
   One Section C/211   "   " One Section B/157th.
   One Section D/211   "   " One Section D/157th.

   May 29th/30th.

   2 Sections C/210 relieved by 2 Section A/157th.
   2 Sections C/211   "   " 2 Sections B/157th

   O.C. 157th Bde R.F.A. will get in touch with O.C. Right Group 42nd D.A. at Q.27.c.5.3. and make all necessary arrangements with him.

   (b) O.C. 157th Bde R.F.A. will also reconnoitre positions for C/157th and the remaining 2 Sections D/157th and move them into position on the night May 28th/29th.

   (c) As they are relieved the above units of the present Right Group 42nd D.A. will rejoin their own Brigades and move into positions selected by O.C's 210th & 211th Bdes. respectively.

   (d) 157th Bde R.F.A. will move to their new Wagon Lines in VALLULART WOOD in P.33.a. on 27-5-17.
   They should bring all available tents and shelters with them.

2. 157th & 211th Bdes will form the Right and Left Groups covering the eventual 59th Divnl Front.
   They will be under the orders of C.R.A. 42nd Division until 6 a.m. on June 1st when they will come under the orders of C.R.A. 59th Division.

3. O.C. 210th Bde R.F.A. will arrange to form his Brigade (less D/210) into two Groups to cover the Right and Left halves of the 42nd Divisional Front.

4. Group Commanders will arrange schemes for mutual support with the Groups on their Right and Left.

5. All information, maps & existing communications will be handed over to incoming Batteries.

6. Battery Positions, Arcs of Fire, Positions of O.Ps. etc. will be notified to this office as soon as possible.

7. No.2 Section, 42nd D.A.C. will proceed to VALLEES COPSE in V.9.a. under orders of 59th D.A. to be issued later.
They will supply 211th Bde R.F.A.

8. 211th Bde R.F.A. Wagon Lines will remain in VALLULART WOOD.
210th Bde R.F.A. Wagon Lines will move to BERTINCOURT as as soon as the water supply is developed.

9. The present 42nd A.R.P. at NEUVILLE will be handed over to 59th D.A. at noon 1st June, when a new dump will be opened at RUYAULCOURT P.15.b.69. for supply of ammunition to 210th Bde R.F.A.
The Ammunition supply will continue to be maintained by Battery wagons as at present until further notice.

10. Ammunition at gun positions will be handed over to relieving batteries. All echelons will be kept full by drawing from A.R.P. Statements of Ammunition handed over are to reach this office by 9 a.m. on morning following completion of relief of each Battery.
211th Bde R.F.A. will render usual ammunition returns to this office up to and including the return due on June 1st, after which date they will render them to 59th D.A.
157th Bde R.F.A. will render usual daily ammunition returns to this office up to return due on June 1st. Subsequent returns will be sent to 59th D.A.

11. ACKNOWLEDGE.

Issued at...10 pm......
On......30/5/17.........
By......Hand...........

P.R. Mitchell
Major.R.A.
Brigade Major.R.A.
42nd Division.

Copy No. 1 to 3 to 210th Bde R.F.A.
    4 to 6 to 211th Bde R.F.A?
    7 to 8 to 42nd D.A.C.
    9 to 12 to 157th Bde R.F.A.
    13   to 42nd Division 'G'
    14   to 35th D.A.
    15   to 40th D.A.
    16   to 59th D.A.
    17   to R.A. XV CORPS.
    18 to 19 to Right Group 42nd D.A.
    20   to S.C.,R.A. 42nd Division.
    21   to S.S.O. 42nd Division.
    22   to D.T.M.O. 42nd Division.
    23   to WAR DIARY.
    24   to FILE.

Vol 5

CONFIDENTIAL

WAR DIARY

— OF —

HEADQUARTERS R.A
42ⁿᵈ DIVISION.

FROM 1.6.17   TO 30.6.17.

VOLUME 4.

Army Form C. 2118.

HDQRS R.A.
42nd Division.
SHEET 1.

WAR DIARY
INTELLIGENCE SUMMARY
(Erase heading not required.)

Place	Date	Hour	Summary of Events and Information	Remarks and references to Appendices
YPRES.	1.6.17		REFERENCE MAP FRANCE 1/40,000 Sheet 57.C.	
			DISPOSITION OF 42nd DIV ARTY as set out in attached Disposition Report dated 1.6.17.	APPENDIX No 1.
			B.G.R.A. departed on 10 days leave to ENGLAND. Lt Col. A. BIRTWISTLE C.M.G. 210th Bde R.F.A assumed temporary command of 42nd Div Artillery. MAJOR T.C. BROWNING D.S.O assumed temporary command of 210th Brigade R.F.A.	n.T.R.
	4.6.17		C.R.A. attended conference at III Corps Headquarters regarding defence of front in event of an offensive. Instructions as to disposition of Artillery and preparation of new positions received. Copy attached.	APPENDIX No 2. n.T.R.
	5.6.17 to 9.6.17		C.R.A. selected positions in consultation with B.S.F.R.A. and 39th Division. Working party of 110 men detached from Units and placed under command of LIEUT. H.B. ECCLES for preparation of new positions. Work commenced 9.6.17.	n.T.R.
	6.6.17. 8.6.17. 9.6.17.		X/42 T.M.B. (1 Officer 22 O.R.) proceeded to conort at Trench Mortar School YPRIX-LEZ-RAMICOURT. Y/42 T.M.B. rejoined 42nd Division from attachment to 2nd Cavalry Division and billeted at BERTINCOURT. Personnel of Trench Mortar Batteries (X, Y and Z) moved from BERTINCOURT to new quarters in HAVRINCOURT WOOD (P.18.B.18). Work commenced on emplacements for medium batteries at K32 a 85, K32 a 96, Q3 B central, Q3 B 4325 and Q3 a 77.2. Also on preparation of emplacement for heavy trench mortar at K32 a 2.4. LIEUT E. NOTTALL 210th Brigade R.F.A. attached HdQrs R.A	n.3.R.

Army Form C. 2118.

WAR DIARY
or
INTELLIGENCE SUMMARY

HD Qrs RA 42nd Div.

SHEET 2

(Erase heading not required.)

Place	Date	Hour	Summary of Events and Information	Remarks and references to Appendices
ANDENNE YPRES	11.6.17		STAFF CAPT R.A. proceeded on 10 days leave. LIEUT E NUTTALL 210th Bde R.F.A. took over duties as acting Staff Captain.	m.7.70.
IBW	13.6.17		B.G.R.A. rejoined from leave and assumed command of 42nd Div. Arty.	m.7.70.
	19.6.17		Y 42 T.M. Battery rejoined from 4th Army School of Instruction VAUX-EN-AMIENOIS. Y 42 T.M. Battery proceed to same School for course of Instruction.	m.7.70.
	20.6.17		MAJOR H.E. BOONE D.S.O. R.A. posted to command D Battery 211th Bde R.F.A.	m.7.70.
	22.6.17		STAFF CAPT R.A. rejoined from leave.	
	30.6.17.		Preparation of replacement for second Army Trench Burlaw Command at P.3 L.68.	m.7.70.
			DRAFTS received during month -- 143 Other Ranks REMOUNTS " -- 100 Horses L.D. and 64 mules. 1 Section C Battery 296th Brigade R.F.A. posted to D Battery 211th Bde R.F.A. to complete this Battery to 6-gun establishment. To Strong 1R. 2 Officers 65 other ranks 17 Horses 4 Ammunition Wagons 4.5, 1 double cart, 1 Cooks Cart, 1 G.S. Wagon. Section remained at 4th Army Artillery School at disposal of the Commandant and did not join Unit. 1 Section of a 4.5" Battery (PERSONNEL ONLY) transferred from First Army and posted to "D" Battery 210th Brigade R.F.A. to complete the establishment to 6 gun Battery. Joined 25.6.17.	m.7. Staff Capt for BGRA 42 Div

2449 W. W14957/M90 750,000 1/16 J.B.C. & A. Forms/C.2118/12.

APPENDIX No. 1

SECRET.
++++++++

42nd DIVISIONAL ARTILLERY

DISPOSITION REPORT   JUNE 1st 1917.   COPY NO........5.

UNIT	POSITION.	O.Ps.	WAGON LINES.	REMARKS.
HEADQUARTERS. R.A.	P.26.b.3.0.			(1). At present there is only one Group covering the whole of 42nd Divisional Front.
GROUP R.A. (LIEUT. COL. A. BIRTWISTLE. C.M.G).				
Headquarters.	P.10.a.2.8.			(2) 211th Bde R.F.A. (less D/211) at present functioning with 50th Div.
A/210 Bde (5 guns	Q.7.a.1.4.	Q.7.a.1.4.		
(1 gun	T.36.d.9.9.	Q.1.b.5.4.		
B/210 Bde (4 guns	Q.1.a.3.2.	Q.1.b.6.4.	VALLULART WOOD..	(3) Position of Group Wireless Mast:- ~~P.10.b.2.8.~~
(2 guns	Q.1.a.2.7.	Q.9.c.4.4.	(P.33.a & b.)	
C/210 Bde	P.12.d.25.25.	K.52.d.8.0.		(4) D/210 at present attached to 2nd Cavalry Division.
D/211 Bde (2 How's	Q.8.d.8.6.	Q.1.b.6.4.		
(2 How's	Q.7.c.10.45.	Q.9.a.4.4.		(5) A.R.P. at RUYAULCOURT,
		Q.1.d.3.6.		(P.15.b.7.8.)
TRENCH MORTAR BATTERIES.				
V/42. (no guns).	LEBUCQUIERE.			(6) T.M.B. Y/42. attached to 2nd Cavalry Division.
X/42.	(P.7.b.)			
Z/42.				
42nd D.A.C. H.Q.	BUS. (O.24).			
No.1. Section.				
No.2. Section.	ROCQUIGNY(O.27)			
'B' Echelon.				

DISTRIBUTION:- Copies to :-

No.1. C.R.A.   No.8. 42nd Division 'Q'.   No.15. 59th D.A.
No.2. B.M., R.A.   No.9. R.A., IIIrd Corps.   No.16. Counter Batteries.
No.3. S.C., R.A.   No.10. H.A., IIIrd Corps.   No.17. 52nd Squadron R.F.C.
No.4. R.O.   No.11. Group R.A.   No.18. 15th Balloon Co.
No.5. War Diary.   No.12. D.T.M.O.   No.19. D.A.D.O.S.
No.6. 42nd Division 'G' 13½ 42nd D.A.C.   No.20. I.O.M., IIIrd Corps.
No.7. Defence Scheme 14.   48th D.A.

1-6-1917.

P.R. Mitchell
Major, R.A.
B.M., R.A., 42nd Division.

APPENDIX

SECRET.
Headquarters,
III Corps.
No. R.A./01/303.

42nd Division.
----

1. In the event of an offensive, the present IIIrd Corps front will be taken over by two Corps.

2. Each Corps will have three Divisions in the front line.

3. Each Division will be covered by four Brigades of Field Artillery formed into two sub-groups of two brigades each.

4. The Heavy Artillery covering each Corps will consist of:-

    6" Gun Batteries 3
    60-pdr Batteries... ... 8
    12" How. (piece) 1
    9.2" or 8" How. Batteries ... 10.
    6" How. Batteries. ... 12.

5. Boundaries between Corps and Divisions and Divisional and Infantry Brigade Headquarters are shewn on the attached map.

6. The map shews approximate, suggested positions which are subject to alteration by the C.R.A's concerned.

    GREEN and RED positions are for the SOUTHERN Corps.
    BLUE and PURPLE   "   "   "   " NORTHERN   " .

7. 35th and 40th Divisional Artilleries will be responsible for the Southern Corps F.A. positions.
    42nd and 59th Divisional Artilleries for the NORTHERN Corps F.A. positions.

8. Sufficient positions to accomodate batteries as in paras. 2,3,and 4 will be selected by Divisional Artilleries and 21st H.A.G.
    Where F.A. and H.A. positions are close together they will be sited under arrangements to be made between the Divisional Artillery concerned and the Heavy Artillery.

9. 42nd Divisional Artillery will reconnoitre positions for two 18-pdr Batteries in the Eastern edge of HERMIES to enfilade HAVRINCOURT. These batteries would not open fire until the commencement of the attack.

10. C.R.As of the Divisions concerned will arrange in conference, as soon as possible, the allotment of O.P's to battery positions and the grouping of batteries on their Corps front to allow of the scheme for cable being commenced.
    Positions for batteries to enfilade the enemy's positions will be taken into consideration.

11. Reports giving the O.P's, Battery positions, and grouping of batteries will be forwarded to the G.O.C.,R.A., IIIrd Corps as early as possible.

- 2 -

12. The positions selected will be marked out and work commenced in the following order:-

    (a) O.Ps (two for each Brigade)
    (b) Trenches for the personnel.
    (c) Protection for the ammunition.

Work will be pushed on as soon as possible and no attempt will be made in (b) or (c) to build elaborate positions.

13. The positions of Sub-Group Headquarters should be close to the Infantry Brigade Headquarters.

14. Two or more officers will be struck off other duties to superintend the work on each Corps front. One of these will be a Battery Commander or an officer senior to a Battery Commander.

These officers will, if necessary, be provided for the NORTHERN Corps front by the Divisional Artillery covering the 59th Division and for the Southern Corps front by the 40th Divisional Artillery.

As many men as can be spared will be employed on this work.

15. The work will be carried out under the supervision of the C.R.As of Divisions as in para.7.

16. ACKNOWLEDGE.

                          (Sgd) M.H.DENDY, Major., R.A.
                              for Brigadier-General,
                                  General Staff,
4-6-17.   IIIrd Corps.

        Copies to:- IIIrd Corps "G"
                   IIIrd Corps "Q"

Vol 6

CONFIDENTIAL

WAR DIARY

OF

HEAD QUARTERS R.A. 42nd DIVISION.

FROM 1 7 17 TO 31 7 17

VOLUME 3.

Army Form C. 2118.

WAR DIARY
or
INTELLIGENCE SUMMARY

(Erase heading not required.)

HD QRS R.A.
42nd DIVISION

SHEET 1.

Place	Date	Hour	Summary of Events and Information	Remarks and references to Appendices
YPRES.			REFERENCE. MAP FRANCE 1/40000. SHEET 57d.	
	1.7.17		Disposition of 42nd Div. Artillery as set out in attached Disposition Report dated 25.6.17.	APPENDIX No 1. m.7.70
	3.7.17.		Preliminary Orders received as to taking over of 42nd Divisional Front by 58th Division. 42nd Div Artillery (less the Small Arm Section of R.A.C.) to remain in present positions. Command of 42nd Divisional Front and Area to be handed over to 58th Division at 10 a.m. on 9th instant. (42nd Reinforcement Order No.27 dated 3.7.17 copy attached)	APPENDIX No 2. m.7.70.
	5.7.17. 4.p.m		Destructive shoot carried out by batteries of 42nd Div Arty in accordance with 42nd Div Artillery Order No 15 copy attached.	APPENDIX No 3. m.7.70.
	6.7.17		Orders issued for move of S.A.A. Section 42nd D.A.C. to new area. Copy attached	APPENDIX No 4. m.7.70.
	9.7.17. 10 a.m.		Command of 42nd Div Artillery handed over to C.R.A. 58th Division. All ammunition in charge of 42nd Div Artillery transferred to 58th Div Arty. 42nd Div A.R.P at Ruyaucourt handed over to 58th Div Arty.	m.7.70.
	10.7.17		HQ R.A. 42nd Div? moved from LITTLE WOOD YPRES (P.26.C.30) to new Headquarters at P.20.C.36.(YPRES). S.A.A Section 42nd D.A.C. moved to new Divisional Area.	m.7.70.

Army Form C. 2118.

WAR DIARY
INTELLIGENCE SUMMARY

HQRS R.A.
SHEET 2
42nd DIVISION

(Erase heading not required.)

Instructions regarding War Diaries and Intelligence Summaries are contained in F. S. Regs., Part II. and the Staff Manual respectively. Title Pages will be prepared in manuscript.

Place	Date	Hour	Summary of Events and Information	Remarks and references to Appendices
YPRES	10/7/17	10 am	Northern half of existing 3rd Corps area passes to 4th Corps. Artillery of 42nd Division now administered as follows :-	
			210th Bde R.F.A. (less D/210) by 58th Division 4th Corps 3rd Army	
			D/210 Bde R.F.A. by 35th Division 3rd Corps 3rd Army.	
			211th Bde R.F.A. by 58th Division 4th Corps 3rd Army.	
			42nd D.A.C. (less S.A.A. section) by 58th Division 4th Corps 3rd Army	
			S.A.A. Sect. 42nd D.A.C. by 42nd Division 6th Corps 3rd Army.	
			42nd Div Trench Mortar Batteries by 58th Division 4th Corps 3rd Army.	
	24/7/17	5 p.m.	210th Bde R.F.A. (less D/210) and one section D/211 Bde R.F.A attached to 3rd Divl R.A. 58th Divl Artillery orders No 2 dated 21.7.17 copy attached.	Appendix No 5
				" " "
	31/7/17		58th Division relieved by 9th Division. 211th Bde R.F.A. (less one section D/211) 42nd D.A.C (less S.A.A section) and 42nd Divl Trench Mortar Batteries came under command of C.R.A. 9th Division. Bgde R.A. 42nd Division remains at YPRES P.20.c.56.	" " "
			DRAFTS from Base during month 12 Other Ranks.	
			REMOUNTS received during month 4 Chargers	
			1 Riding Horse	
			114 Light Draught Horses	
			57 Mules.	
			Two H.5 Hows received from Ordnance to complete B/211 Bde R.F.A. to 6 guns.	

Sgd W Michael Thompson
Lt Col
for Brig Genl R.A.
42nd Division

2449 Wt. W14957/M90 750,000 1/16 J.B.C. & A. Forms/C.2118/12.

APPENDIX No 1.

SECRET.

42nd DIVISIONAL ARTILLERY.

DISPOSITION REPORT.

JUNE 25th 1917.

UNIT.	POSITION	O.Ps.	WAGON LINES.	REMARKS.
Headquarters.R.A.	P.26.b.3.0.			(1) At present there is only one Group covering the whole of 42nd Divisional Front.
Group.R.A. (Lieut Col.A.BIRTWISTLE.,C.M.G.)				
A/210 Bde (5 guns	Q.1.a.0.8.	Q.7.a.1.4.		(2) 211th Bde R.F.A. (less D/211) at present functioning with 59th Divn.
(1 gun	Q.7.a.1.4.	Q.1.b.5.4.		
B/210 Bde (4 guns	J.36.a.9.9.	Q.1.b.6.4.	0.24.d.6.8.	
(2 guns	Q.1.a.3.2.	Q.9.a.4.4.		
C/210 Bde -	Q.1.a.2.7.	K.32.d.8.0.		(3) Position of Group Wireless Mast:- Q.1.c.39. attached to B/210 Battery. Q.1.a.0.9.
D/211 Bde (2 Hows	Q.8.d.55.75.	Q.9.a.4.4.		
(2 Hows	Q.7.c.10.45.	Q.1.d.3.6.	VALLULART WOOD.	
TRENCH MORTAR BATTERIES. (Headquarters)	P.18.b.1.8.			(4) D/210 at present attached to 2nd Cavalry Division.
42nd D.A.C.,H.Q.	BUS. (0.24)			(5) 1 Section D/211 attached Arty School at VAUX.
No.1.Section.				
No.2.Section.	ROCQUIGNY (C.27).			(6) T.M.B. Y/42 at Arty School VAUX.
'B' Echelon.				
A.R.P.	RUYAULCOURT. (P15.b.7.8.)			

DISTRIBUTION:- Copies to :-

C.R.A.	WAR DIARY	R.A.,IIIrd Corps.	L.O.M., IIIrd Corps.
B.M.R.A.	42nd DIVISION.	H.A.,IIIrd Corps.	42nd Div.Signals.
S.C.R.A.	DEFENCE SCHEME.	Group.R.A.(5)	211th Bde R.F.A.
R.O.	42nd DIVISION'Q'	D.T.M.O.	
42nd D.A.C.	40th D.A.	48th D.A.	
		59th D.A.	
		Counter Batteries.	
		59th Squadron R.F.C.	
		15th Balloon Co.	
		D.A.D.O.S.	

25th June 1917.

P.R.Mitchell
Major,R.A.
B.M.,R.A., 42nd Division.

SEEN BY:-
B.G., R.A. ....
B.M., R.A. ....
S.C., R.A. ....
R.O., R.A. ....

APPENDIX No 2.
Extracts to

SECRET

Copy No. 7.

42nd DIVISION ORDER No. 27.

Reference: 1/40,000, Sheet 57c.   3/7/17.

1.   The 58th Division will take over the 42nd Divisional Front and Area on the 7th/8th and 8th/9th inst. and will arrive in the Divisional Area as follows :-

   175th Inf. Brigade Group on the 6th inst., distributed :- Brigade Group (less two Battalions and Field Amb.) at YTRES, two Battalions at BERTINCOURT, and Field Amb. at RUYAULCOURT.

   173rd Inf. Brigade Group on the 9th inst. after 5 p.m., distributed :- Brigade H.Q. and one Battalion at NEUVILLE, one Battalion at RUYAULCOURT, one Battalion at YTRES, and one Battalion in 59th Divisional Area.

2.   The 125th Inf. Brigade Group will march from present Divisional Area on the 6th inst. in accordance with the attached March Table.

3.   The 126th and 127th Inf. Brigade Groups will be relieved by the 175th Inf. Brigade Group on the night 7th/8th and 8th/9th inst. respectively, and, on completion of relief, will march in accordance with the attached March Table.

   Special instructions regarding relief have been issued to those two Brigades.

4.   All maps, papers, defence schemes, intelligence summaries, etc., will be handed over to the incoming units.

5.   The 42nd Division R.A. (less S.A.A. portion D.A.C.) will remain in its present positions until further orders. This includes personnel of the Medium and Heavy Trench Mortar Batteries.

   The S.A.A. Section D.A.C. will march on 10th inst. in accordance with March Table attached.

   Sufficient portion of the Divnl. Train to administer the R.A. will remain at BUS.

- 2 -

6. Command of the 42nd Divisional Front and Area will be handed over to the 58th Division at 10 a.m. on the 9th inst., at which hour Divisional H.Q. will close at LITTLE WOOD, YTRES. It will re-open at ACHIET-LE-PETIT at 2 p.m. same day.

7. ACKNOWLEDGE on attached slip.

Bryan Curling
Lt. Colonel,
General Staff,
42nd Division.

Issued by D.R. at 6 p.m. 3/7/17.
Orderly

Distribution as follows :-

Copy No.		Copy No.	
1.	File.	13.	Supply Column.
2.	War Diary.	14.	A.A. & Q.M.G.
3.	" "	15.	D.A.Q.M.G.
4.	125th Inf. Bde.	16.	A.P.M.
5.	126th Inf. Bde.	17.	S.S.O.
6.	127th Inf. Bde.	18.	D.A.D.O.S.
7.	Divnl. Arty.	19.	Camp Comdt.
8.	Divnl. Engrs.	20.	III Corps.
9.	Signal Coy.	21.	59th Division.
10.	A.D.M.S.	22.	58th Division.
11.	A.D.V.S.	23.	3rd Division.
12.	Divnl. Train.	24.	IV Corps.

MARCH TABLE TO ACCOMPANY 42nd DIVISION ORDER No. 27.

Item No.	Date.	Unit.	From.	To.	Route.	Remarks.
1.	July. 6	125th Inf. Bde. Group, consisting of 125th Inf.Bde., 428th Field Coy. R.E., and 1/2nd E.Lancs.F.Amb.	YTRES and RUYAULCOURT.	GOMIECOURT.	BUS - ROCQUIGNY - LE TRANSLOY - BAPAUME - SAPIGNIES.	Relieved by 175th Inf. Bde. Group. H.Q. and 2 Sections, 428th F.Coy.R.E. will be detached from 125th Inf.Bdo. Column on the march at BAPAUME, and proceed to BIHUCOURT. 1/2nd E.Lancs.F.Amb. to join Group under orders of 125th Inf. Bde.
2.	Night 7/8	H.Q., 126th Inf. Bde. 1 Battn. M.G. Coy. T.M. Btty. 429th F.Coy.R.E.	Line.	YTRES.	Via NEUVILLE.	Relieved by H.Q. and 2 Battns., M.G.Coy., and T.M. Btty., 175th Inf. Bde. If rail accommodation can be arranged for any of these units they will be railed to BUS for Camp at 0.16.
3.	-do-	3 Battns, 126th Inf. Bdo.	Line.	Camp at 0.16.	Rail.	
4.	8	126th Inf. Bde. Group less 3 Battns. at 0.16.	YTRES.	Camp at 0.16.	BUS.	Move to be completed by 7 p.m.
		1/1st E.Lancs. Field Amb.	RUYAULCOURT.	Camp at 0.16.	Via BERTINCOURT.	—do— Under orders of 126th Inf. Bde. to join 126th Inf. Bde. Group.

Item No.	Date.	Unit.	From.	To.	Route.	Remarks.
5.	July. Night 8/9.	127th Inf. Bde. Group less 2 Battns.	Line.	YTRES.	Rail.	Relieved by 2 Battns., 175th Inf. Bde. and detachment of H.G.Coy. and T.M.Bty. If fine, to BUS (instead of YTRES) where they will bivouac until 126th Inf. Bde. Group clears, and then take over their accommodation in Camp O.16. at O.16.
6.	Night 8/9.	1 Battn., 127th Inf. Bde.	Line.	BERTINCOURT.	via RUYAULCOURT.	
7.	9.	126th Inf. Bde. Group.	O.16.	BIHUCOURT.	VILLERS-AU-FLOS – BAPAUME.	To be clear of O.16 by 10 a.m. 429th F.Coy.R.E. will leave column at BAPAUME and march via ACHIET-LE-GRAND & ACHIET-␣-PETIT.
8.	9.	42nd D.H.Q.	YTRES.	ACHIET-LE-PETIT.	VILLERS-AU-FLOS – BAPAUME – ACHIET-LE-GRAND.	
9.	9.	127th Inf. Bde. Group less 2 Battns.	YTRES or BUS.	O.16.		To be clear of YTRES, BERTINCOURT, and RUYAULCOURT by 5 p.m.
10.	9.	1 Battn., 127th Inf. Bde.	BERTINCOURT.	O.16.		
11.	9.	1 Battn., 127th Inf. Bde.	RUYAULCOURT.	O.16.	BUS.	

- 3 -

Item No.	Date	Unit.	From.	To.	Route.	Remarks.
12.	July 10.	127th Inf. Bde. Group.	0.16.	ACHIET-LE-PETIT	VILLERS-AU-FLOS — BAPAUME — ACHIET-LE-GRAND.	427th F.Coy.R.E. will march as far as BAPAUME with the 127th Inf. Bde. Group, whence it will march via SAPIGNIES to GOMIECOURT, to be affiliated with 125th Inf. Bde. Group. 1/3rd E.Lancs.F.Amb. will join column from BUS under orders of G.O.C., 127th Inf. Bde. Group.
13.	10.	2 Sections, 423th F.Coy. R.E.	GOMIECOURT.	BIHUCOURT.		To be affiliated with 125th Inf. Bde. Group.
14.	10.	S.A.A. portion D.A.C.	BUS.	Destination and route to be notified later.		

N.B. The intervals to be kept between Units (i.e. Coys., etc.) on the march as far as 0.15. is left to the discretion of G.O's.C., Inf. Brigade Groups.

On the march beyond 0.15., Battalions, Field Coy/s. R.E., and Field Ambs. will march with their 1st Line Transport closed up. Coy. Trains will march as laid down in Fourth Army Standing Orders.

An interval of 400 yards will be kept between units.

War Diary　　　　　　　　　　　　　　　　　APPENDIX No 3
SECRET.   Copy No.......

42nd DIVISIONAL ARTILLERY ORDER No.15.

Reference: Map 57c.N.E. 1/20,000   5-7-17.

1. Patrols report large enemy working parties and much activity in and around DEAN COPSE (K.32.b.85.70) each night.

2. A destructive shoot will be carried out on this area on the night 5th/6th July.

3. Action of 42nd Divisional Artillery:-

Trench Mortars.

Unit.	Time	Objective	Ammunition.
One Heavy Trench Mortar.	Zero to Zero+ 75	DEAN COPSE. (K.32.b.85.70)	20 rds as quickly as possible -(no fire after Zero + 75)
Two Medium Trench Mortars.	-ditto-	(1) ETNA (K.26.d.9.1.) and vicinity. (2) Eastern Extremity of slag heap (YORKSHIRE BANK) in K.32.a.and.b.	25 rounds per Mortar.

Group.R.A. 42nd Divn.			
A/210.	Zero +½ to Zero +3½	4 Guns - K.33.a.0.4. to K.32.b.60.55. 1 Gun - K.32.b.65.70.	4 rounds per gun per minute. Shrapnel
B/210.	-ditto-	1 Gun - K.27.c.05.50. 1 Gun - K.26.d.95.20.	-ditto-
C/210.	-ditto-	3 Guns- K.33.a.0.8. to K.32.b.75.80. 1 Gun - K.32.b.80.95.	-ditto-
D/211	-ditto-	1 How - K.33.a.8.5. 1 How - K.33.a.20.45 1 How - K.33.a.0.8. 1 How - K.27.c.0.3.	2 rounds per How per minute.

In addition to above batteries will fire bursts of fire at the following times:-
Zero +6, Zero +12, Zero +19, Zero +21, Zero +29, Zero +40, Zero +43, Zero +52, Zero +57, and Zero +74.

  18-pounders -- -- -- 3 rounds per gun (Shrapnel)
  4.5" Hows   -- -- -- 2 rounds per How.

4. Zero Hour is fixed at 11.p.m. July 5th.

5. <u>1st Australian Divn Arty.</u> are also co-operating and will fire 500 rounds of 18 pdr and 100 rds of 4.5" How Ammunition from Zero to Zero + 75 on K.27.c.8.8. to K.26.d.9.8.

6. IIIrd Corps Heavy Artillery are co-operating and will fire salvoes at intervals from Zero to Zero + 60 on :-
(a) K.27.c.8.8. to K.26.d.9.8.
(b) K.33.a.8.5. to K.33.a.0.5.

7. Watches will be synchronized from this office at 7.p.m. 5th July.

8. ACKNOWLEDGE.

                                                          P.R.Mitchell

Issued at... 7 p.m.   Major., R.A.

By.................   B.M.,R.A., 42nd Division.

Copies to:- 42nd Division.
            Group.R.A., 42nd Division.
            D.T.M.O., 42nd Division.
            127th Inf.Brigade.
            R.A., IIIrd Corps.
            21st H.A.G.
            1st Australian Div.Arty.
            59th Div.Arty.
            War Diary. ✓
            File.

SECRET.

APPENDIX No 4

O.C., 42nd D.A.C.

P.R.M.

Reference 1/40,000 Sheet 57c.

(1). The S.A.A. Section of the 42nd D.A.C. will march to the new Divisional Area on the 10th inst. and will camp at ACHIET-LE-PETIT. Route to be taken will be notified later. Captain F. SOWLER will command all S.A.A. details.

(2). Advance party of 1 Officer and 6 other ranks will rendezvous at ROCQUIGNY at 7.30 a.m. on the 9th inst and will proceed with the advance party of the 19th Mobile Veterinary Section by motor lorry to ACHIET-LE-PETIT. Town Major ACHIET-LE-PETIT will point out camp. This party should take two days rations. The Officer in Charge of the advance party will arrange to meet the unit on its arrival and conduct it to the camp.

(3). A rear party of 1 Officer and 10 men will be left to see that the camp is left thoroughly clean and tidy and the Officer i/c will obtain a certificate to this effect from the Town Major before re-joining the unit.

(4). The detached S.A.A. Section now at YTRES under Lieut BEARD will rejoin its unit on 8th inst. The ammunition belonging to this Section which is now dumped at the A.R.P. will be picked up before rejoining.

(5). The following ammunition should be taken :-

	Infantry Bde Reserve	S.A.A.	264,000 rounds.
D.A.C.	For "A" Echelon.	S.A.A.	600,000 rounds.
		Grenades.	4,140.
"	For "B" Echelon.	S.A.A.	680,000 rounds.
	"	Grenades.	1,380.
	"	Stokes Mortar.	720 rounds.

Sufficient wagons will be sent to carry above ammunition, the limbered G.S. Wagons being withdrawn from "A" Echelon if required. In addition, the 3 G.S. Wagons allotted to Infantry Brigades for carriage of Stokes Mortars and ammunition must be taken unless these have previously been sent to join the Infantry Brigades.

and 3 Limbered G S Wagons

(6). Supplies will be drawn at ACHIET-LE-GRAND the day after arrival in the new area.

(7). 58th Division will take over the S.A.A. portion of the A.R.P. at 2 p.m. on the 8th July. Instructions as to taking over the gun ammunition will be issued later. On relief the Infantry details employed at the A.R.P. will be withdrawn and will join No.3. Section 42nd D.A.C. They will accompany this Section to the new area.

(8). Instructions as to disposal of tents etc., will be issued later.

(9). The strictest march discipline will be observed. Distances of 25 yards will be kept between groups of six wagons and 4 yards between all vehicles in the groups. These distances will be carefully watched. Officers and N.C.Os will be continually moving up and down their own portions of the column for this purpose. Outriders will not ride on the left of their vehicles, but in gaps in front or behind them. If a vehicle falls out of its place, it will remain behind the nearest group of six and never close up to its own place until arrival in camp.

P.R. Mitchell
Major, R.A.

6-7-1917.

B.M., R.A., 42nd Division.

Copies to :- 42nd Div. "G", 42nd Div "Q" & O.C., 42nd Div Train.A.S.C.

SECRET.   Copy No. ...5...

58th DIVISIONAL ARTILLERY ORDER NO. 2.

1. The 210th Brigade R.F.A., less D Battery, with 1 Section D/211th Battery R.F.A., will reinforce the 3rd Divisional Artillery on the nights 21st/22nd, 22nd/23rd, 24th/25th and 25th/26th July 1917.

2. The reinforcement will be carried out as follows :-

   (a) Night of 21st/22nd July.

   1 Section B/210th Battery will move to the position vacated by 6th Battery.

   1 Section A/211th Battery will move to the position vacated by B/210th Battery.

   (b) Night of 22nd/23rd July.

   Remainder of B/210th Battery will move to the position vacated by 6th Battery.

   Remainder of A/211th Battery will move to the position vacated by B/210th Battery.

   (c) At 5.0 p.m., 24th July.

   A/210th Battery will come under the command of the 3rd Divisional Artillery.

   Lt. Col. A. Birtwistle, C.M.G., Commanding 210th Brigade R.F.A. will relinquish command of the Left Group, and, with his Headquarters, will come under the command of the 3rd Divisional Artillery.

   Major H.G. Boone, D.S.O., temporarily commanding 211th Brigade R.F.A. will assume command of the remaining batteries of the Left Group.

   (d) Night of 24th/25th July.

   1 Section C/210th Battery will move to the position vacated by 23rd Battery.

   1 Section D/211th Battery will move to the position vacated by 130th Battery.

   (e) Night of 25th/26th July.

   Remainder of C/210th Battery will move to the position vacated by 23rd Battery.

3. All positions will be left camouflaged by the Batteries vacating them.

4. All telephone wires will be left in position and labelled by outgoing Batteries.

5. Orders for re-distribution of the Divisional Front will be issued later.

6. Ammunition /

2.

6. Ammunition left by B/290th Battery will be handed over to A/211th Battery.
Ammunition left by C/210th Battery will be collected by 42nd Divisional Ammunition Column and returned to the Dump at RUYAULCOURT.
Officers Commanding the Batteries concerned and the 42nd Divisional Ammunition Column will report to this office by wire, the amounts handed over or received.

7. ACKNOWLEDGE.

S. H. Hurst
Major,
for Brigade Major, R.A.,
58th Divisional Artillery.

H.Q.R.A.,
21st July 1917.
Issued at 8 p.m.

Copies to :-   Copy No. :-

290th Bde. R.F.A.   1
291st Bde. R.F.A.   2
210th Bde. R.F.A.   3
211th Bde. R.F.A.   4
42nd Div. Artillery.   5
42nd Div. Amm Column.   6
R.A., IVth Corps   7
H.A., IVth Corps   8
No. 14 H.A. Group   9
58th Division "G"   10
174th Infy. Bde.   11
175th Infy. Bde.   12
3rd Divisional Artillery   13
40th Divisional Artillery   14
Staff Captain, R.A.   15
War Diary   16 - 17
File   18 - 19

Vol 7

CONFIDENTIAL.

WAR DIARY

of

H.Q. R.A. 42nd Division.

From 1-8-17 to 31-8-17

Vol VI.

WAR DIARY or INTELLIGENCE SUMMARY

Army Form C. 2118.

(Erase heading not required.)

Instructions regarding War Diaries and Intelligence Summaries are contained in F. S. Regs., Part II. and the Staff Manual respectively. Title Pages will be prepared in manuscript.

Place	Date	Hour	Summary of Events and Information	Remarks and references to Appendices
YPRES	August 1917		Ref. Map 20,000 57O N.E. & S.E. Sheet I.	
			H.Q. R.A. 42nd Div't at YPRES – R.20.c.5.7.6.	R.P.M.
			210th Bde R.F.A. attached to 3rd Div. Arty	
			211th " " " " "	
			42nd T.M.Bde " " " "	
"	4th		211th " " attached to 40th D.A.	P.R.M.
"	5th		210th " " attached to 9th D.A.	P.R.M.
"	19th		210th Bde to wagon lines at BUS	P.R.M.
"	22nd		211th " to wagon lines at YPRES	P.R.M.
"	25th		210th " entrained at BAPAUME for PROVEN, 211th at PERONNE for GODEWAERSVELDE	P.R.M.
"	26th		42nd Div. Arty concd in WATOU area – B.G.R.A. 42nd Div'n assumed command of 42nd D.A. again.	P.R.M.
"	28th		210th Bde relieves 70th Bde } in the line, East of YPRES, coming under	
" & 29th			211th " " 71st Bde } command of 13th Div. Arty.	P.R.M.

P.R. Whitelock
Maj. B.M. R.A. 42nd Div.
1–9–17.

CONFIDENTIAL

WAR DIARY

of

H.Q. R.A. 42nd Divn.

From 1-9-17 to 30-9-17

Vol. VII.

WAR DIARY or INTELLIGENCE SUMMARY

Army Form C. 2118.

Sheet I.

Place	Date	Hour	Summary of Events and Information	Remarks and references to Appendices
YPRES	Sept 1		Ref^{ce} Map 20,000 57. C.N.E. & S.E. 42nd Div^l. Art^y. settle under command of 15th Div. Art^y.	App^x I.
	2nd		C.R.A. 42nd Divⁿ assumes command of H.A.R. Div. Art^y. H.Q.R.A. at BRANDHOEK 210th B^{de} R.F.A. } in action East of YPRES in POTIZE Road. 211th " " }	
	3rd 4th 5th 6th		Captⁿ H.B. Eccles attached to H.Q.R.A. as Acting Reconnaissance Officer. Continuous harassing fire & barrages on the enemy. Attack by 165 B^{de} on IBERIAN, BECKHOUSE & BORRY FARM. - Our troops driven out by enemy counterattack in afternoon.	App^x II.
	7th 6 19th		Constant Harassing fire carried out with practice barrages & bombardments. On the night 16/17 & 17/18. the 9th Divⁿ relieved the 42nd in the line.	App^x III.
	20th		At 10 a.m. command of the Art^y covering the 9th Divⁿ front passed to C.R.A. 9th Div.	
	30th		42nd D.A. come out of the line & marches to WORMHOUDT.	App^x IV.

P.R. Mitchell
Major. Bn. R.A.
1-10-17

SECRET. App I.   Copy No. 15   File

15th DIVISIONAL ARTILLERY ORDER NO.92.

Headquarters,
15th Divl. Artillery,
28th August 1917.

1. The 15th Divisional Artillery will be relieved in the line on 28th, 29th and 30th August.
   Reliefs to be completed by 6 am. 30th instant.

2. On relief 15th Divisional Artillery will march to WATOU area. March Table to follow.

3. The 70th Brigade R.F.A. will be relieved by 210th Brigade R.F.A., and 71st Brigade R.F.A. by 211th Brigade R.F.A., as follows:-

Relieving Unit.	Unit relieved.	Gun Position.	Wagon Lines.
H.Q. 210th Bde. R.F.A.	H.Q., 70th Bde. R.F.A.	I.8.d.1.8.	
A/210th Bde.RFA.	A/70th Bde.R.F.A.	I.3.d.45.75.	)
B/210th Bde.RFA.	B/70th Bde.R.F.A.	I.3.d.45.80.	) G.10.b.
C/210th Bde.RFA.	C/70th Bde.R.F.A.	I.3.a.50.10.	)
D/210th Bde.RFA.	D/70th Bde.R.F.A.	I.3.d.80.40.	)
H.Q., 211th Bde. R.F.A.	H.Q., 71st Bde. R.F.A.	I.8.d.1.8.	
A/211th Bde.RFA.	A/71st Bde.R.F.A.	I.4.c.55.40.	G.15.b.5.6.
B/211th Bde.RFA.	B/71st Bde.R.F.A.	I.4.c.95.60.	G.15.b.5.7.
C/211th Bde.RFA.	C/71st Bde.R.F.A.	I.4.c.90.75.	G.11.c.3.1.
D/211th Bde.RFA.	D/71st Bde.R.F.A.	I.5.d.57.39.	G.12.c.0.0.
42nd D.A.C.	15th D.A.C.	G.17.a.9.4.	

4. Guns will not be exchanged.
   All aeroplane and panorama photographs, log books, maps, telephone lines, etc. will be handed over on relief.

5. One Officer and 3 telephonists from each Battery of 42nd Divisional Artillery will arrive at Battery positions of 15th Divisional Artillery on 28th instant.

6. One section per battery will be relieved on night of 28th/29th. Reliefs will be completed on night of 29th/30th. Hour of relief each night will be notified later.
   On relief personnel and guns will withdraw to their wagon lines.
   No guns of 15th Divisional Artillery Batteries will be withdrawn until the relieving guns have arrived on the position.

7. Ammunition.
   Vehicles will march full of ammunition - 75% shrapnel, 25% H.E.

8. On completion of relief Lt. Col. C.E. Walker, D.S.O, RFA. will assume command of Right Sub-group.

9. All other details will be arranged between Brigade Commanders concerned.

10. The 15th Divisional Trench Mortar Batteries will be relieved by those of 42nd Division on 29th instant, under arrangements to be made between Divisional Trench Mortar Officers concerned.
    The 15th Divisional Trench Mortar Officer will hand over two 9.45" Trench Mortars (one is in action at C.30.b.2.0) and three 6" trench mortars.

1.

11. Completion of each portion of the relief will be reported by wire to this Office.
   Code word:- BRISTOL.

12. The G.O.C.,R.A.,15th Division will remain in command of the Artillery covering the 15th Division till further orders.

E Boyce
Major R.A.,

28/8/17.   Brigade Major 15th Divisional Artillery.

DISTRIBUTION:-
Copy No. 1. to 70th Brigade R.F.A.
         2. to 71st Brigade R.F.A.
         3. to 15th D.A.C.
         4. to 15th Divl.T.M.O.
         5. to 15th D.A.Signals.
         6. to 15th Division.
         7. to 15th Division "Q".
         8. to A.D.M.S.,15th Divn.
         9. to A.P.M.,15th Divn.
        10. to D.A.D.V.S.,15th Divn.
        11. to D.A.D.O.S.,15th Divn.
        12. to 15th Divnl.Train.
        13. to S.S.O.,15th Divn.
        14. to 15th Divn.Signals.
        15. to 42nd Divl.Arty.
        16. to XIX Corps R.A.
        17. to XIX Corps H.A.
        18. to Staff Captain.

APPENDIX A.

MARCH TABLE TO ACCOMPANY 15th DIVISIONAL ARTILLERY ORDER NO.92.

Date.	Units in order of march.	From.	To.	Route.	Starting Point.	Time.	Remarks.
28th.	Gun Limbers of 1 Secn. per Bty. of 71st Bde.R.F.A.	Wagon Lines.	Gun Position.	YPRES Main Road.	Cross Roads, H.7.c. 5.5.	6 pm.	Guns of 211th Bde.R.F.A. march up in rear of 71st Bde.R.F.A.
	Gun Limbers of 1 Secn. per Bty. of 70th Bde.R.F.A.	-do-	-do-	-do-	-do-	6.25 pm.	Guns of 210th Bde.R.F.A. march up in rear of 70th Bde.R.F.A. 300 yards will be maintained between Sections.
29th.	Gun Limbers of 2 Secns. per Bty. of 71st Bde.R.F.A.	-do-	-do-	-do-	-do-	6 pm.	
	Gun Limbers of 2 Secns. per Bty. of 70th Bde.R.F.A.	-do-	-do-	-do-	-do-	6.50 pm.	

MARCH TABLE TO ACCOMPANY 15th DIVISION L ARTILLERY ORDER NO.92.

APPENDIX B.

Date.	Units in order of March.	From.	To.	Route.	Starting Point.	Time.	Remarks.
29th.	1 Secn.per Bty.of 70th Bde.R.F.A.	Wagon Lines	WATOU Artillery Area	Cross Roads G.17.c.3.9 BUSSEBOOM G.15.b.1.6	Cross Roads G.17.c.3.9.	8 am.	300 yards will be maintained between sections or sub-sections of D.A.C.
	1 Secn.per Bty.of 71st Bde.R.F.A.	-do-	-do-	G.20.a.4.5 HOPOUTRE HILLHOEK	-do-	8.30 am.	
	15th D.A.C.	-do-	-do-	L.14.b.2.1. K.24.b.9.0.	-do-	11 am.	(To move by sub-sections, move to be completed by (4 pm.
30th.	70th Bde.R.F.A. less 1 Secn.per Battery.	-do-	-do-	Cross Roads G.5.d.0.2 Switch Rd.N.of POPERINGHE	Road Junction G.11.c.6.2.	10.15 am.	
	71st Bde.R.F.A. less 1 Secn.per Battery.	-do-	-do-	ST.JANS-TER-BIEZEN.	-do-	10.55 am.	

SECRET.   Copy No.........

                    42nd Divisional Artillery Warning Order No.3.

                                                            3rd Sept. 1917.

Reference: FREZENBERG SHEET, 1/10,000.
----

1. The 125th Infantry Brigade will attack and capture the strong points in the neighbourhood of BORRY FARM, BECK HOUSE and IBERIAN on 'Z' Day. The 61st Division is attacking GALLIPOLI on the same day and at the same time.

2. Details of Heavy Artillery bombardment, of the creeping and protective barrage, and of the smoke screens to be put up by the R.F.A. and the Special Cos.R.E. on 'Z' day, are given in Programme A. Appendix A, and the barrage map. Appendix B.
The barrage map will be issued later.

3. A Staff Officer of the 42nd Divisional R.A. will visits Formation 'Y' day at times to be notified later for the purpose of synchronising watches.

4. 'Z' day and Zero hour will be notified later.

                                                    P.R. Mitchell
                                                    Major., R.A.
                                                    B.M., R.A., 42nd Division.

Issued by... D R L S...
at.. 1100 .... 4-9-17.

Distribution as follows:-

Copy No.1.- 5 RIGHT GROUP.
        6 - 10 CENTRE GROUP.
        10 -15 LEFT GROUP.
            16 S.C.R.A.
            17 D.T.M.O., 42nd Divn.
            18 D.T.M.O., 5th Aust.D.A.
            19 61st D.A.
            20 FILE.

APPENDIX A.

P R O G R A M M E A.

1st Day.	2.30.a.m.	Projection of gas on to BORRY FARM, BECK HOUSE and IBERIAN by Special Cos.R.E.
	4.30 a.m. to 6.30 a.m.	Occasional gas shell by 4.5" Hows on objectives to be attacked, and on other targets in the vicinity.
	7.0 a.m.	Bombardment of selected targets by flanking Corps artillery.
	Zero - 15 to Zero.	Intensive bombardment of three objectives with 6" Hows.
	Zero - 15 for 1 hour.	Smoke barrage on line D.26.a.35.70. - BILBEN REDOUBT - D.20.a.5.5., from D.26.d.0.0. towards Brick Kiln and Yard, and also to blot out PIT WORK and VAMPIR.
	Zero	Creeping barrage comes down in front of our trenches and lifts 100 yards every 5 minutes, eventually forming protective barrage beyond objectives.
	Zero	6" Hows lift to form a protective barrage beyond the line on which the 18-pdr. protective barrage will eventually rest.
	Zero.	4.5" Hows. Bombardment of certain selected points too close to objectives for 6" Hows to shoot at.
	Zero.	Smoke Screen on and just beyond BORRY FARM, BECK HOUSE and IBERIAN from mortars of Special Cos.R.E.

SECRET.   Copy No. 52

42nd DIV ARTY GROUP ORDER No 22.

(Reference 42nd D.A. Warning Order No.3.)

Reference: FREZENBERG SHEET 1/10,000, Edition 3,

---

1. (a) <u>The "Creeping" Barrage</u>, (Map attached) will be carried out by the 18-pdr batteries of Right, Centre and Left Sub-Groups, less the 5th Aust. D.A.

   Right Sub-Group.   J.2.c.75.85. to D.25.b.75.02.

   Centre Sub-Group. D.25.b.75.02 to D.19.d.05.05.

   Left Sub-Group.   D.19.d.05.05. to D.19.b.00.35.

   (b) The "Creeping" Barrage will be put down at Zero and will make the first lift at Zero plus 5 minutes.
   Thereafter lifts will be as shown on the map (approximately 100 Yards each lift) every 5 minutes until the Protective Barrage line is reached.

   (c) It will be noted, with regard to the barrage map, that owing to the kicking off point of the Infantry attacking BECK HOUSE being further withdrawn from the main barrage line than is the case with the attacks on IBERIAN and BORRY FARM, a seperate small barrage about 120 yards long, is superimposed on the main barrage and starting 100 yards in rear of it.
   This will be formed by one Battery of the Left Sub-Group.

   (d) <u>Ammunition "Creeping" Barrage.</u>

   Time Shrapnel with long corrector (60% on graze)

   <u>Protective Barrage.</u>

   $\frac{1}{2}$ Time Shrapnel with long corrector.
   $\frac{1}{2}$ H.E.

   (e) <u>Rates of Fire.</u>

   Zero to Zero +10   -   - 4 rounds per gun per minute
   Zero +10 to Zero +20 -   - 3 rounds per gun per minute
   Zero +20 onwards   -   - 2 rounds per gun per minute.

2. <u>A Standing Barrage</u> will be formed by the 4.5" How Batteries of all Brigades in accordance with Appendix A.

3. <u>A Smoke Barrage</u> will be formed by the 18-pdr Batteries of the 13th and 14th Bdes Aust F.A. as follows:-

   (a) 14th Bde.   D.26.c.30.90. to D.26.a.70.85.
       (2 Batteries)

   (b) 13th Bde.   D.26.a.70.85. to D.20.a.5.5.
       (3 Batteries)

para 3 cont/d

    (c) 14th Bde   Blotting out BIT WORK and VAMPIR.
        (1 Section)

    (d) 14th Bde   D.26.d.20.15. to D.26.d.9.4.
        (1 Section)

    (e) 14th Bde.   D.27.c.7.7. to D.27.b.2.1.
        (1 Section)

TIME   Zero - 15 to Zero + 45 for all the above Smoke barrages.

AMMUNITION. (a) 1800 rds Smoke shell
               (b) 2600 rds   "   "
               (c) 200 rds   "   "
               (d) 200 Rds   "   "
               (e) 200 rds   "   "

    Care will be taken to screen the actual lines indicated which may necessitate range or line being altered slightly according to which way the wind is blowing.

4.   Three 9.45" T.Ms will fire as many rounds as possible within the limits of time laid down as follows:-

1 H.T.M. Zero - 15 to Zero + 5 - - - D.25.b.1.5.
1 H.T.M. Zero - 15 to Zero + 5 - - - BECK HOUSE.
1 H.T.M. Zero - 15 to Zero +15 - - - BORRY FARM.

5.   REGISTERING.

Sub-Groups and T.Ms will register carefully on 5/9/17.

6.   Zero day and time will be notified later.

7.   ACKNOWLEDGE.

                                          P.R. Mitchell
                                              Major., R.A.
                                     B.M., R.A., 42nd Division.

Issued by.. D.R.L.S.
At. Barr. on 5/9/17
Copies as under.
  Nos.1 to 10   Right Sub-Group.
     11 " 24   Centre Sub-Group.
     25 to 38   Left Sub-Group.
     39 to   42nd Division.
     40 to   R.A.XIX Corps.
     41 to   XIX Corps H.A.
     42 to 44   125th Inf Bde.
     45 to   S.C.R.A.
     46 to   61st D.A.
     47 to   25th D.A.
     48 to   D.T.M.O. 5th Aust D.A.
     49 to   D.T.M.O. 42nd Div.
     50 to   H.A. Liaison Officer.
     51 to   42 Div (Spare copy)
     52 to   War Diary
     53 to   File.

Appendix A.

Programme of 4.5" How. Standing Barrages.
(to accompany 42nd D.A.G. Order No.22.)

UNIT.	No of Batteries.	Task	Time From	Time To	Rates of Fire	
Right Sub-Group.	1 Battery	POTSDAM (D.26.c.4.8.)	Zero	Zero + 60	2 rds p.h.p.m. till Zero 30 - 1 rd p.h.p.m. onwards.	
Centre Sub-Group.	1 Battery	VAMPIR	Zero	Zero + 60	As above	
	1 Battery	BIT WORK	Zero	Zero + 60	As above	
	1 Battery	(a) Dug-outs at D.25.b.87.75	Zero	Zero + 20	2 rds p.h.p.m.	3 Hows on each.
		(b) " " " D.25.b.95.63	Zero	Zero + 20	2 rds p.h.p.m.	
Left Sub-Group.	1 Battery	Dug-outs at D.19.d.60.75	Zero	Zero + 30	2 rds p.h.p.m.	
	1 Battery	DELVA FARM	Zero	Zero + 60	2 rds p.h.p.m. till Zero 30 - 1rd p.h.p.m. onwards.	

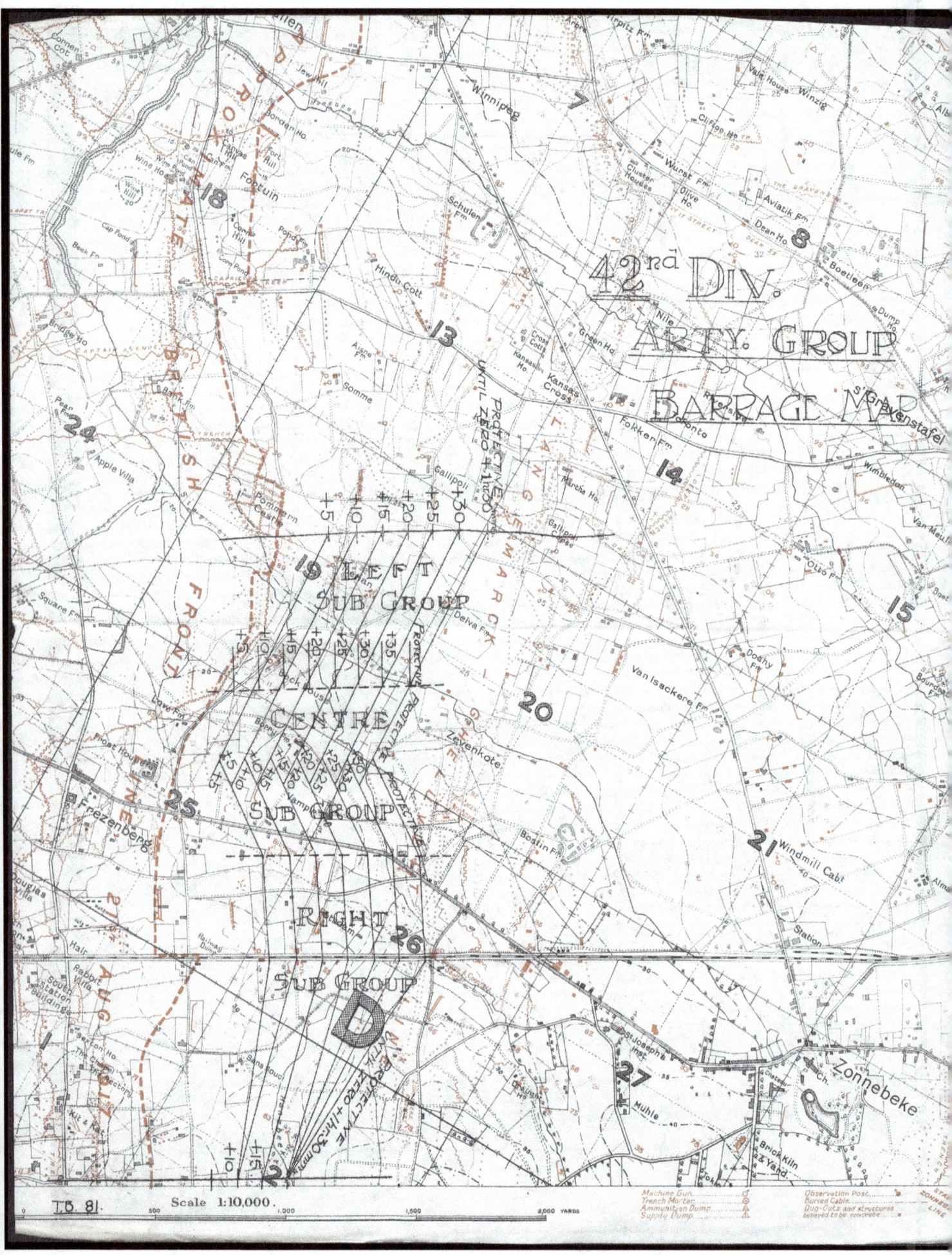

SECRET.

A/L × 3

EXTRACT FROM 42nd DIVISION ORDER NO:36.

13th Sept. 1917.

Reference : FREZENBERG Sheet.
$\frac{1}{20,000}$ Map. 28 N.W.

1. x x x x x x x x

2. On the night 16th/17th and 17th/18th Sept., the 9th Division will relieve the 42nd Division in the line.

3. As a preparatorary measure to this relief, the 125th Infantry Brigade will hand over to the 55th Division on their left that portion of their line North of XXX ZONNEBEKE Stream, from D.19.c.80.73 to D.19.a.70.15.
   On the same night, the 125th Infantry Brigade will also hand over to the 126th Infantry Brigade that portion of their front line from the YPRES-ROULERS Railway (exclusive) to the Road which runs from D.26.a.3.0. to D.25.d.40.45. inclusive.
   The Inter-Brigade Boundary will then run from D.25.d.40.45. to the Centre of WILDE WOOD at I.6.b.6.2. and thence to GULLY FARM.
   The details of these adjustments are to be arranged between the G.Os.C., Infantry Brigades concerned.

x x x x x x x x

sd. BRYAN CURLING. Lt-Colonel.
General Staff, 42nd Division.

G.C.
   No.1 Sub-Group.
   No.2 Sub-Group.
   No.3 Sub-Group.
   No.4 Sub-Group.

HEADQUARTERS,
42ND
DIVL. ARTILLERY.

For your information. Liaison Officers should inform Sub-Groups when the adjustment marked // takes place.

P R Mitchell
Major. R.A.

14-9-17.   Brigade Major., 42nd D.A. Group.

SECRET   App* 4   Copy No. :......

42nd Divisional Artillery Operation Order No.38.

29th Sept 1917.

Reference maps BELGIUM and FRANCE 1/40,000 Sheets 27 and 28.

1. 42nd Divisional Artillery and No.1 Coy, 42nd Divisional Train A.S.C. will march on 30th inst from present location to WORMHOUDT area.

2. ROUTE.   Cross Roads G.5.d.1.2. Sheet 28 -
             Switch road North of POPERINGHE - PROVEN Road -
             Fork Roads L.4.b.9.2. Sheet 27 - ST JAN-TER-BIEZEN -
             Cross roads E.30.c.4.5. Sheet 27 - HOUTKERQUE - HERZEELE -
             WORMHOUDT.

3. Order of March -
         Headquarters, 42nd Divisional Artillery
         210th Brigade, R.F.A.
         211th Brigade, R.F.A.
         42nd Divisional Ammunition Column.
         No.1 Coy, 42nd Divisional Train A.S.C.

4. Starting point - Cross Roads G.5.d.1.2. Sheet 28.

5. Time of March. Head of 210th Brigade, R.F.A. to reach starting point at 8.0 a.m.
         Head of 211th Brigade R.F.A. to reach starting point at 8.45 a.m.
         Head of 42nd Divisional Ammunition Column to reach starting point at 9.30 a.m.
         Head of No.1. Coy, 42nd Divisional Train to reach starting point at 10.30 a.m.

6. Distances. 500 yards to be maintained between batteries, Sections and similar units.
         50 yards between each group of 6 vehicles.
         These distances to be maintained both when on the move and when halted.

7. Halts. No halts are to take place East of HOUTKERQUE. Leading Units will halt sufficiently far West of HOUTKERQUE to enable units in rear to clear the village before halting. Greatest care to be taken not to block either roads or railways when halted.
         If possible units should draw clear of main roads into fields to water or feed.

8. Ammunition Echelons will be full.
         Units will report to D.A.H.Q. on arrival at WORMHOUDT, quantities of ammunition and number of guns on charge.

9. Receipts will be obtained for all area stores handed over to N.Z. Units and duplicates forwarded to D.A.H.Q.

10. Mechanical Transport. Motor lorries from 42nd Ammunition Sub-Park will report as follows at 8.0 p.m. 29-9-1917.-
         2 lorries D.A.H.Q.
         14 lorries Fork Roads G.11.c.6.3. (of these 5 for
            210 Bde R.F.A.
            5 for 211th Bde
            4 for 42nd D.A.C.
         6 lorries Farm H.8.c.8.8. for D.T.M.O.

         Units will arrange for these lorries to be met at the above rendezvous and guided to various camps. Lorries when loaded will proceed independently under orders of Unit concerned. All lorries are to be retained by units until further orders. Units will arrange to ration and billet M.T. personnel.

11. **Supplies.** No supplies will be drawn on morning 30th Sept 17.
Rations for consumption on 1/10/17 will be delivered to units in WORMHOUDT Area by Divisional Train on conclusion of march on 30/9/17.
Each unit will send guides to Town Square WORMHOUDT to guide Supply wagons to billets.
Refilling arrangements for 1/10/17 will be notified later.

12. **Billets.** Billeting parties from each unit should report to Commandant Staging Area WORMHOUDT (Office in Town Square) by 9. a.m. 30/9/17.
The most convenient arrangement would be for billeting parties to travel by lorry. Area Commandant is in possession of Unit Strengths and will have detail of billeting prepared.

13. Headquarters, 42nd Divisional Artillery closes at POPERINGHE at 7 a.m. 30/9/17 and opens at WORMHOUDT 12 noon 30/9/17.

14. Please acknowledge by wire.

                                                  Captain, R.A.
S.C., R.A., 42nd Division.

Issued at ;...... on 29-9-17.
by Orderly
D.R.

```
Copy No. 1      R.A., II ANZAC.
         2      R.A., XV Corps.
         3      42nd Division.
         4      3rd Div. Arty.
         5      N.Z., Div Arty.
         6      66th Div. Arty.
     7 to 11    210th Bde R.F.A.
    12 to 16    211th Bde R.F.A.
    17 to 20    42nd B.A.C.
        21.     42nd D.T.M.O.
        22.     No.1. Coy 42nd Div Train A.S.C.
        23.     D.A.D.O.S., 3rd Div.
        24.     D.A.D.Q.S., 42nd Division.
        25.     D.A.D.P.S., II ANZAC.
        26.     Area Commandant BRANDHOEK, No.2.
        27.     Commandant Staging Area WORMHOUDT.
        28.     42nd Ammunition Sub-Park.
    29 - 35     War Diary and Spare.
```

CONFIDENTIAL.

WAR DIARY.

of

H.Q.R.A. 42nd Divn

From 1 – 10 – 17
To 31 – 10 – 17.

VOL. VIII.

WAR DIARY / INTELLIGENCE SUMMARY

Army Form C. 2118.

Sheet 1.

Place	Date	Hour	Summary of Events and Information	Remarks and references to Appendices
Ref. to FURNES MAP (PROVISIONAL) 1/40,000	Oct 1st 2nd		42nd D.A. marched from WORMHOUDT to TETEGHEM. 42nd D.A. marched from TETEGHEM to 42nd Div. area near COXYDE.	P.R.M. Appx I. P.R.M.
	3rd/4th		42nd D.A. relieved 66th D.A. in NIEUPORT BAINS section, with hrs. on right on 2/3rd & 3/4th. Lt. 6 a.m. Oct 4th command of the Arty. covering the 42nd Div's Front passed to C.R.A. 42nd Div. (Lt. Col. A. BATTWISTLE C.M.G.)	
	11th		42nd D.A. relieved on the Left Div'l. Front by 41st D.A. - 42nd Div. relieving 32nd D.A. in the line on the Right Div'l. Front.	P.R.M.
	12th			
	13th		The command of the Arty. covering the Right Div'l. Front passed to C.R.A. 42nd Div. at 12 noon Oct 13th.	Appx II. P.R.M. P.R.M.
	14th		Oct 12th Gen. WALSHE D.S.O., C.R.A. 42nd Div. returned from Hospital to duty.	
	15th		Gen. WALSHE D.S.O., C.R.A. 42nd Div., proceeds to England on 14 days leave. Lt. Col. BATTWISTLE C.M.G. takes over u/C.R.A.	P.R.M.
	16th		The following B.sdes. R.F.A. constitute the Right Div'l. Arty.:- 210th & 211th B.sdes. R.F.A. (T), 14th & R.F.A. (T), 14th (Army) B.de R.H.A., 72nd (Army) B.de R.F.A., 175th (Army) B.de R.F.A. & 2nd (Army) B.de N.Z. F.A.	P.R.M.
	25th		2nd (Army) B.de N.Z. F.A. transferred to Left Div'l. Artillery.	Appx III. P.R.M.
	29th		Gen. WALSHE, C.R.A. 42nd Div., returns from leave.	P.R.M.
	31st		Disposition of 42nd Div. Arty., with attached F.A. B.des., as per attached Disposition Return.	Appx IV. P.R.M.

P.R. KENDELLS
Major, B.M.R.A.
42nd Div.

1-11-17.

SECRET.   Copy No.......

42nd Divisional Artillery Operation Order No.39.

30-9-1917.

Reference Map Sheets 27 & 19, 1/40,000 BELGIUM & FRANCE.

1. 42nd Divisional Artillery and No.1 Coy, 42nd Divisional Train A.S.C. will march on 1st October from WORMHOUDT Area to TETEGHEM Area.

2. ROUTE. WYLDER - MAISON BLANCHE - Cross Roads O.17.d.5.3. Sheet 19.
   (Note:- The latter point is not named on Sheet 5A. On this map it is Cross Roads on BERGUES - REXPOEDE Road ½ mile S.E. of S in BERGUES).

3. Order of March.
   211th Brigade, R.F.A.
   210th Brigade, R.F.A.
   42nd D.A.C.
   No.1 Coy, 42nd Div. Train A.S.C.

4. STARTING POINT. - Cross Roads C.17.a.5.8. Sheet 27.

5. TIME OF MARCH.
   Head of 211th Bde R.F.A. to reach starting point at 10 a.m.
   Head of 210th Bde R.F.A. to reach starting point at 10-45 a.m.
   Head of 42nd D.A.C. to reach starting point at 11-40 a.m.
   Head of No.1 Coy 42nd Div. Train, A.S.C. to reach starting point at 12.50 p.m.

6. DISTANCES. 500 yards between Batteries, Sections and similar Units to be maintained.
   Not less than one mile between Brigades and similar Units.
   Gaps of 50 yards between Sections of Batteries and equivalent portions of other units.
   Particular attention to be paid to maintainance of distances.

7. HALTS. The whole column will halt as follows:-
   11-0 a.m. to 11-10 a.m.
   12 noon to 12-10 p.m.
   1-0 p.m. to 1-10 p.m. and so on every hour.

8. MECHANICAL TRANSPORT will proceed independently under orders of Units to whom attached.

9. SUPPLIES. will be delivered to units in TETEGHEM by Divisional Train on conclusion of days march. Each unit will send guides to office of Area Commandant to guide supply wagons to billets.

10. BILLETS. Billeting parties from each unit will report at 9 0 a.m. to Area Commandant TETEGHEM.

11. Headquarters, 42nd Divisional Artillery closes at WORMHOUDT at
    10-0 a.m. 1/10/17. and opens at TETEGHEM at same hour.

12. Please acknowledge by bearer.

                                                                                               Captain, R.A.
                S.C., R.A., 42nd Division.

Issued at ...... p.m. 30/9/17.
By D.R.

Distribution.
          Copy No. 1 to 5. 210th Brigade, R.F.A.
                   6 to 10. 211th Brigade, R.F.A.
               11 to 14. 42nd D.A.C.
                     15. 42nd D.T.H.O.
                     16. No.1 Coy, 42nd Div.Train, A.S.C.
                     17. Area Commandant WORMHOUDT.
                     18. Area Commandant, TETEGHEM.
                     19. R.A., XVth Corps.
                     20. 42nd Division.
                     21. 66th Div. Arty.
                     22. War Diary.

W 3 - 210
T 4 - DAC
F 5 - DIMO
S 6   210
S 7   211
M 8   DAC
T 9   210
W 10 DAC
T 11 DIMO
F 12 210
S 13 211
S 14 DAC

SECRET.   Copy No. 21

42nd Divisional Artillery Operation Order No. 40.

1-10-1917.

Reference Maps 1/40,000 Sheets 19 & 11.

1. The 42nd Divisional Artillery will march from TETENGHEM Area to 42nd Division Area, near COXYDE, on 2nd inst, and will relieve the 66th Divisional Artillery in the line on the nights 2nd/3rd and 3rd/4th

2. ROUTE. Pont de ZUYDCOOTE (D.13.b.3.1). - Canal Road. - ADINKERKE.

3. STARTING POINT. Road junction D.25.c.2.8.
   Heads of units will pass the starting point as follows:-

H.Q., R.A.	9-0 a.m.
210th Bde R.F.A.	9-15 a.m.
211th Bde R.F.A.	10-0 a.m.
42nd D.A.C.	10-45 a.m.

4. MINIMUM distances will be maintained as follows :-
   Between batteries and sections D.A.C.   200 yards.
   Between Sections of batteries and equivalent portions of D.A.C.   50 yards.
   When limitations of time and space permit, distances between batteries and Sections D.A.C. should be increased.

5. On arrival in 42nd Divisional Area, batteries and Sections of D.A.C. will proceed to the wagon lines of the units they are relieving and will bivouac alongside ready to move in to 66th Divisional Artillery wagon lines as soon as they are vacated.
   A certain number of tents and trench shelters are being drawn which will be divided up pro rata and conveyed to the wagon lines of the various R.A.Units of 66th Divisional Artillery.
   These will be returned to D.A.D.O.S. 42nd Division on the 4th inst.

6. Details of relief in the line are as follows :-
   (a) Night 2nd/3rd Oct.
      1 Section per bty 42nd D.A. relieves
      1 Section per bty 66th D.A.

   Night 3rd/4th Oct.
      Remaining 2 Sections per bty 42nd D.A. relieve
      Remaining 2 Sections per bty 66th D.A.

   (b) 210th Brigade, R.F.A. relieves 330th Brigade, R.F.A.
                                    ('C' Group).
      211th Brigade, R.F.A.(less D/211 Bty) relieves 331st Brigade, R.F.A. ('D' Group).
      D/211 Bty will be grouped with 'A' Group (158th Bde R.F.A), and not with 'D' Group.
      Batteries relieve opposite numbers.

   (c) Command of 'C' Group will pass to O.C. 210th Bde R.F.A. and of 'D' Group to O.C. 211th Bde R.F.A. at 5-30 a.m. Oct 4th.

   (d) At 6 a.m. 4th Oct. the Command of all the Artillery covering the 42nd Divisional Front will pass to the a/C.R.A., 42nd Division (Lieut-Colonel A.BIRTWISTLE, C.M.G).

   Brigades will notify 42nd D.A.H.Q. each night by wire of completion of relief.
      Code word "JAKE" will be used meaning 'relief complete".

7.

7. Brigade Commanders, D.A.C.Commander, Brigade Signal Officers and D.T.M.O. will meet B.M.,R.A., 42nd Division at the Cross Roads at E.9.b.6.9. at 9 a.m. on 2nd inst. Guides will be provided to conduct them to their Group and D.A.C. Headquarters.
   They will make all arrangements as to the detail of reliefs of their units.

8. One officer per battery and Section D.A.C will meet B.M.,R.A., 42nd Division at the ADINKERKE Cross Roads at E.9.b.6.9. at 9 a.m. 2nd inst.
   Guides will be provided and after being shown their respective wagon lines these officers will return to the Cross Roads at E.9.b.6.9. to guide their units to their new wagon lines.

9. Guns will not be exchanged.

10. Guns of 42nd Divisional Artillery will be drawn into action by 66th D.A. teams.

11. Ammunition at gun positions, camouflage in positions, gun registers, log books, aeroplane photos, battery and O.P.boards, secret and trench maps, defence scheme and all instructions relating to the 42nd Division Front will be taken over on relief, receipts being given.
    All area stores will be taken over.

12. Amounts of ammunition taken over will be reported to S.C., R.A., 42nd Division by 9 a.m. 4th Oct.

13. Responsibility for ammunition supplies will pass to 42nd Div. Arty. at 6 a.m. on 4th Oct.

14. TRENCH MORTARS. T.M.Batteries of 42nd D.A. will relieve T.M.Btys of 66th D.A. (in reserve) at 2 p.m. 3rd Oct at which time Command of the T.M.Group covering 42nd Division will pass to D.T.M.O., 42nd Division.

15. D.A.C. O.C., 42nd D.A.C will, in consultation with O.C.66th D.A.C., arrange all detail with regard to taking over ammunition dumps, relief of Sections D.A.C. etc.

16. A table of Map-spottings of R.A.Units 66th D.A. is attached.

17. ACKNOWLEDGE.

F. E. Morgan
Captain, R.A.
for B.M., R.A., 42nd Division.

Issued at 8.30 p.m 1-10-17.
by D.R.

Distribution:-
Copy No. 1.   R.A., XVth Corps.
         2.   66th D.A.
         3.   42nd Div. 'G'.
         4.   42nd Div. 'Q'.
     5 to 9   210th Bde R.F.A.
    10 to 14. 211th Bde R.F.A.
    15 to 18 42nd D.A.C.
        19   42nd D.T.M.O.
        20.   Area Commandant TETEGHEM.
        21.   War Diary.

SECRET.   Copy No......14......

AIF II

ADDENDUM NO:1
to
42nd DIVISIONAL ARTILLERY ORDER NO:41.   10-10-17

1. The command of 'B' Group, Right Divisional Artillery will pass from O.C. 161st Brigade R.F.A. to O.C. 211th Brigade R.F.A. at 12 noon, October 13th.

2. D/211th will take over the Hows. of D/161st in the line.
   As D/211 have only 5 Hows., D/161 are taking one gun out of the line.
   D/211 will withdraw their 2 Hows. to their Wagon Lines on night 11th/12th and the remaining 3 Hows. to their Wagon Lines on night 12th/13th.
   They will deliver the 5 Hows. to the Wagon Lines of D/161st on the morning of 13th October.
   B.Cs. concerned will make all arrangements regarding exchange or otherwise of sights and small stores.

3. The Command of the Trench Mortars on the Left Divisional Front will pass from D.T.M.O. 42nd Division to D.T.M.O. 41st Division at 12 noon, October 12th.

4. L.T.M.O. 42nd Division will arrange to take over the quarters vacated by 32nd T.M.Bde. at COXYDE.

5. ACKNOWLEDGE. (211th Bde & D.T.M.O. 42nd Div. only).

P.R. Mitchell
Major. R.A.
Brigade Major. R.A., 42nd Division.

Issued at...7 am........
By D.R. on ...11-10-17...

Copies to :-
- No.1. — 210th Brigade R.F.A.
- 2 — 211th Brigade R.F.A.
- 3 — 42nd D.A.C.
- 4 — 42nd D.T.M.O.
- 5 — S.C., R.A. 42nd Division.
- 6 — 32nd D.A.
- 7 — 41st D.A.
- 8 — 42nd Div. 'G'
- 9 — R.A. XV Corps.
- 10 — 42nd Div. 'Q'
- 11 — D.A.D.C.S., 42nd Division.
- 12 — O i/c R.A. Sigs.
- 13 — R.O., R.A.
- 14 — War Diary.
- 15 — File.
- 16 — 42nd Div. Train.
- 17 — 41st Div. 'G'
- 18 — 41st Div. 'Q'.

SECRET.   Copy No. 27

42nd Divisional Artillery Order No. 41

Reference Map Sheets 4 & 5 1/10,000.

1. The 42nd D.A. will be relieved in the line on the Left Divisional Front by the 41st D.A. and will relieve the 32nd D.A. in the line on the Right Divisional Front on the nights 11th/12th, 12th/13th & 13th/14th October.
   Details of the above double relief are shown in the attached table.

2. All moves East of the line COXYDE - COXYDE BAINS, and any movement in a Westerly direction will take place during hours of darkness only.

3. Guns and How. will not be exchanged.
   Units will retain their own equipment.

4. The Command of the Left Divisional Artillery will pass from C.R.A. 42nd Division to C.R.A. 41st Division at 12 noon October 12th.
   The Command of the Right Divisional Artillery will pass from C.R.A. 32nd Division to C.R.A. 42nd Division at 12 noon October 13th.
   The Command of Groups, T.M.Bdes and D.A.C's will pass on completion of relief.

5. 42nd D.A. will move with all Echelons full, less G.S. Wagons which ordinarily carry boxed ammunition.

6. During all moves minimum distances will be maintained as follows:-

   Between Btles. and between Sections D.A.C. ... 200 yards.

   Between Sections of Batteries and equivalent
   portions of D.A.C. .... 50 yards.

   When limitations of time and space permit, distances between batteries and Sections D.A.C. should be increased.

7. (1) All log-books, intelligence, aerial photographs, panoramas, map boards, copies of standing orders, etc, etc., will be handed over to incoming units and will similarly be taken over from outgoing units.
   (2) One Camera obscura and one 12 ft. Ross periscope will be handed over by 210th Bde to 190th Bde R.F.A. - receipts being obtained.

8. All camouflage will be left standing.

9. All tents, shelters and bivouacs will be left standing.

10. All area stores will be handed over to incoming units and taken over from outgoing units - receipts passing in each case.

11. 42nd D.A. will afford every facility to the 41st D.A. to bivouac alongside their present wagon lines until the withdrawal of 42nd D.A. from the Left Divisional Area is completed.

- 2 -

12. Copies of 32nd D.A.Disposition Report have been issued to all concerned.

13. The details of the double relief of the 42nd D.A.C. and the 42nd T.M.Bde will be arranged between O.C's concerned.

14. 210th Bde.R.F.A., on arrival at their new wagon lines, will remain out of the line for some 10 days.
    They will arrange for the adequate policing of battery positions now occupied by 168th Bde, daily patrolling and testing of communications and supervision of ammunition at gun positions.
    They will also take over the items mentioned in para 7 (1) from 168th Bde.
    The work of overhauling and calibrating the guns of 210th Bde will proceed as rapidly as possible.

15. 210th Bde will send forward 1 Officer and 2 signallers per battery and Bde H.Q. for attachment to 168th Bde on October 9th.
    211th Bde will send a similar advance party to 161st Bde on October 10th.

16. S.C. R.A. 42nd Division will arrange for all necessary transport.

17. Progress and completion of reliefs will be wired to this office

18. The amounts of ammunition taken over and handed over will be wired to S.C.,R.A., 42nd Division on completion of relief.

19. H.Q.,R.A. 42nd Division will close at St.IDESBALDE at 12 noon on October 12th and will re-open at COXYDE BAINS (W.6.a.6.4.) at 12 noon on October 13th.
    From 12 noon October 12th to 12 noon October 13th H.Q.,R.A., 42nd Division will be established (for administrative purposes only) at No.3.BILLET,St.IDESBALDE where reports will be sent during this period.

20. ACKNOWLEDGE.

P.R.Mitchell
Major.,R.A.
Brigade Major.,R.A. 42nd Division.

Issued at 2.30 p.m.

By D.R. on 9/10/17.

Copies to:-   1 to 5   210th Bde.,R.F.A.
              6 to 10   211th Bde R.F.A.
             11 to 14   42nd D.A.C.
             15 to 17   42nd D.T.M.O.
                  18   S.C.,R.A., 42nd Division.
                  19   32nd D.A.
                  20   41st D.A.
                  21   42nd Div.'G'
                  22   R.A. XV Corps.
                  23   42nd Div.'Q'
                  24   D.A.D.O.S. 42nd Divn.
                  25   O.i/c R.A.Sigs.
                  26   R.O.,R.A.
                  27   War Diary
                  28   File.
                  29   42 Div Train.
                  30   41 Div. G.
                  31.   41 Div Q

SECRET

TABLE OF RELIEFS

DATE.	DETAIL OF RELIEF.	REMARKS.
Night 10th/11th October.	168th Bde.R.F.A., Right Divnl.Arty., will withdraw from action to wagon lines.	210th Bde will make all arrangements for policing Bty positions, maintaining existing communications, and taking over Ammunition at Battery positions prior to the withdrawal of 168th Bde from the line.
Night 11th/12th October.	One Section of each Battery, 187th Brigade R.F.A., 41st Divisional Artillery, will relieve one Section of each Battery, 211th Bde.R.F.A. in action on Left Divisional Front. Those Sections of 211th Brigade R.F.A. will then relieve one Section of each Battery of the 161st Brigade... 32nd Divisional Artillery, in action on the Right Division Front. The Section of 161st Bde R.F.A. after being relieved will withdraw to wagon lines. 168th Bde.R.F.A., will march from wagon lines to camp in GHYVELDE Area. There will be no movement on night 11th/12th October, East of the OOST DUNKERKE – OOST DUNKER E BAINS Road till after 10 P.M.	210th Bde will detail a sufficient party to arrive at the wagon lines of 168th Bde. on the evening of the 11th to take over all tents, bivouacs, area stores, etc, when 168th Bde. move out. This party will remain till the arrival of 210th Bde on night 13th/14th.
Night 12th/13th October.	Remainder of 187th Bde R.F.A. will relieve the remainder of 211th Bde R.F.A. on Left Division Front. The latter will relieve remainder of 161st Bde R.F.A. on Right Division Front. Remainder of 161st Bde R.F.A., (after being relieved), will withdraw to wagon lines.	
Morning 13th October.	42nd T.M.Bde will relieve the 32nd T.M.Bde in the line under arrangements to be made between D.T.M.O. 42nd & 32nd Divns	Relief to be completed by 12 noon
Night 13th/14th October.	210th Bde will withdraw from action to wagon lines vacated 32nd D.A.(less 168th Bde) march from wagon lines to camp in GHYVELDE Area. by 168th Bde..	
Morning 14th October	211th Bde and 42nd D.A.C. will march from their present wagon lines to the wagon lines vacated by 161st Bde and 32nd D.A.C. respectively. 32nd D.A. (less 168th Bde) march from wagon lines to camp in GHYVELDE area.	To clear present wagon lines by 8.30 a.m. 211th Bde and 42nd D.A.C. will detail a sufficient party to arrive at the new wagon lines on the evening of 13th to take over bivouacs, tents, area stores, etc, when 161st Bde and 32nd D.A.C. move out.

App* III.

War Diary

SECRET.

42nd Divisional Artillery Order No. 43.

1. The 210th Bde R.F.A. will relieve the 2nd (Army) Bde N.Z.,F.A. (SYKES GROUP) in the line on the nights October 23rd/24th, 24th/25th.

    The 2nd (Army) Bde N.Z.,F.A. will relieve the 158th (Army) Bde R.F.A. in the line on the same two nights.

    A Table of Reliefs is attached.

    On completion of the above relief the 2nd (Army) Bde N.Z.,F.A. will be transferred to the Left Divisional Artillery and will come under the orders of the 41st D.A.

2. Guns and Hows will not be exchanged.

3. All reliefs will be carried out during the hours of darkness.

4. Details of the double relief will be arranged between Brigade Commanders concerned.

5. Command of Brigades and Batteries will pass on completion of relief when 210th Bde.R.F.A. will be known as 'F' Group.

6. 210th Bde.R.F.A. will take over S.O.S. and Counter Preparation tasks at present performed by 2nd (Army) Bde.N.Z.,F.A.

    They will maintain the same liaison and man the same O.P's.

7. All O.P's, Ammunition at gun positions, existing communications, trench and area stores, standing camouflage, maps, panoramas, log-books, intelligence, aerial photographs, duties, Instructions and Standing Orders will be taken over by relieving Brigades. 210th Bde.R.F.A. will render all returns at present rendered by the 2nd (Army) Bde N.Z.,F.A.

8. 2nd (Army) Bde N.Z.,F.A. will retain their present Wagon lines.

    The re-allotment of wagon lines to 210th and 211th Brigades R.F.A. and to 42nd D.A.C. are shown in 42nd D.A.memo's S.C.24/25 and S.C.24/26 already issued.

9. Advanced parties of One Officer and 2 Signallers per Bde H.Q. and per Battery of 210th Bde.R.F.A. and 2nd (Army) Bde N.Z.,F.A. will proceed to their "opposite numbers" on the morning of October 22nd.

10. Units will move with echelons full.
    On completion of relief 210th Bde.R.F.A. will notify the S.O.,R.A. 42nd Division the amount and nature of ammunition taken over.

cont/d.

cont/d.

-2-

11. The 9th Divisional Artillery are arriving at GHYVELDE on 22nd October and will come under the orders of 42nd Division with a view to going into action on Right Division Front.

One Brigade, 9th D.A., will take over the policing and maintenance of the Battery Positions, communications, O.P's, etc., at present policed and maintained by 210th Bde.R.F.A.

Detailed orders with regard to the above will be issued later.

210th Bde.R.F.A. will continue to police and maintain these positions, communications, O.P's, etc until they are handed over.

12. Progress and completion of reliefs will be wired to this office.

13. ACKNOWLEDGE. ('A' & 'SYKES' Groups only)

P.R. Mitchell
Major., R.A.
Brigade Major, 42nd Divisional Artillery.

Issued at..7 a.m.
By.D.R. on 22/10/17.

Distribution: Copies to:-

SYKES and 'A' Group. (5 Copies each)
B., C., D., & E Groups (1 each)
42nd D.T.M.O.
42nd D.A.C.
41st D.A.
42nd Division 'G'.
R.A., XV Corps.
S.C.,R.A., 42nd Division.
R.O.,R.A., 42nd Division.
Major BRIDGE, Liaison Officer with 3rd Belgian Divn.
125th Inf.Bde
126th Inf.Bde
127th Inf.Bde
War Diary.
Defence Scheme.
File.

SECRET.

TABLE OF RELIEFS.

(Issued with 42nd L.A. Order No.43)

ITEM	DATE	UNIT	FROM	TO	REMARKS
1.	Night of Oct 23/24th	1 Section each Btt'y 210th Bde R.F.A.	Wagon Lines	Line, in relief of 1 Section of each Btt'y of the 2nd (Army) Bde N.Z., F.A.	A/210 relieves 2nd Btt'y B/210 " 5th " C/210 " 9th " D/210 " 6th "
2.	Night of Oct 23/24th	1 Section each Btt'y 2nd (Army) Bde N.Z., F.A.	Present Battery Positions	Line, in relief of 1 Section of each Btt'y of the 158th (Army) Bde.R.F.A.	2nd Btt'y relieves D/158 5th Btt'y " B/158 9th " " C/158 6th Btt'y goes into positions recently occupied by 30th Btt'y R.F.A. at M.25.d.1.1.(2 Sections) & M.25.b.7.3.(1 Section)
3.	Night of Oct 24/25th	Remaining 2 Sections of each Btt'y of 210 Bde R.F.A.	Wagon Lines	Line, in relief of remaining 2 Sections of each Btt'y of the 2nd (Army) Bde N.Z., F.A.	
4.	Night of Oct 24/25th	Remaining 2 Sections of each Btt'y of 2nd (Army) Bde N.Z.,F.A.	Present Battery Positions.	Line, in relief of remaining 2 Sections of each Btt'y of 158th Army Bde R.F.A.	

NOTE :- No portion of the 2nd (Army) Bde N.Z., F.A. will move from its present position until it has been relieved by the corresponding portion of 210th Bde.R.F.A.

SECRET.

AM x IV

RIGHT DIVISIONAL ARTILLERY.

LOCATION STATEMENT, 12 noon 26th October, 1917.

Reference Map FURNES 1/40,000

RIVET. HEADQUARTERS: 42nd Divisional Artillery, COXYDE BAINS (W.6.a.6.4)

			POSITION	WAGON LINES.
	50th Bde.R.F.A.	O.C., Lieut.Col, C.W.W.MACLEAN, D.S.O.		
	Headquarters.		S.3.a.7.3.	
'A'	A/50	(5)	S.3.a.75.00	)
GROUP.		(1)	M.35.a.25.25	)
	B/50	(5)	M.33.a.05.10	) Policed only
		(1)	M.33.d.50.85	)
	C/50	(5)	M.34.d.47.81	)
		(1)	M.32.a.7.0	)
	D/50		M.33.c.4.0.	)

RIDGE. 211th Bde.R.F.A. O.C., Lieut.Col, E.J.INCHES, D.S.O.

	Headquarters.		M.32.b.7.6.	X.13.d.6.8.
	A/211		M.32.a.0.8	X.13.d.0.3.
'B'	B/211	(4)	M.33.a.8.4.	W.15.d.2.2.
GROUP.		(2)	M.32.a.25.75	
	C/211		M.32.b.55.30	X.13.d.6.8.
	D/211		M.20.a.0.3.	V.26.c.8.8.

CARD. 14th Bde.R.H.A. O.C Lieut.Col, T.E.P.WICKHAM, D.S.O.

	Headquarters.		S.8.b.2.9.	GHYVELDE.
	'F' Btty		S.4.b.1.8	"
'C'	'T' "	(5)	S.3.d.97.65	"
GROUP.		(1)	S.3.d.46.66	
	400th Btty	(5)	M.33.c.90.08	"
		(1)	M.34.c.10.25	
	401st "	(3)	S.3.b.4.1.	"
		(3)	S.3.b.7.3.	

CARDINAL, 72nd Bde R.F.A. O.C, Lieut.Col.F.W.RICHEY.

	Headquarters.		M.33.c.0.0.	
	A/72	(5)	S.3.a.58.82	)
		(1)	M.33.d.58.12	) Rear at I.12.b.& 1.
'D'	B/72	(5)	S.3.b.12.52	)
GROUP.		(1)	M.33.d.62.22	) Advanced at X.14.c.
	C/72	(5)	M.33.c.62.48	)
		(1)	M.33.d.45.32	)
	D/72	(5)	S.3.a.85.40	)
		(1)	S.4.a.05.31.	)

CARPET. 175th Bde.R.F.A. O.C., Lieut.Col.W.FURNIVALL.

	Headquarters,		X.5.b.8.0	W.22.d.30.30
	A/175		S.2.a.35.78	W.16.d.3.2.
	B/175	(4)	S.2.a.63.99.	W.16.d.5.2.
'E'		(2)	S.2.b.35.80	
GROUP.	C/175	(4)	M.32.c.12.64	W.16.d.7.2.
		(2)	S.2.d.60.73	
	D/175	(4)	M.32.d.28.10	W.16.d.55.40
		(2)	S.2.b.39.62	
	175th B.A.C.			D.17.d.5.2.

- 2 -

		POSITION	WAGON LINES.
RING. 210th Bde.R.F.A.(.C.,Major.D.J.Mason,			
Headquarters		R.30.a.85.85	X.14.a.2.9.
A/210	(3)	M.26.a.28.20	X.14.a.2.9.
	(3)	M.26.a.48.32	
'F' B/210	(3)	M.32.a.80.90	X.20.a.0.7.
GROUP.	(3)	M.26.c.69.80	
C/210	(1)	M.20.d.00.55	X.20.b.2.2.
	(5)	M.20.c.05.25	
D/210	(2)	M.20.c.30.85	W.26.b.2.0
	(2)	M.20.c.05.90	
	(2)	M.20.a.25.15	

RIPPLE. Headquarters, 42nd Divisional Ammunition Column. W.23.a.4.3.

No.1.Section   W.21.a.5.6.
No.2.Section   W.21.a.5.6.
No.3.Section ('B'Echelon)   W.23.a.4.3.

RUPEE. D.T.M.O. 42nd Division. X.13.b.7.8.

X/42 T.M.Btty NEW PARADE M.21.d.40.06)
Y/42 " " " BRICKWORKS M.29.b.6.8.   ) Rest Billets
Z/42 " " "   M.36.b.45.60) X.13.b.7.8.
V/42 " " " NIEUR RT   M.28.c.58.43)

A.R.P.   HULL DUMP   X.8.b.4.3.
  "   CANAL DUMP   X.27.a.9.8.

9th Divisional Artillery   at rest in   GHYVELDE.

P.R.Mitchell
Major, R.A.
Brigade Major, 42nd Divisional Arty.

WAR DIARY

of

H.Q.R.A. 42nd Divn

From 1-11-17

To 30-11-17

Vol. ~~VIII~~ IX

WAR DIARY or INTELLIGENCE SUMMARY

Army Form C. 2118.

R/Hugh FURNES 40,000 RAMSCAPELLE 12 SW 3 10,000

Place	Date	Hour	Summary of Events and Information	Remarks and references to Appendices
COXYDE BAINS	1/11/17		Capt BLEWITT GHQ (& 42nd DA from IV Army AMS School for "training" course. (BM) (SG)	
	3rd		Shell ENTINKELLE ..... 42nd DAC.	App. I
	5th		C.I. BIRTNWHISTLE away on a months leave.	
	6th		N°3 Sect-STC. (B Eclair) Become "S.M.A. Section"	
	9th		405th BE. take the place under E. Group	
	12th	3.30 am	Raid by 3rd Belgian Division on TERSTILLE FM. 405th C/175 and N/175 cooperated. few prisoners taken.	App. II
	11.15		Major MITCHELL to ENGLAND for MG Course at GRANTHAM and a months leave.	
	15/16	night	175 Brigade (Lieut C.884) withdrawn to prepare Division to return to Italy. C/175 B/210 and	
			405th BE come under B Group.	
	19/20	night	42nd DA Relieved by half battalion by 265th Regt French Artillery, covering 133rd French Division.	App. III
	20/21	night		
	21st	6 am	2nd A2 (Army) JA 884 from under Command D.95 Division.	
		pm	42nd DA march to GHYVELDE. DAHQ to GHYVELDE.	App. IV
	23rd		" " " WORMHOUDT (A) " WORMHOUDT	
	24th		" " " (B) " ZERMEZEELE	
	25		" " " STAPLE area ST MARIE CAPPELL	
	26		" " " AIRE FME ST ANDRE LITTERNESSE	
			During the march from GHYVELDE to the Infantry Defence (Maj HOWARTH) 42nd BDE A.S.C. 1 Section 1/2 EL 37 Amb. 1915/14th vet. section.	

Army Form C. 2118.

Sheet 2

WAR DIARY
or
INTELLIGENCE SUMMARY.
(Erase heading not required.)

Place	Date	Hour	Summary of Events and Information Ref. BETHUNE COMBINED 1/40,000	Remarks and references to Appendices
AIRE	30th		42nd D.A. marched to ROBECQ under orders to relieve 25th D.A. in the CANAL and GIVENCHY Sector on nights 1/2 and 2/3, which orders were received to advance all details 24 hrs and the relief to be on nights 30/1 and 1/2. Maj Mitchell returned from leave. Relief of 25th D.A. completed at 7/pm Dec 1st. DA HQ at LOCON	See App V

Rothwell Capt
for ? ? SBNRA 42 Div

WAR DIARY File

SECRET.

Appendix I

H.Q. 42nd Division "Q".
H.Q. 42nd Division "A".
A.D.M.S., 42nd Division.
D.A.D.V.S.   do
C.R.E.   do
O.C., Divisional Train.
D.A.D.O.S.
125th Infy. Bde.
126th Infy. Bde.
127th Infy. Bde.
210th Brigade, R.F.A.
211th Brigade, R.F.A.
D.T.M.O., 42nd Division.
42nd D.A.C.(for information).
Brigade Major.

Please note that, the 42nd D.A.C. having been re-organized in accordance with G.H.Q. letter No. O.B.2065 of 16/10/17, the Section hitherto known as No. 3 Section, or "B" Echelon, 42nd D.A.C., will, with effect from noon 4th instant, be known as S.A.A. Section, 42nd D.A.C.

F. E. Morgan
Captain, R.A.,
for Commanding 42nd Div'l Artillery.

5/11/17.

SECRET.

42nd Divisional Artillery Order No. 48.

14th November 1917.

1. The 175th (Army) Bde. R.F.A. (less C. Battery) will be withdrawn to their Wagon Lines on night 15th/16th inst., when they will come under orders of G.O.C., R.A., XV Corps.

   O.C., 175th Bde. will make all necessary arrangements for the move.

2. The responsibility for the Artillery Defence of the Front at present covered by E. Group will be taken over at 4.30 pm. on 15th inst., by O.C., B. Group.

   At that hour C/175, B/210 and 400th Battery will come under orders of O.C., B. Group.

3. The necessary adjustments of S.O.S. Lines are given in 42nd D.A. Instruction No.29 which have been issued to all concw concerned.

Captain., R.F.A.
issued at..5/n...   A/Brigade Major., 42nd Divisional Artillery.
By....DRLS....

Copies to :- R.A., XV Corps.
             42nd Division.
             E. Group.
             B. Group.
             F. Group.
             War Diary.
             File.

SECRET.

Appendix War Diary
III

42nd Divisional Artillery Order No. 48.

16th November, 1917.

1. The 42nd Division is being relieved by the 133rd French Division, the relief of the Infantry taking place on the nights 17th/18th and 18th/19th November.

2. The batteries of 42nd Divisional Artillery and of 2nd N.Z. (Army) F.A.Bde also 400th and C/175 batteries will be relieved during the nights 19th/20th and 20th/21st inst.

   Half batteries will be withdrawn each night to their Wagon lines during the hours of darkness.

   The relieving French batteries will, in some cases, move into the positions of 42nd D.A. batteries which they relieve and in other cases take over the defence of the line from new positions.

3. All Trench maps, air photos and defence scheme's etc., will be handed over to the relieving units.

4. All telephone wires and cables required by French units will be left down.

5. The following will be handed over to the French:-

   by 211th Bde. - 1 - 75 m.m. Gun in the REDAN.
   by D.T.M.C. - 2 - 240 m.m. T.M's (French pattern)

6. The British 9.45" and 6" Newton T.M's in the line will be relieved on the night 19th/20th, and after relief will be handed in to Ordnance.

7. The British S.O.S. Rifle Grenade (i.e. bursting into two red and two green lights) will remain in force till 12 noon 19th inst.

8. The completion of all the above reliefs will be reported to this office by telephone.

9. Command of the 42nd Divisional Front will pass to the G.O.C. 133rd French Division at 10 AM, 19th November.

10. The 42nd Divisional Artillery and 400th and 6/175 batteries will march on 22nd to GHYVELDE in accordance with a march Table which will be issued later.

cont/d.

-2-

11. 2nd N.Z.(Army) F.A.Bde will at 6.0 am on 21st inst come under orders of 9th Division.

12. The following distances will be maintained on the line of march:-

In the XV Corps Area, minimum distances of 200 yards between batteries, Sections of D.A.C., Companies of Infantry, etc, and Sections of Transport of Equivalent road space.

50 yards will be maintained between Sections of batteries and equivalent portions of D.A.C.

13. ACKNOWLEDGE

Ralph B. Gwalt

Captain, R.F.A.
A/Brigade Major, 42nd Divisional Artillery

Issued at 6.0 p.m.
By D.R.L.S.

Copies to:-   B.Group.   3 copies.
              F.   "   4   "
              SYKES " 5   "
    42nd D.A.C.   5   "
    42nd D.T.M.O. 5   "
    42nd Division.'G' 2 copies.
    42nd Division"Q" 1
    R.A. XV Corps.   1
    9th Division.   1
    C.R.A. 133rd French Division. 1
    42nd Div.Signals. 1
    42nd Div.Train.   1
    428th Coy.A.S.C. 1
    S.C.,R.A. 42nd Div.
    R.O.,R.A. 42nd Div.
    War Diary.
    File.

SECRET.

ADDENDUM to

42nd DIVISIONAL ARTILLERY ORDER NO: 49.

-o-o-o-o-o-o-o-o-o-o-o-o-o-o-

18-11-17.

1. British Artillery will be responsible for the defensive Barrage until 4 p.m. on 19th inst.

    At that hour Liaison Officers with the Infantry will be withdrawn.

    O.C., Groups will make the necessary arrangements for the withdrawal of half batteries after dark.

    Both on nights 19th/20th & 20th/21st, however, guns will be kept in action on their S.O.S. Lines as late as possible consistent with not keeping the teams waiting on the positions.

2. The French S.O.S. Signal is a rocket bursting into three white balls.

    A rocket bursting into six white balls is the Signal for "Longthen Range".

    These Signals come into force at 12 noon, 19th inst.

    In the event of the French S.O.S. being sent up batteries will open fire as laid down in 42nd D.A. Instruction No.11. (S.O.S. Standing Orders).

    After 4 p.m., 19th inst, British F.A. Batteries (or remaining half batteries) will NOT open fire unless specially requested to do so by the French C.R.A. through this office.

3. The responsibility for T.M. Barrages will pass from the D.T.M.O., 42nd Division, at 8 a.m., 19th inst., after which hour he may hand over the French Trench Mortars and withdraw the British ones.

    211th Brigade will make arrangements to hand over the 75 m.m. Gun in the REDAN any time after 8 a.m. on 19th inst.

4. Acknowledge.

                                Ralph Brown
                                Captain. R.F.A.
                                A/Brigade Major., 42nd Divisional Artillery.

Issued at 5 P.M.
On 18-11-17.
By. D.R.L.S.

Copies to :-   'B' Group.   -   8 Copies.
               'F' Group.   -   4 Copies.
               'SYKES' Group.   -   5 Copies.
               42nd D.T.M.O.   -   2 Copies.
               42nd Div. 'G'.   -   2 Copies.
               R.A., XV Corps.   -   1 Copy.
               C.R.A. 133rd French Div. - 1 Copy.
               R.O., R.A.   -   1 Copy.
               War Diary.
               FILE.

SECRET.   XV Corps No. D.398/9.

"B" Group.
"P" Group.
SYKES Group.

Registration by French Field Batteries will not take place before 18th November. This registration will be carried out as carefully as possible, and with the minimum expenditure of ammunition.

F.A. Brigade Commanders will arrange with French Group Commanders that British Batteries fire a few rounds at the same time as the French Batteries, in order, if possible, to prevent the enemy from discovering that French 75's have come into action on this front.

Ralph Blewitt

16/11/17.   Captain, R.F.A.
                         A/Brigade Major, R.A. 42nd Division.

SECRET

42nd Divisional Artillery Order No.51.

19th November, 1917.

1. 42nd Divisional Artillery Order No.50 is hereby cancelled.

2. The 42nd Divisional Artillery, less 42nd Div.T.M's, will march from their Wagon Lines to GHYVELDE on 21st inst, in accordance with attached March Table.

3. Brigade and D.A.C. billeting parties will meet the S.C.,R.A. at the Area Commandants office, GHYVELDE, at 10.0 am 21st inst.
   As most of the accomodation for 42nd D.A. in the GHYVELDE Area is in tents, as much transport as can be spared should be sent forward with billeting parties to draw tents from Area Commandant and to carry them to camping ground.

4. Trench Mortar Batteries and Units attached to 42nd D.A. (Infantry Detachment(Maj.HOWARTH), 428th Coy,A.S.C., 1/3rd E.L. Fld.Amb., and 19th Mob.Vet.Section) will march to GHYVELDE on 22nd inst at the time ordered by their respective Os.C.
   Billeting parties will be sent on in advance and will report to the S.C.,R.A. at GHYVELDE at 10.0 am.

5. 42nd Divisional Artillery and attached troops will march on 23rd inst to WORMHOUDT (A) in accordance with a march table to be issued later.

6. Halts for 10 minutes will be made every clock hour after the starting point. Unit Commanders will synchronise their watches before the start of a march and will ensure that their Units are halted and moved off by the clock independently and irrespectively of any other unit.

7. Refilling point on 22nd inst will be at GHYVELDE Church. Time of refilling will be notified later.

8. On arrival at GHYVELDE on 22nd inst, O.C.Detachment,1/3rd E.L.Fld.Amb will open an Aid Post in GHYVELDE Village to which sick from all units should be sent.

Ralph B Stewart.
Captain.,R.F.A.
A/Brigade Major,42nd Divisional Artillery.

Issued at.. 11:30 pm
On 19-11-17.
By D.R.L.S.
Copies to:-
210th Bde.R.F.A.   O.C.Infantry Detachment (Major
211th Bde.R.F.A.   HOWARTH)
D.T.M.O. 42nd Div. 428th Coy.A.S.C.
42nd D.A.C.   1/3rd E.L.Fld.Amb.
42nd Div.'G'   19th Mob.Vet.Section.
42nd Div.Sigs.   Supply officer,42nd Div.Troops.
XV Corps.R.A.   S.C.,R.A., 42nd Divn.
War Diary   File.

MARCH TABLE for 21st Instant.

Reference Map, FURNES 1/40,000.

UNIT	STARTING POINT.	TIME TO PASS STARTING POINT.	ROUTE.	REMARKS.
210th Bde.less D.Battery	Cross Roads F.2.b.0.2.	5.0 pm	Cross Roads F.2.c.0.3 Bridge F.7.c.1.8. - S.bank of Canal - Cross Road D.15.b.6.6. - GHYVELDE.	
211th Bde.less B & D Batteries	ditto	5.40 pm	ditto	
D/210 D/211	Wagon Lines	4.30 pm	BRAY DUNES - GHYVELDE	
42nd D.A.C.	Cross Roads LA PANNE W.20.b.8.8.	4.30 pm	ADINKERKE Cross Roads D.15.b.6.6. GHYVELDE	
B/211	ditto	5.10 pm	ditto	

ADDENDUM to 42nd D.A.Order No.51.

H.Q., 42nd Divisional Artillery will close at COXYDE BAINS at 10.0 am 22nd inst and open at GHYVELDE at the same hour.

Ralph B____

Captain., R.F.A.
20-11-17.   A/Brigade Major, 42nd Divisional Artillery.

Distribution; as for 42nd D.A.Order No.51.

App. IV

SECRET

42nd Divisional Artillery Order No. 52

23-11-17

1. The 42nd Divisional Artillery, less T.M's, and Units attached to 42nd D.A. will march to WORMHOUDT (A) on November 23rd, 1917, in accordance with attached March Table.

2. Brigade and D.A.C. billetting parties and representatives of attached Units will meet the S.C., R.A. at the Area Commandant's Office, WORMHOUDT, at 9-0 am.

3. Prior to departure from GHYVELDE all tents must be struck and handed in, without fail, to the store from which they were drawn.

4. Refilling point for 23rd instant is the Square at WORMHOUDT.
    Wagons should be sent in as soon as possible after arrival in billets.

5. Railheads will be as follows:-

    On 23rd and 24th inst   ARNEKE
    25th and 26th inst   EBBLINGHEM
    27th inst   AIRE

6. On arrival in billets an orderly from each Brigade 42nd D.A.C., and attached Units will report to H.Q., 42nd D.A. at No.7 Rue de CASSEL, WORMHOUDT.
    It is essential that these orderlies should know the exact location of their own Unit Headquarters.

F. E. Morgan
Captain.
S.C., R.A., 42nd Divisional

Issued at 6.0 pm

By orderly

Distribution: As for 42nd D.A. Order No. 51.

MARCH-TABLE for 23rd inst

Map Reference 1/100,000 DUNKERQUE and HAZEBROUCK.

UNIT.	STARTING POINT	TIME TO PASS STARTING POINT.	ROUTE	REMARKS
H.Q., 42nd D.A.	Cross Roads ½ mile S of GHYVELDE	9.0 a.m	LES MOERES KROMM'HOEK WEST CAPPELL WILDER BILLETS	
210th Bde		9.10.am		
211th Bde		9.50 am		
42nd D.A.C.		10.40 am		
Infantry Detachment		11.20 am		
1/3rd Fld Amb		11.30 am		
19th Mot Vet Section		11.35 am		
428th Coy. A.S.C.		11.40 am		

Note: Minimum distances of 200 yards between batteries, Sections of D.A.C. Companies of Infantry, etc, and Sections of Transport of equivalent road spaces. 50 yards will be maintained between Sections of batteries and equivalent portions of D.A.C.

SECRET

42nd Divisional Artillery Order No. 53.

23rd November, 1917.

1. The 42nd Divisional Artillery (Less T.M.Batteries) and Units attached will march to billets in WORMHOUDT (B) Area on 24th inst in accordance with March Table attached.

2. Billeting parties will meet S.C.,R.A. at Area Commandant's Office ZERMEZEELE at 9.0 am.
   It is essential that at least one representative from each Unit should be in possession of a map.
   Billeting parties should proceed either mounted or on cycles. Motor lorries should not be taken into the new Area until the roads have been thoroughly reconnoitred.

3. Refilling point, 24th inst On WORMHOUDT - CASSEL Road in I.23.b. Wagons should report at Refilling Point as soon as possible after arrival in billets.

4. In WORMHOUDT (B) area, 1/3rd E.L.Fld Amb will establish an Aid Post at Farm 1/3 mile S of 4th E in ZERMEZEELE and 19th Mob. Vet Section will be at FARM ½ mile W of ZERMEZEELE Church.

5. H.Q., 42nd Div.Arty closes at WORMHOUDT at noon 24th inst and will open at same hour at Farm ½ mile N of ZERMEZEELE Church.

Ralph Stewart

Captain., R.F.A.
A/Brigade Major, 42nd Divisional Artillery.

Issued at 8.0 pm
by orderly.

Distribution; as for 42nd D.A.Order No. 52.

MARCH TABLE for 24th November.

Map Reference HAZEBROUCK, 1/100,000

UNIT.	STARTING POINT.	TIME TO PASS STARTING POINT.	ROUTE	REMARKS.
210th Bde	Bridge on WORMHOUDT-CASSEL ROAD over PEENE BECQUE	9.30 am	WORMHOUDT-CASSEL Road to Cross Roads ½ mile N of H* in HARDIFORT - L'ANGE - BILLETS	About 7 miles
Infantry	ditto	10.20 am	3 miles along WORMHOUDT-CASSEL Road to Billets.	Not before the tail of 211th is clear.
428th Coy R.S.C.	Present Lines	As ordered by O.C.	To Billets on WORMHOUDT-CASSEL Road	
19th Mob.Vet Section	As for 210th Bde	10.30 am	WORMHOUDT-CASSEL Road - Cross Road RIETVELD - S.W. through H of LEDRINGHEM to Road Junction on 50 Contour ⅝ mile E of 2nd E in ARNEKE	About 5 miles.
1/3rd E.T.Fld Ambulance	ditto	10.45 am	As for 210th Bde	
211th Bde	ditto	11.30 am	WORMHOUDT-CASSEL Road - Cross Roads RIETVELD	Not to pass these Cross Roads till met by Guides.
42nd D.A.C.	Present Lines	As ordered by O.C?	About 2 miles along WORMHOUDT-STEENVOORDE Road	

SECRET

42nd Divisional Artillery Order No. 54.

24th November, 1917.

1. The 42nd Divisional Artillery (less T.M.Batteries) and attached Units will march to the STAPLE Area on 25th instant, in accordance with attached March Table.

2. Billeting parties will meet S.C.,R.A. at Area Commandant's Office STAPLE at 9.0 am.
   These parties should travel if possible in lorries.

3. The maps issued herewith will be returned without fail to H.Q.,R.A. by 8.0 pm on 25th instant.

4. Billeting certificates for both ZERMEZEELE and STAPLE Areas should be dealt with by Units concerned and NOT handed to Area Commandant.

5. Refilling point on 25th instant will be at Church at WALLON CAPPEL (U.23.c.).

6. H.Q.,R.A. will close at ZERMEZEELE at 9.30 am and will open at ST MARIE CAPPEL at the same hour.

   Mobile Vet.Section and Field Ambulance will be at HONDEGHEM.

7. ACKNOWLEDGE.

Ralph Stewart
Captain., R.F.A.
A/Brigade Major, 42nd Divisional Artillery

Issued at 7.30 pm
By orderly.
Copies to:-
    210th Bde.R.F.A.
    211th Bde.R.F.A.
    42nd D.A.C.
    42nd Division. 'G'
    O.C.Infantry Detachment. (Major HOWARTH)
    128th Coy.A.S.C.
    1/3rd E.L.Fld.Ambulance.
    19th Mob.Vet.Section.
    Supply Officer, 42nd Div.Troops.
    Area Commandant, STAPLE.
    S.C.,R.A. 42nd Division.
    Officer i/c R.A.Sigs.
    War Diary
    File.

MARCH TABLE for 25th November, 1917.

Map Reference Sheet 27, 1/40,000

UNIT.	STARTING POINT.	TIME TO PASS STARTING POINT	ROUTE	REMARKS
210th Bde.	LEVEL CROSSING O.8.a.1.3.	9.30 am	Road Junction O.8.a.1.1. - Cross Roads O.15.d.4.8. - Cross Roads O.15.d.5.0 - Road Junction U.5.a.5.5. - LONGUE CROIX - Billets.	About 6 miles.
Infantry Detachment	ditto	10.30 am	Cross Roads O.7.d.6.6. - T Road in N.29.a. - Corner N.29.c.2.0 - Billets.	About 4 miles.
R.A., H.Q.	Cross Roads L'ANGE	9.50 am	Cross Roads I.29.b.5.7. - Main Road to CASSEL - Cross Roads O.12.d.5.9. - St MARIE CAPPEL.	Not to pass starting point till tail of Infantry Detachment is clear (about 5 miles)
211th Bde	As for 210th Bde	10.45 am	As for 210th Bde to LONGUE CROIX then to Road Junction U.16.b.8.0 - Billets	Will follow H.Q., R.A. to Cross Roads L'ANGE (about 7 miles.)
1/3rd E.L.Fld Ambulance	ditto	11.40 am	As for 210th Bde to Road Junction U.5.c.4.8. to Road Junction P.32.a.9.0 - Billets.	About 7 miles.
19th Mob.Vet Section	ditto	11.45 am	ditto	ditto
428th Coy. A.S.C.	ditto	11.50 am	ditto	ditto
42nd D.A.C.	Cross Roads in J.8.a.	10.30 am	CUDEZEELE - Cross Roads J.31.b.1.9. - Road Junction P.2.c.9.5. - Cross Roads P.7.a.4.9. - CASSEL-CAESTRE Road to Billets.	About 7 miles.

SECRET.

42nd Divisional Artillery Order No. 55.

25th November, 1917.

1. The 42nd Divisional Artillery (less T.M. Batteries) and attached Units will rejoin 42nd Division in the AIRE Area on 26th November in accordance with attached March Table.

2. HALTS. In order to avoid halting in the town of AIRE, clock hour halts will not be made after 11.0 am. After this hour a halt for 10 minutes will be made as the head of 211th, 210th Bdes and 42nd D.A.C. respectively reach the Railway Crossing just outside AIRE. Units in rear will conform to these halts.

3. Billeting parties from 210th, 211th Bdes and 42nd D.A.C. will report to S.C., R.A. at office of Area Commandant LAMBRES at 10.0 a.m.
   Billeting party from 428th Coy. A.S.C. will proceed direct to ST. MARTIN.
   Billeting party from Section 1/3rd Fld. Amb. will report to H.Q. 1/3rd E.L. Fld. Amb. at THIENNES.
   Billeting party from 19th Mob. Vet. Section will report to D.A.D.V.S. 42nd Division office at AIRE.
   Guides from Units will meet the Infantry Detachment at BLARINGHEM CHURCH at 11.0 am.

4. H.Q., 42nd D.A. will close at ST. MARIE CAPPEL at 9.0 am and open at ST. ANDRE FARM 200 yards N of 2nd S in LES TOURBIERES just north of WITTERNESSE at 11.0 am.

Ralph Blewitt.
Captain., R.F.A.
A/Brigade Major, 42nd Divisional Artillery.

Issued at 5.30 pm
By orderly.
Distribution; as for 42nd D.A. Order No. 54 less Area Commandant ZERIEZEELE and plus Area Commandant LAMBRES.

MARCH TABLE for 26th November, 1917.

Map reference HAZEBROUCK, 1/100,000.

UNIT.	STARTING POINT.	TIME TO PASS START- ING POINT.	ROUTE	REMARKS.
211th Bde	Cross Roads 1/3 mile N.E. of 3rd L in WALLON CAPPEL	9.10 am	LA BELLE HOTESSE Cross Roads 1/3 mile N of 3rd E in BOESEGHEM. BOESEGHEM - AIRE - LAMBRES - FONTES	
210th Bde	ditto	9.55 am	As for 211th Bde to LAMBRES then to WITTERNESSE.	
R..,H.C.	ditto	10.50 am	ditto	
42nd.D.A.C.	ditto	10.55 am	As for 211th Bde to LAMBRES then to QUERNES.	
428th Coy. A.S.C.	ditto	11.35 am	As for 211th Bde to BOESEGHEM then to GUARLINGHEM - ST.MARTIN	
19th Mob.Vet. Section	ditto	11.40 am	As for 211th Bde to AIRE	Report to D.A.D.V.S. 42nd Division.
1/3rd Fld.Amb.	ditto	11.45 am	As for 211th Bde to Cross Roads 1/3 mile N of 3rd E in BOESEGHEM then to THIENNES	
Infantry Detachment.	Cross Roads ½ mile N.E. of M in EBBLINGHEM	3.30 am	EBBLINGHEM - LYNDE - BLARINGHEM	On arrival at BLARINGHEM O.C., Detachment will direct parties from each battalion to join their units.

SECRET.

App V

42nd Divisional Artillery Order No. 56. 28th November, 1917.

Reference Sheet 36.A 1/40,000.
----

1. The 42nd Division is relieving the 25th Division in the line.

2. 42nd Divisional Artillery will march to the CALONNE ROBECQ Area on 30th inst and will relieve the 25th Divisional Artillery in the line on 1st and 2nd prox.
   Reliefs will take place by day.

   210th Bde will relieve 110th Bde
   211th Bde will relieve 112th Bde.

   A March Table and Table of Reliefs will be issued later.

3. Representatives (1 Officer & 2 Telephonists) from each Battery and Bde H.Q. will proceed forward on 29th inst and will remain with batteries to be relieved.
   In addition to above each Bde will send a working party of 20 men to renew old battery positions to be occupied by batteries of 42nd D.A.
   The above parties will parade at Cross Roads FONTES (N.29.a 4.2) at 8.0 am on 29th instant to proceed by lorry.
   Rations will be taken for 1st December.
   Arrangements have been made with the 25th D.A. for the accommodation of all advanced parties.

4. Separate orders for the relief of T.M's will be issued later.

                                            Ralph Bruin Lt
                                            Captain., R.F.A.
                                A/Brigade Major, 42nd Divisional Artillery

Issued at 8.0 am
By D.R.L.S.
Copies to :-   210th Bde.R.F.A.   (5)
               211th Bde.R.F.A.   (5)
               42nd D.A.C.   (4)
               42nd D.T.M.O.   (2)
               42nd Divn. 'G'   (2)
               42nd Divn. 'Q'
               R.A. XV Corps
               25th D.A.
               42nd Div. Train.
               Area Commandant's ROBECQ & LAMBRES.
               S.O.,R.A., 42nd Division.
               R.O.,R.A. 42nd Division.
               Officer i/c R.A.Signals.
               War Diary.
               File.

Secret. Urgent.

H.Q. 42nd D.A.C.

HEADQUARTERS, 42ND DIVL. ARTILLERY.
No. SC 74/143
Date.........

War Diary

1. The S.A.A. Section, 42nd D.A.C. will relieve the S.A.A. Section, 25th D.A.C. in the Line on the 29th inst.
   Headquarters, S.A.A. Section, 25th D.A.C. is at F.8.b.8.4. Bethune Sheet.

2. The Section will march independently, there being no restriction as to time of march or route to be followed.

3. The O.C., S.A.A. Section, will take over from his opposite number, 25th Div'l Artillery, all dumps which are manned by personnel of the S.A.A. Section, and will also take over all standing fatigues. duties, etc. found by S.A.A. Section, 25th D.A.C.

4. The S.A.A. Section will draw rations as usual from Refilling point at LAMBRES on the 29th inst.. Refilling point for the 30th will be notified later.

5. Completion of the relief will be wired by O.C. S.A.A. Section, 42nd D.A.C. direct to S.C.R.A., 42nd Division.

Morgan
Captain, R.A.
S.C.R.A., 42nd D.A.

28/11/17.

SECRET.

42nd Divisional Artillery Order No. 57.

29th November, 1917.

1. 42nd Divisional Artillery and 428th Coy A.S.C. will proceed to ROBECQ Area in accordance with attached March Table on 30th instant.
    Billeting Parties will meet S.C., R.A. at Area Commandants Office at ROBECQ at 9.30 am.

2. 42nd Divisional Artillery will relieve part of 25th Divisional Artillery in the CANAL and GIVENCHY SECTORS on the 1st and 2nd December, in accordance with attached Table of Reliefs.

3. The 25th Divisional Artillery will withdraw all 18-pdr guns.
    The 25th Divisional Artillery will withdraw all 4.5" Hows in action, except two in each How Battery which will be taken over in situ by 42nd D.A. Batteries stripped except for sights.

4. One gun of each battery in the detached section, and one gun in the main position will be relieved on the first night.
    The remaining guns will be relieved on the second night.

5. Incoming batteries will take over the present normal Zones and S.O.S. Lines from batteries relieved.
    Special Orders will be issued later for the two batteries of 211th Bde not relieving batteries of 25th D.A.

6. Maps, Aeroplane photos and map boards will be taken over.
    All ammunition at gun positions, also trench and area stores, will be taken over and returns made out and forwarded to Staff Captain, 42nd Divisional Artillery.

7. Command of Groups will pass on completion of reliefs on the night 2nd/3rd December.

8. Attached Table gives the allotment of Wagon Lines to the 42nd Divisional Artillery.

9. A/211 and B/211 batteries complete will move into action on evening 1st prox, their teams returning to the ROBECQ Area.
    176 rounds per gun will be dumped at their new battery positions.
    In the case of the relieving portions of other batteries, after relief teams will return to new Wagon Lines.

10. The 42nd D.A.C. (less S.A.A. Section) will relieve 25th D.A.C. on 2nd prox.
    42nd D.A.C. will take over Gun Ammunition Dump and the accounting of ammunition from 12 noon on 2nd December.

11. Refilling Point on November 30th and December 1st, will be in the village of ROBECQ.

12. A March Table for 1st and 2nd prox will be issued later.

13. The command of the Artillery covering CANAL and GIVENCHY Sectors will pass to C.R.A. 42nd Division on completion of reliefs.
    42nd D.A., H.Q. will remain at AIRE (Fm. ST. ANDRE, N.2.d.2.9.) until it moves to LOCON on 2nd prox.

14. ACKNOWLEDGE.

Captain., R.F.A.
A/Brigade Major, 42nd Divisional Artillery.

Issued at 7.30 pm
by D.R.L.S.
Copies to:-
210th Bde (5)   42nd Divn. 'G'   R.A. XV Corps.
211th Bde (5)   42nd Divn. 'Q'   S.C., R.A. 42nd Divn.
42nd D.A.C. (4) 25th D.A.   Off i/c R.A. Sigs.
D.T.N.O. (2)   Area Com'dt. ROBECQ A.D.M.S. 42nd Divn.
428th Coy. A.S.C.   LAMBRES 42nd Div. Train.
War Diary   File.

MARCH TABLE for 30th Instant.

Reference 42nd D.A.Order No.57.

ITEM	UNIT.	STARTING POINT	TIME TO PASS STARTING POINT.	ROUTE.	REMARKS.
1.	211th Bde.	Road Junction N.29.c.8.1.	9.10 am	ST.HILAIRE - LILLERS - L'ECLEME - Road Junction V.9.b.9.9. - ROBECQ - Billets.	
2.	210th Bde.		10.15 am.		
3.	42nd D.A.C.		11.20 am.		
4.	428 Coy. A.S.C.		11.55 am.		
5.	T.M's.	T.M.,H.Q. FONTES.	As ordered by D.T.M.O.		Any except that taken by Batteries.

TABLE OF RELIEFS to accompany 42nd Divisional Artillery Order No.

No.	Unit	Relieving	Position Number	No. of Gun Pits.	Map Co-ordinates.	O.P.
1.	H.Q., 219th Bde.	H.Q., 110th Bde.			F.10.b.5.2.	
2.	A/210	B/110	F.24/6 G.7/2.	4 2	F.24.a.4.8. G.7.b.80.50.	FOUR HUNDRED
3.	B/210	C/110	F.17/1. F.18/1.	4 2	F.17.a.1.2. F.18.a.2.1.	B HOUSE SPOIL BANK
4.	C/210	B/112	F.11/2. A.14/5	4 2	F.11.d.25.45 A.14.a.1.9. (unoccupied)	
5.	D/210	D/110	A.20/1.	4 1	A.20.c.4.7. A.20.c.5.8. (Camouflage)	KINGSCIENE
6.	H.Q., 211th Bde.	H.Q., 112th Bde.			X.28.a.7.8.	
7.	A/211		F.5/3 F.5/4	6	F.5.d.2.9. (unoccupied) F.5.b.45.15	V HOUSE A.8.c.95.35. SAPPER HOUSE A.9.c.70.25.
8.	B/211	B/112	X.24/6 F.4/1	2 3 1	X.24.a.9.6. (unoccupied) about F.4.d.2.8. (unoccupied) about F.5.c.2.2.	GUN HOUSE S.20.d.15.15. BREWERY S.20.d.30.25.

- 2 -

No.	Unit.	Relieving.	Position Number.	No of Gun Pits	Map Co-ordinates.	C.P.
3.	C/211	C/112	X.30/2	4 2	X.30.c.5.3. A.13.b.42.42	GIRLS SCHOOL S.25.d.65.10. CANOT EE.
10.	D/211	D/112	A.1/1 X.24/4	4 2	A.1.b.0.2. X.24.c.2.6.	BELL HOUSE S.20.c.85.25. HEYTESBURY HOUSE A.8.a.75.75.

29-11-17.

TABLE showing allotment of Wagon Lines to
42nd Divisional Artillery to accompany 42nd D.A.
Order No. 57.

			Now occupied by
210th BRIGADE.	H.Q.	F.10.b.5.2.	H.Q. 110 Bde.
	A.	E.18.b.8.2.	B/110
	B.	F.14.b.8.1.	C/110
	C.	F.13.a.8.2.	A/110
	D.	F.14.b.7.3.	D/110
211th BRIGADE.	H.Q.	X.26.a.7.8.	H.Q. 112 Bde.
	A/211	X.25.a.9.7.	A/112
	B/211	X.19.c.2.9.	B/112
	C/211	W.24.c.5.0.	C/112
	D/211	W.30.b.8.2.	D/112

Wagon Lines of 42nd D.A.C.

H.Q.	W.23.c.90.15.
No.1.Section	W.18.a.2.6.
No.2. "	W.18.a.5.7.
No.3(S.A.A.)	F.8.b.9.7.

SECRET & URGENT.

O.C.

    210th Bde. R.F.A.
    211th Bde. R.F.A.

Reference 42nd D.A. Order No.57. para.3.

CANCEL that portion of the para. relating to transfer of 4.5" How. Equipment.

25th D.A. will withdraw all 4.5" Hows. which will be relieved in action by all 4.5" Hows. of 42nd D.A.

[signature]
Captain. R.F.A.
Staff Captain., 42nd Divnl. Artillery.

30-11-17.

SECRET & URGENT.

> HEADQUARTERS,
> 42ND
> DIVL. ARTILLERY.
> No. Bm 1/46
> Date...........

O.C.

211th Brigade R.F.A.

----

1. Under orders from XV Corps, 42nd D.A. will hand over to 25th D.A. 9 - 18pdr. Guns.

2. These guns will be furnished by 211th Bde R.F.A. as follows :-

    6 guns of A/211 Battery.
    3 guns of B/211 Battery.

    The personnel of A/211 Battery will therefore remain in Wagon Lines until further orders and B/211 Battery will occupy position X.24/6 and man one gun in position F.4/1.

3. The 6 guns of A/211 will be marched to ANNEZIN (BETHUNE Sheet E.9.) on the morning of December 1st. and there handed over to A/112 Battery at the Recreation Ground.

    B/211 Battery will march to Wagon Lines of B/112 Battery (X.19.c.2.9.) on the morning of December 1st. where 3 guns will be handed over to B/112 Battery and whence the remaining 3 guns will be taken into action on the afternoon of December 1st.

    [signature]

30-11-17.

Captain. R.F.A.
Staff Captain., 42nd Divnl. Artillery.

Copies to :-

   25th D.A.
   R.A., XV Corps.
   42nd Division. 'G'.
   War Diary.
   File.

<u>CONFIDENTIAL</u>

WAR DIARY

OF

H.Q., R.A. 42nd Division

Volume X

From 1-12-17
To. 31-12-17.

Ref: BETHUNE (Combined Sheet) 1/40,000

WAR DIARY
or
INTELLIGENCE SUMMARY.

Army Form C. 2118.

Vol. X. SHEET I

(Erase heading not required.)

Place	Date	Hour	Summary of Events and Information	Remarks and references to Appendices
LOCON.	Dec 1st	7pm.	Relief of 25th D.A. completed and command passed from CRA 25th Div to CRA 42nd Div.	App I
"	4th		Definition of Batteries Re.	
"	13th		Lieut H.W.L. Kearns (A/211) att'd DAHQ for transit. Evans Cowns (S.C.)	
"	20th	10 am	Capt MORGAN (SCRA) to England on leave.	App II
"	"		42nd Division transferred from XV Corps to I Corps.	
"	"		Lieut D Malcolm to Arras with R.F.C. at BERTANGLES.	
"	24th	7.30 onwards p.m.	Concentration by 18 pdrs and Gen bombardment by 4.5" Hows in connection with Gas Projection on CANAL LEFT SECTOR	App III
"	26th		Major P R Mitchell to I Corps RA vice Maj Douglas Jones (on leave)	
"	27th		Lieut Malcolm returned from R.F.C. Course.	
"	28th		Capt Morgan " " leave.	App IV
			Definition report 27th Dec.	App V
			Present Policy	

Ashworth
Col W R? 3? R.A.
CoW 42? 18? 3? R?

Appendix I

42nd Divisional Artillery.

DISPOSITION REPORT.

UNIT.		POSITION	WAGON LINES.
HEADQUARTERS.R.A.		LES CAUDRONS. W.6.d.5.5.	W.6.d.5.5.
210th Bde.R.F.A.			
Headquarters.		F.10.b.5.2.	F.10.b.5.2.
'A' Btty.	(4)	F.24.a.4.8.	E.18.b.8.2.
	(2)	G.7.b.80.50	
'B' "	(4)	F.17.a.1.2.	F.14.b.8.1.
	(2)	F.18.a.2.1.	
'C' "	(4)	F.11.d.25.45	F.13.a.8.2.
	(2)	A.14.a.1.9.	
'D' "	(4)	A.20.c.4.7.	F.14.b.7.3.
	(2)	A.20.c.5.8.	
211th Bde R.F.A.			
Headquarters,		X.28.a.7.8.	X.28.a.7.8.
'A' Btty.		F.5.d.2.9.	X.25.a.9.7.
'B' "	(2)	X.24.a.9.6.	X.19.c.2.9.
	(3)	F.4.d.2.8.	
	(1)	F.5.c.2.2.	
'C' "	(4)	X.30.c.5.3.	W.24.c.5.0
	(2)	A.13.b.42.42	
'D' "	(4)	A.1.b.0.2.	W.30.b.8.2.
	(2)	X.24.c.2.6.	
42nd Div.Amm.Col.			
Headquarters,			W.23.c.90.15.
No.1.Section.			W.13.a.2.5.
No.2.Section.			W.18.a.5.7.
S.A.A.Section.			F.8.b.9.7.
42nd T.M.B's.			
D.T.M.O.		BEUVRY. F.21.a.10.10	
V/42 T.M.Btty.		A.26.b.35.40	
X/42 T.M.Btty.		A.14.d.37.75.	Rest Billets for Bde.
Y/42 T.M.Btty		A.9.c.10.75.	F.21.a.10.10
Z/42 T.M.Btty.		A.14.d.35.75.	

P.R.Mitchell

4-12-17.   Major.,
Brigade Major, 42nd Divisional Artillery.

"War Diary"

HEADQUARTERS, 42ND DIVL. ARTILLERY.
No. B.M.S. 1/25
Date.

A/M II

S E C R E T.   Copy No. 9

42nd DIVISION ORDER No: 53.

Reference: 1/10,000 Trench Map, LA BASSEE.

18th December 1917.

1. The 42nd Division will be transferred from XV Corps to I Corps from 10 a.m., 20th December 1917.

2. No alteration will for the present be made in Divisional Boundaries.

3. ACKNOWLEDGE on attached slip.

Bryan Curling
Lieut Colonel,
General Staff,
42nd Division.

Issued by D.R. at ..11.30.. a.m. 18/12/17.
    Orderly
Copies to :-

Copy No.1. G.O.C.	13. 'Q'
2. War Diary.	14. XV Corps.
3. War Diary.	15. XV Corps.
4. 125th Inf.Bde.	16. XV Corps R.A.
5. 126th Inf.Bde.	17. XV Corps H.A.
6. 127th Inf.Bde.	18. 45th H.A.G. (through
7. No.4 Special Coy.R.E.	XV Corps H.A.)
8. D. Special Coy. R.E.	19. 46th Division.
9. C.R.A.	20. 1st Portuguese Divn.
10. C.R.E.	21. Capt. Warner, 1st
11. A.D.M.S.	Portuguese Divn.
12 'A'	22. D.G.O.
	23. D.M.G.O.
	24. I Corps.
	25. File.

SECRET.

42nd Divisional Artillery Order No. 59.

Reference: 1/10,000 Trench Map, LA BASSEE.

Dec. 13th 1917.

1. Reference 42nd Divisional Artillery Warning Order No. 10 dated 15/12/17.

   On a night and at a time to be notified later R.E. Special Coys. are projecting gas on the "CANAL LEFT" and "GIVENCHY I" Sectors.

   42nd Divisional Artillery will co-operate as shown on attached Table.

   45th Heavy Artillery Group is requested to co-operate as shown on the same Table.

2. D.T.M.O. will report objectives chosen and number of T.Ms. firing to this Office.

3. **Communications.** Os. C. D. Special Company, R.E. and M. Section, No. 4 Special Company, R.E. will be located at "KINGSCLERE" (Battn. H.Qrs., Left Battn. Canal Sector,) and will send "priority" wires to 42nd Division, 45th H.A.G., 210th and 211th Bdes., R.F.A., 126th, 127th and 138th Inf. Bdes., and Right Front and Support Battns., 127th Inf. Bde., 2 hours before zero to say whether or not their gas attacks are to take place, and another wire after each gas attack, when all is clear.

4. **Special Precautions.**
   (a) In the area East of the Line A.16.c.2.0., A.15.d.3.3., A.15.b.9.2., all sentries will be specially warned to be on the look out for any rounds that may fall short: all other personnel will wear their box respirators and gas curtains will be closed from zero till zero plus 10, zero plus 1 hour 40' to zero plus 1 hour 50', and zero plus 4 hours 10', to zero plus 4 hours 20'.

   (b) In the areas A.15.b. and A.9.c. (Eastern half) and d., all gas curtains will be closed and all personnel will wear box respirators from zero - 5, until the message "all clear" is received, except that sentries in the saps may take off their respirators at zero plus 10'.

5. Watches will be synchronised by a General Staff Officer at Inf. Bde. Headquarters before 12 noon on a date to be notified later for the Inf. Bdes., and Bdes. R.F.A., and under Bde. arrangements for other units.

   The D.T.M.O. will arrange to obtain the time from Right Group R.F.A. H.Q.,

   Right Group R.F.A. will arrange to give the time to 45th H.A.G. at their H.Q. at F.14.c.5.2,

/ para. 6.

-- 2 --

6. <u>Codes</u>.

    Operation will take place as ordered ..... First O.K.
    Operation put off for 3 hours and
    will take place commencing at zero plus 3 hrs. Second O.K.
    First Gas attack completed .... First HOGIA.
    Second gas attack completed .... Second HOGIA.
    Third gas attack completed .... Third HOGIA.
    Operation postponed for the night .... KARAB.

7. Every precaution will be taken to prepare against enemy gas shelling in retaliation.

8. Acknowledge.

Issued at 2 p.m.

P.R. Mitchell
Major, R.A.
Brigade Major, 42nd Div'l Arty.

On 16/12/17.

By D.R.L.S.

Copies to:-
    210th Bde. R.F.A. (4)
    211th Bde. R.F.A. (5)
    42nd D.T.M.C. (2)
    45th H.A.G. (2)
    42nd Div. "G". (2)
    R.A. XV Corps.
    H.A. XV Corps.
    S.C.R.A. 42nd Div.
    R.O.R.A. 42nd Div.
    File.
    War Diary.

Table to accompany 42nd Div. Artillery Order No. 59.

Item.	TIME. From.	TIME. To.	UNIT.	OBJECTIVE.	Remarks.
1.	ZERO.	Zero plus 5.	45th H.A.G.	H.Q. at A.23.c.55.05; A.23.b.70.42; A.17.b.32.30. and A.11.c.90.45.	One 6" How. on each point. One round per How. per min. H.E.
			D.Bty.210th Bde.	A.23.c.55.05. and A.23.b.70.42.	2 - 4.5" Hows. on each point. 3 rds. per How. per Min. Lethal Shell.
			D.Bty.211th Bde.	A.17.b.32.30. and A.11.c.90.45.	-- ditto. --
			T.M. Bde.	Enemy T.Ms. in area between: Southern limit. A.13.c.25.25. to A.13.c.95.25. Northern limit. A.10.b.30.00 to A.10.b.85.00 and at A.13.d.30.05.	H.E. Rapid rate.
2.	Zero plus 2.	Zero plus 5.	Right Group R.F.A. (18-pdrs. only).	Concentration "CANAL LEFT."	Shrapnel, 25´ graze. 5 rds. per gun per min.
3.	Zero plus 2.	Zero plus 5.	Left Group, R.F.A. (18-pdrs. only).	Concentration "GIVENCHY I".	Shrapnel, 25´ graze. 5 rds. per gun per min.

- 2 -

ITEM.	TIME.		UNIT.	OBJECTIVE.	REMARKS.
	From.	To.			
4.	Zero plus 5	Zero plus 20.	45th H.A.G. D/210 } D/211 }	As in Item 1. As in Item 1.	Slow bombardment. ½ rd. p.h. p.m. H.E. } (½ round per How. Lethal. (per min.
5.	Zero plus 1 hr. 40 min.	Zero plus 1 hr. 45 mins.	45th H.A. } D/210. } D/211. } T.M.Bde.		Repeat Item 1.
6.	Zero plus 1 hr. 42 mins.	Zero plus 1 hr. 45 mins.	Right Group R.F.A. (18-pdrs. only.)		Repeat item 2.
7.	Zero plus 1 hr. 45 mins.	Zero plus 2 hrs.	45th H.A. } D/210. } D/211. }		Repeat Item 4.
8.	Zero plus 4 hrs. 10 mins	Zero plus 4 hrs. 15 mins.	45th H.A.G. } D/210. } D/211. } T.M.Bde. }		Repeat Item 1.
9.	Zero plus 4 hrs. 12mins.	Zero plus 4 hrs. 15mins.	Right Group, R.F.A. (18-pdrs. only.)		Repeat Item 2.
10.	Zero plus 4 hrs. 15 mins.	Zero plus 4 hrs. 30 mins	45th H.A.G. } D/210. } D/211. }		Repeat Item 4.

16/12/17.

SECRET.

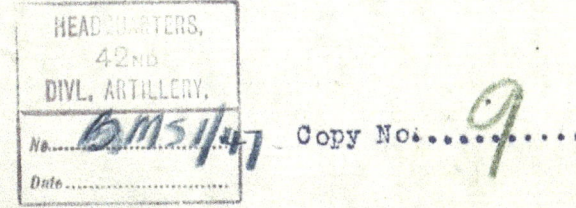 Copy No. 9

ADDENDUM No: 2 to
42nd DIVISION ORDER No: 52.

24th December 1917.

1. Reference paras.1 and 5 of the above mentioned order, the date will be the 24th instant, (to-day).

2. Zero hour will be 7.30 p.m.

3. Reference para.3 of the above mentioned order, the 125th Inf. Brigade will be substituted for the 127th Inf. Brigade, and the 125th M.G. Coy will be added to the list of units to whom the wire therein ordered is to be sent.

4. ~~ACKNOWLEDGE on attached slip.~~

Bryan Cusling
Lieut Colonel,
General Staff,
42nd Division.

Issued by ~~D.R.~~ at 10.30 a.m., 24/12/17.
        Orderly

Distribution :-

  To all recipients of 42nd Division Order No:52, except XV Corps.

  Copies Nos.14 & 15 to I Corps.
  Copy No: 16 to I Corps R.A.
  Copy No: 17 to I Corps H.A.

Appendix IV

SECRET.

42nd Divisional Artillery.

LOCATION STATEMENT.   27th December, 1917.

Reference Map; BETHUNE, Sheet 36 1/10,000

UNIT.		POSITION.	WAGON LINES.
Headquarters, R.A. LES CAUDRONS.		W.6.d.5.5.	W.6.d.5.5.

RIGHT GROUP.(CANAL) 210th Bde.R.F.A. O.C., Major.D.J.MASON.

		POSITION.	WAGON LINES.
Headquarters,		F.10.b.5.2.	F.10.b.5.2.
A/210	5 guns	F.24.a.36.84	E.18.b.8.2.
	1 gun	F.24.c.78.39	
B/210	4 guns	F.17.a.1.2.	F.14.b.8.1.
	2 "	F.18.a.2.1.	
D/210	4 Hows	A.20.c.32.71	F.14.b.7.3.
	2 "	F.23.b.25.80	

LEFT GROUP.(GIVENCHY) 211th Bde.R.F.A. O.C., Lieut.Col.E.J.INCHES,D.S.O.

		POSITION.	WAGON LINES.
Headquarters.		X.28.a.7.8.	X.28.a.7.8.
A/211	4 guns	F.4.d.2.8.	X.25.a.9.7.
	2 "	X.24.a.9.6.	
B/211	4 "	F.5.b.1.1.	X.19.c.2.0.
	2 "	F.5.b.5.3.	
C/211	2 guns	X.30.c.5.3.	W.24.c.5.0.
	2 "	A.13.b.42.42	
D/211	6 Hows	A.5.c.1.9.	W.30.b.8.2.
C/210	4 guns	F.11.d.25.45	F.13.a.8.2.
(attached)	2 "	A.7.d.7.1.	

42nd Divisional Ammunition Column. O.C., Lieut.Col.A.E.JOLLIFFE, V.D.

Headquarters.		W.23.c.9.1.
No.1.Section.		W.18.a.2.6.
No.2.Section.		W.18.d.5.7.
S.A.A.Section.		F.8.c.9.7.

42nd Trench Mortar Brigade. D.T.M.O. Capt. H.L.LEVITT.

	POSITION.	WAGON LINES.
Headquarters BEUVRY	F.20.a.5.9.	
V/42 T.M.Btty	A.14.d.35.75.	
X/42 " " "	A.14.d.35.75.	Host Billets for
Y/42 " " "	A.9.c.10.75	Brigade BEUVRY
Z/42 " " "	A.14.d.35.75	F.20.b.10.45.

A.R.P. ROBEY DUMP.   W.18.b.8.1.

G.H.Clemey Lieut.
for Brigade Major, 42nd Divn. Artillery.

No. 1/CA/1303 25th Dec. 1917

Appendix V

SECRET.

1. In view of the present cessation of hostilities on the Russian Front it is essential that special attention be paid to the DEFENSIVE POLICY, to be adopted on this front. The enemy reinforced as they must be, may embark upon an offensive against any portion of the Allied Fronts. It is therefore necessary that every precaution be taken and adequate preparations made to meet a hostile offensive at short notice. Instructions as to the action of the Artillery in the event of a strong hostile Attack are contained in I Corps Instructions No. 9 dated 25th November, 1917.

A policy of PASSIVE DEFENSIVE is of no value, and, although stress is at present laid upon defensive measures, yet the possibility of assuming the offensive must be considered and arrangements made accordingly.

It is further necessary in dealing with Defensive Policy that thorough preparations are made to launch strong and determined counter-attacks, in which the role of the Artillery will be one of bold and energetic support of the Infantry.

2. Schemes for Artillery Support to meet every situation will be prepared by Divisional Artilleries and Heavy Artillery I Corps. Only the general lines along which preparations will be made can be given. Much depends upon local conditions. An outline of the general policy and requirements is as follows :-

(i) Artillery will be distributed in depth, so that forward guns may be withdrawn under cover of rearward batteries. The main line of resistance will not be less than 3,000 yards for Field Artillery and 4,000 yards for Heavy Artillery, from the front line, and the reinforcing line 4,000 yards and 7,000 yards respectively.

(ii) A proportion of Heavy and Field Guns and Howitzers will be so sited that fire can be brought to bear upon the hostile front system of defence at long range only. These guns and howitzers may not always be manned. In the event of suspicious action by the enemy, the personnel of Divisional and Heavy Artilleries billeted in back areas for training, to whom the guns belong, will be sent up in buses and lorries.

(iii) Wide arcs of fire must be obtained so that every battery may cover as broad a portion of front as possible. Small arcs mean limited zones of fire and therefore considerable restriction in the usefulness of batteries.
Platforms will be prepared outside each gun pit in all Field Artillery positions, so that guns may be run out at short notice and utilized on objectives outside their normal arc of fire.

(iv) Should an hostile offensive appear probable on this front, the Artillery at present in the line must be prepared to be reinforced. It will therefore be necessary for reinforcing positions to be selected and work commenced on them forthwith, so that they may be ready for occupation at short notice.
These positions will be numbered and a notice board placed in No. 1 Pit of each position. The board will shew the number of the position and the sign of the formation to which it belongs. A list of reinforcing positions will be submitted to I Corps by 30th inst. Brigadier-Generals Commanding Divisional and Heavy Artilleries will have prepared to following information, equipment, etc., which will be kept ready for immediate issue to each reinforcing battery :-

2. (iv) contd.

(a) Co-ordinates of all guns - or directing gun.
(b) Map Boards with arcs of fire, and dead ground within the arc clearly shewn.
(c) Description of true bearings of aiming points and description of suitable datum points.
(d) Co-ordinates of O.Ps.
(e) Diagram of communications.
(f) Latest maps 1/20,000 and 1/10,000.
(g) Local traffic map.
(h) Corps Artillery Standing Orders. (To be issued later).
(i) Map locations of
    Group H.Q.   Nearest Water Supply.
    Refilling Point.   Nearest Dressing Station.
    Source of Supplies.   R.F.C. Squadron covering front.
    Nearest K.B. Section.

(v) Divisional Artilleries and Heavy Artillery I Corps will select positions to cover the several intermediate systems of defence enumerated in the I Corps Defence Scheme. These positions and the approaches to them are to be thoroughly reconnoitred by the batteries allotted to them. A list of positions selected will be forwarded to I Corps by the 30th inst. All positions so selected will be signboarded as in para. (iv) above.

(vi) Further to the instructions contained in I Corps No.1/C.A./1271 dated 9th December, 1917, it will be necessary for special arrangements to be made in the 42nd Division area for the protection of personnel. Battery positions in the 42nd Division area are to a great extent situated in orchards or gardens belonging to small houses. With care and forethought these positions may be made strong points for our Infantry. Wiring must be judiciously done, so that it may be covered by a good field of fire from the battery position.

Infantry Officers are to be encouraged to visit battery positions so that they may know the situation of localities that might be of value to them.

The wiring of Battery positions of 42nd Divisional Artillery must be completed by the 30th inst.

(vii) The enemy has frequently feigned ignorance of the exact location of our batteries prior to an attack. Yet, at a moment most suitable to his offensive plan, he has opened very heavy and accurate neutralizing fire upon our batteries. Concealment and deception, thus become most important factors. Arrangements must be made for the preparation of alternate positions.

Divisional and Heavy Artilleries must arrange for the construction of "Dummy Batteries", and will also detach "roving" actions to occupy new sites for short periods only, thus multiplying the positions earmarked by the enemy for neutralization during his offensive and thereby weakening his fire on those positions that will actually be occupied during operations.

para.3./-

3. Observation Posts will be selected as follows :-

   (i) Sufficient reserve Observation Posts to meet the requirements of reinforcing batteries.

   (ii) Suitable O.Ps. to overlook each intermediate line of Defence. These O.Ps. will be marked by a notice board and a general plan of communications will be prepared. The Map Locations of these O.Ps. will be forwarded to I Corps by the 5th January 1918.

   (iii) Over and above the "NORMAL" system of Observation Posts that overlook the present front occupied by the enemy,,the following Observation Posts must be reconnoitred and earmarked :-

   (a) "Intermediate O.Ps."to cover the ground over which the enemy may advance after it has been necessary to quit the NORMAL O.P.

   (b) "HOME O.Ps." to be selected in close proximity to the battery position to enable guns to be fought up to the last possible moment.

4. Arrangements will be made for single "silent" guns to be sited well forward to deal with hostile tanks. These guns are to have as wide an arc as possible and will be provided with 200 rounds AX per gun. Sufficient "silent" guns will be used to ensure the whole front being covered.

5. In the event of a forced retirement, batteries will withdraw by Sections, the last section will remain, and if necessary fight to the finish.

6. One machine gun will be issued to each Field Battery to be manned by Battery Personnel. Sites for placing machine guns must be selected with great care, due regard being paid to the possibility of enfilade fire.
Arrangements must be made to train sufficient Field Artillery personnel in the handling of machine guns.

7. Preparations will be made to receive, at battery positions, double the amount of ammunition at present kept at the guns.

25th December 1917.

CONFIDENTIAL 9/A/12

WAR DIARY.

OF

R.A. H.Q., 42nd Divn.

From 1st January 1918.

To 31st January 1918

Volumn XI

42nd Div Arty. H.Q.

Army Form C. 2118.

WAR DIARY
or
INTELLIGENCE SUMMARY.

Vol XI Sheet I.

(Erase heading not required.)

Instructions regarding War Diaries and Intelligence Summaries are contained in F.S. Regs., Part II. and the Staff Manual respectively. Title pages will be prepared in manuscript.

Place	Date	Hour	Summary of Events and Information	Remarks and references to Appendices
LOCON	Jan. 1st		Ref BETHUNE (Combined Sheet) 1/40000	Bn. Appx I
	5th		Disposition Report	Div.
	6th		Reduction in H.Q.R.A. Staff to economize in man-power	
	7th		Instructions sent out to reduce Artillery Activity in accordance with I Corps Instructions	Div. Appx II
	8th		The 84th Army Brigade RFA - Lt-Col Corna attached 42nd Division from 4th Army arrived Mt BERNENCHON and ANNEZIN (1 Battery)	Bn. Appx III
	10th		Lieut HWL Kearns attached H.Q.R.A proceeded on course to GHQ 3rd Echelon	Bn.
	13th		Disposition Report	Bn. Appx IV
	14th		Lieut HWL Kearns returned H.Q.R.A. from course at GHQ 3rd Echelon	Bn.
	15th		Period of Arctic Spell broke up	Bn.
	17th		84th Army Bde commenced preparing positions	Div.
	19th		Disposition Report	Bn. Appx V
	20th		Lt-Col Robart, B. McBride, Chief of Staff 30th Inf Div U.S.A. Army and Capt. B.F. Hoge 10th Cavalry U.S.A. Army visited H.Q.R.A. 42nd Division for instruction.	Div.
	21st		Brig-Gen F.W.H. Walshe D.S.O. C.R.A. 42nd Div. Arty took over command 42nd Div during absence of Maj.-Gen. A. Solly-Flood C.M.G. D.S.O on leave to England	Div.
	23rd		Lt-Col McBride and Capt Hoge left for 126th Inf Bde H.Q at VENDIN-LES-BETHUNE	Bn.
	24th		Bank C Batteries 84th Army Bde came into Action	Bn.
			Disposition Report	Bn. Appx VI

Army Form C. 2118.

WAR DIARY
or
INTELLIGENCE SUMMARY.

(Erase heading not required.)

Instructions regarding War Diaries and Intelligence Summaries are contained in F. S. Regs., Part II. and the Staff Manual respectively. Title pages will be prepared in manuscript.

Place	Date	Hour	Summary of Events and Information	Remarks and references to Appendices
	Jan 26th		84th Bde HQ from Locon relieved 211th Bde HQ at LOISNE	RWL
	27		211th HQ moved to LOCON	RWL
	31st		A and D batteries 84th Bde came into Action. Disposition Report	RWL App. VII
			To Watson Lt. for B C RA 78th Div.	
			10228	

Appendix I

SECRET.

42nd Divisional Artillery.

LOCATION STATEMENT.   27th December, 1917.

Reference Map: BETHUNE, Sheet 36 1/10,000

UNIT.		POSITION.	WAGON LINES.
Headquarters, R.A. LES CAUDRONS.		W.6.d.5.5.	W.6.d.5.5.

RIGHT GROUP. (CANAL) 210th Bde.R.F.A. O.C., Major.D.J.MASON.

Headquarters,		F.10.b.5.2.	F.10.b.5.2.
A/210	5 guns	F.24.a.36.84	E.18.b.8.2.
	1 gun	F.24.c.78.30	
B/210	4 guns	F.17.a.1.2.	F.14.b.8.1.
	2 "	F.18.a.2.1.	
D/210	4 Hows	A.20.c.32.71	F.14.b.7.3.
	2 "	F.23.b.25.80	

LEFT GROUP. (GIVENCHY) 211th Bde.R.F.A. O.C., Lieut.Col.E.J.INCHES, D.S.O.

Headquarters.		X.28.a.7.8.	X.28.a.7.8.
A/211	4 guns	F.4.d.2.8.	X.25.a.9.7.
	2 "	X.24.a.9.6.	
B/211	4 "	F.5.b.1.1.	X.19.c.2.0.
	2 "	F.5.b.5.3.	
C/211	2 guns	X.30.c.5.3.	W.24.c.5.0.
	2 "	A.13.b.12.12	
D/211	6 Hows	A.5.c.1.0.	W.30.b.8.2.
C/210	4 guns	F.11.d.25.45	F.15.a.8.2.
(attached)	2 "	A.7.d.7.1.	

42nd Divisional Ammunition Column. O.C., Lieut.Col.A.E.JOLLIFFE, V.D.

Headquarters.		W.23.c.9.1.
No.1.Section.		W.18.a.2.6.
No.2.Section.		W.18.d.5.7.
S.A.A.Section.		F.8.c.9.7.

42nd Trench Mortar Brigade. D.T.M.O. Capt. H.L.LEVITT,

Headquarters BEUVRY	F.20.a.5.5.	
V/42 T.M.Btty	A.14.d.35.75.	Rest Billets for
X/42 " " "	A.14.d.35.75.	Brigade BEUVRY
Y/42 " " "	A.9.c.10.75	F.20.b.10.45.
Z/42 " " "	A.14.d.35.75	

A.R.P. ROBBY DUMP.		W.18.b.8.1.

G.H.Clemy Lieut.
for Brigade Major, 42nd Divn. Artillery.

LIST OF T.M's in Position

Ready to fire.

NORTHERN SECTOR.

SOLLY.	1 Long Heavy 9.45"	A.2.c.25.65.
Birdcage.	1 6" Newton.	A.9.c.2.4
Ware Road	1 6" "	A.9.c.5.9
Upper Cut.	1 6" "	A.9.a.8.1.
Avenue	1 2" M.T.M.	A.9.c.3.8.
Elephant.	1 2" M.T.M.	A.9.d.1.5.

SOUTHERN SECTOR.

Ikey	1 Short Heavy	A.15.d.5.5.
No.Bon.	1 " "	A.21.a.9.5.
CUINCHY	2 6" Newton	A.21.a.7.4.
Braddell Cut.	2 6" "	A.21.c.55.5
Esperanto.	1 6" " (Banbury X)	A.15.d.2.35.
Cabbage Patch.	2 2" M.T.Ms	A.15.d.6.1.
Lovers Redoubt.	1 2" M.T.M.	A.15.d.8.25.

S E C R E T. B.M.S.1/69.

O.C.
    210th Brigade R.F.A.
    211th Brigade R.F.A.
    42nd D.T.M.O.

Appendix II

    In accordance with the present policy, apart from defensive Barrages, Artillery Fire will be limited to the following :-

1. Registration and Calibration.
2. "Sniping" at movement or work in progress.
3. Fire on request of Infantry Brigadiers.
4. "Punishment" Scheme.
5. "Destroy T.M." Scheme.

    Wire cutting and Night Firing will therefore cease till further orders.

5-1-18.

SD/) Ralph BLEWITT., Capt. R.F.A.
A/Brigade Major., 42nd Divisional Artillery.

S E C R E T .
First Army No. G.S.957.
42nd Division. G.S.35/1/21.
R.A., 42nd Division. B.M.S.5/9.

I Corps.

Reference First Army Instructions for Defence,

In order to carry out the Policy of improving our defences without undue interference by the enemy, artillery activity on the Corps Front may be allowed to die down.

It will be limited to what is considered necessary for the defence on the line.

First Army.   SD/-   W.H.ANDERSON., Maj. Gen.
27th December 1917.   General Staff., First Army.

-2-

11th Division.
42nd Division.
46th Division.
55th Division.

No. 321. (G.C.) dated 28th December 1917.
----

1.   Reference above, this reduction of acitvity will be a gradual process, less and less ammunition being expended each day.

    Trench Mortar fire should be limited to an efficient reply to enemy Trench Mortar activity.

2.   The Corps Commander is of the opinion that this easing down of fire will probably give great opportunities for improving our front wire. He wants special efforts directed to this and definite parties should be kept steadily at work nightly.

    SD/-   Richard REED. Captain. G.S. for
            Brigadier-General., G.S.
            I Corps.

SECRET.

42nd Division G.S.120/4/46.
R.A. 42nd Division No. B.M.S.1/70.

appx III

84th Army Brigade, R.F.A. (c/o Area Cmdt. MORBECQUE.).
42nd Division.

No.1/C.A./1317 dated 5th Jan. 1918.

1. 84th Army Brigade R.F.A. will be transferred to I Corps in accordance with attached move table.

2. The distance of 500 yards will be maintained between Batteries and B.A.C.

3. 84th Army Brigade R.F.A. will be attached to 42nd Division from 7th inst. but will not be employed in the line or be moved from MT BERNENCHOM and ANNEZIN without reference to I Corps H.Q.

4. Billetting parties from 84th Army Brigade R.F.A. will report as follows :-

   For Bde H.Q.   )   to Sub Area Commandant of HINGHES Sub Area
   3 Batteries and   )   at 10 a.m. 7-1-18. at MT BERNENCHOM Church.
   B.A.C.   )   (Area Commandant Reserve Area will arrange
                         for the attendance of the Sub Area Commandant,
                         HINGHES Sub Area).

   For 1 Battery   To Town Major ANNEZIN at 11 a.m. 7-1-18.

5. 42nd Division will report by wire to I Corps "Q" the amount of ammunition by classes, brought in by the 84th Army Brigade R.F.A.

6. Acknowledge.

                              SD/- C.V.HORDERN? Brigadier-General.,
   Copies to :-   General Staff I Corps.

        First Army.
        Portuguese Corps.
        Area Commandant, Reserve Area.
        R.A.
        "Q"

M O V E.

Unit.	Date	From	to	Route	Railhead.
84th Army Bde. R.F.A.	7-1-18.	MORBECQUE Area.	MT BERNENCHON and ANNEZIN (1 Battery)	via ST VENANT.	4th Army on 7-1-18. 42nd Divn. 8-1-18.

SECRET.

42nd DIVISIONAL ARTILLERY.

LOCATION STATEMENT.   10th January, 1918.

UNIT.	POSITION.	CODE NAME.	POSITION CALL.	O.P.	WAGON LINES.
Headquarters, R.A.	LES CAUDRONS. W.6.d.5.5.	RIVET.	CK.6.		W.6.d.5.5.

RIGHT GROUP (CANAL) Lieut.Colonel L.J.MASON, D.S.O.

Headquarters.	F.17.b.5.2.	AIM.	CL.15.		F.10.b.5.2.
A/210	F.24.c.36.84 (5) F.24.c.78.30 (1)	RIBAND	CB.15.	SKIDELL & STEE.A20.d.42.60	E.18.b.3.2.
B/210	F.17.c.1.2. (4)	RIVAL	CC.35	TRAIL BANK. A.15.c.3.9.	F.14.b.8.1.
D/210	F.18.a.2.1. (2) A.2C.c.32.71 (2) F.23.b.35.65 (4)	RISSOLE	CB.17	KINGSCLERE. A.15.c.6.3.	F.14.b.7.3.

LEFT GROUP. (GIVENCHY) Lieut.Colonel E.J.INCHES, D.S.O.

Headquarters.	X.28.c.7.8.	RIDGE	CF.2.	"V" HOUSE O.P. A.8.c.92.35	X.23.a.7.5.
A/211	F.4.c.2.8. (4)	RIFT.	CE.10.		X.25.c.3.7.
B/211	X.24.c.9.6. (2) F.5.b.5.3. (6)	RIOT.	CE.22.	GIRLS SCHOOL.S.25.d.66.22	X.19.c.2.9.
C/211	F.5.c.6.3. (3) A.13.b.42.12 (1)	RINSE	CE.17.	HEYTESBURY HOUSE. A.8.a.8.7.	W.24.c.5.0.
D/211	A.1.b.0.2. (1) F.5.c.3.8. (5)	RIB.	CE.26	"V" HOUSE O.P. A.8.c.92.35	W.30.b.8.2.
C/210 (att'd)	F.11.d.25.45 (4) A.7.c.7.1. (2)	RIDDLE	CL.20.	SAPPERS HOUSE. A.9.c.72.22.	F.13.a.2.2.

42nd DIVISIONAL AMMUNITION COLUMN. Lieut.Colonel A.E.JOLLIFFE, V.D.

Headquarters.   W.29.a.9.3.   RIPPLE
No.1 Section   W.18.a.1.5.
No.2 Section   W.19.d.5.4.
S.A.A. Section. F.8.b.5.7.
A.R. REEFY DUMP W.18.b.8.1.
T.M.Ammn.Dump. F.13.b.2.2.
S.A.A.Dump.   F.2.c.9.2.

84th Army Bde R.F.A. Lieut.Col.CORNE., D.S.O.   At Mt.BERNENCHON and ANNEZIN.
att'd 42nd Div.Arty.

UNIT.	POSITION.	CODE NAME.	
42nd Trench Mortar Brigade.	D.T.M.O.	Captain. H.L. LEVITT.	
Headquarters.	F.10.b.5.2.	RAVE.	Brigade Rest
V/42 H.T.M.Btty.	A.14.d.35.75	RUSSET.	Billets. BEUVRY.
X/42 M.T.M. "	A.14.d.35.75	RACE.	F.20.b.10.45.
Y/42 " "	A.9.c.10.75	RUNG.	
Z/42 " "	A.14.d.35.75.	RUCK.	

LIST OF T.M's

RIGHT GROUP.

CUINCHY.	2	6" Newtons.	A.21.a.7.4.	
BRAIDEIL CUT	2	6" "	A.21.c.55.50	
ESPERANTO	1	6" "	A.15.d.20.35	(In preparation)
CABBAGE PATCH.	2	2" M.T.M's	A.15.d.5.1.	
LOVERS RETREAT	1	2" " " "	A.15.d.80.25	
IKEY	1	Short Heavy 9.45"	A.15.d.5.5.	
NO DON	1	" " "	A.21.a.9.5.	
MOSES	1	Long Heavy 9.45"	A.14.b.7.6.	

LEFT GROUP.

BIRD CAGE	1	6" Newton	A.9.c.2.4.
WARE ROAD	1	6" "	A.9.c.5.9.
UPPER CUT	1	6" "	A.9.c.8.1.
ELEPHANT	1	2" M.T.M.	A.9.d.1.5.
AVENUE	1	2" " " "	A.9.c.8.8.
NEW CUT	1	2" " " "	A.9.c.75.30
SOLLY	1	Long Heavy 9.45"	A.2.c.25.65.

Malcolm (?) Captain., R.F.A.
A/Brigade Major, 42nd Divisional Artillery.

App. V.   appx V.

SECRET.

42nd DIVISIONAL ARTILLERY.

LOCATION STATEMENT.   17th January, 1918.

UNIT	POSITION	CODE NAME	POSITION CALL	O.P.	WAGON LINES
Headquarters.R.A.	LES CAUDRONS. N.6.d.5.5.	RIVET	CL.6.		N.6.d.5.5.
RIGHT GROUP. (GR.1) Lieut.Col.D.J.MASON.,D.S.O.					
Headquarters. A/210	F.10.b.5.2. F.24.a.36.80 (5) F.24.c.78.30 (1)	KING RIBAND	CL.15. CB.15.	BRADELL CASTLE A.20.d.0.60	F.10.b.5.2. E.18.b.8.2.
B/210	F.17.a.1.2. (4) F.18.a.2.1. (3)	RIVAL	CC.35	SPOIL BANK A.15.c.9.9.	F.14.b.8.1.
D/210	A.20.c.32.71. (2) F.23.b.35.65 (4)	RISSOLE	CB.17.	KINGSCLERE A.15.c.6.3.	F.14.b.7.3.
LEFT GROUP. (GIVENCHY) Lieut.Col.A.J.INGHES.,D.S.O.					
Headquarters. A/211	X.28.a.7.8. F.4.d.2.8. (2) X.24.a.9.6. (3)	RIDGE RIFT.	CF.2. CE.10.	"V"House O.P. A.8.a.92.35.	X.28.a.7.8. X.25.a.9.7.
F/211 C/211	F.5.b.5.3. (6) F.5.c.6.3. (5) A.13.b.42.42 (1)	RIOT. RINSE	CE.22. CE.17.	GIRLS SCHOOL B.25.d.66.22. HEYTESBURY HOUSE A.8.a.3.7.	X.19.c.2.9. W.24.c.5.0.
D/211 (How.)	A.1.b.0.2. (1) F.5.a.3.8. (5)	RIM.	CE.26.	"V"HOUSE O.P. A.8.a.92.35	W.30.b.8.2.
C/210 (att'd)	F.11.d.25.45 (4) A.7.d.7.1. (2)	MIDDLE	CL.20.	SAPPERS HOUSE A.9.c.72.22	F.13.a.8.2.
24th Army Bde.R.F.A. Lieut.Col.CORLE.,D.S.O.					
Headquarters. A/84 B/84 C/84 D/84 31th B.A.C.	LOCON.				E.18.a.5.7. F.9.c.1.0. F.20.b.7.7. E.17.b.3.8. E.4.d.7.1.

UNIT.	POSITION	CODE NAME.	REMARKS.
42nd DIV.AMM'n.COLUMN. Lieut.Col.A.E.JOLLIFFE., V.D.		NIPPLE.	
Headquarters.	W.29.a.8.8.		
No.1 Section.	W.18.a.1.6.		
No.2 Section.	W.19.d.5.4.		
No.3 Section.	F.8.b.9.7.		
R.P.			
(ROPEY DUMP)	W.18.c.8.1.		
T.M.Amm.Dump.	F.13.c.2.2.		
S.A....Dump.	F.2.c.9.2.		
42nd TRENCH MORTAR BRIGADE. D.T.M.O. Capt.H.L.LEVITT.			
Headquarters.	F.10.b.5.2.	PAVE.	Bde Rest Billets
V/42 T.M.Btty.	A.14.d.35.75.	RUSSET.	BEUVRY. F.20.b.10.15.
X/42 " "	A.14.d.35.75.	RUNG.	
Y/42 " "	A.9.c.10.75.	RUCK.	
Z/42 " "	A.14.d.35.75.		

LIST OF T.M's in Position.

RIGHT GROUP.

CUINCHY. 2 6"Newtons.	A.21.c.7.4.	
BREDDLL CUT. 2 6" Newtons.	A.21.c.55.50.	
ESPERANTO. 1 6" "	A.15.d.20.35.	
G BRAG. PATCH.2 2" H.T.M's	A.15.d.6.1.	
LOVERS REDOUBT 1 2" "	A.15.d.80.85.	
IKEY. 1 Short Heavy	A.15.d.5.5.	
(9.45")		
NO BON. 1 ditto	A.21.c.9.5.	
MOSES. 1 Long H'vy	A.15.b.7.6.	
(9.45")		
REUBEN 1 ditto	A.15.c.50.44.	

LEFT GROUP.

BIRD CAGE. 1 6" Newton.	A.9.c.2.4.	
HARE ROAD 1 6" "	A.9.c.5.9.	
UPPER CUT. 1 6" "	A.9.c.8.1.	
ELEPHANT. 1 2" M.T.M.	A.9.d.1.5.	
AVENUE 1 2" " "	A.9.c.8.8.	
NEW CUT. 1 2" " "	A.9.c.75.90.	
SOLLY. 1 Long Heavy		
9.45"	A.2.c.25.65.	

Dilalcolm L! Captain. R.F.A.
A/Brigade Major, 42nd Divisional Artillery.

17th January.1918.

App x VI

SECRET.

42nd DIVISIONAL ARTILLERY.

DISPOSITION REPORT.

24th January 1916.

UNIT	POSITION	CODE NAME	POSITION CALL	O.P.	WAGON LINES
Headquarters R.A.	LES CAUDRONS. W.6.d.5.5.	RIVET	O.K.6.		W.6.d.5.5.
RIGHT GROUP. (CANAL) Lieut-Col.I.J.MASON. D.S.O.					
Headquarters.	F.10.b.5.2.	RING	O.D.15.		W.6.d.5.5.
A/210.	F.24.a.36.04. (5) F.24.c.78.36. (1)	RIBARD.	O.B.15.	BRAIDELL CASTLE.A.20.d.9.7.	F.10.b.5.2. E.12.b.3.2.
B/210.	F.17.a.1.2. (4) F.13.c.2.1. (2)	RIVAL.	O.C.35.	SPOIL BANK. A.15.c.97.93.	F.14.b.3.1.
D/210.	A.20.c.32.71. (2)	MISSILE.	O.B.17.	KINGSCLERE A.15.c.6.3.	F.14.b.7.3.
LEFT GROUP (GIVENCHY) Lieut-Col. E.J.INCHES D.S.O.					
Headquarters.	X.23.a.7.8.	RIDGE.	O.F.2.		X.23.a.7.3.
A/211.	F.4.d.2.3. (4) X.24.a.9.6. (2)	RIFT.	O.E.10.	'V' HOUSE O.P. A.3.c.92.35.	X.25.c.9.7.
B/211.	F.5.b.5.3. (6)	RICT.	O.E.22.	GIRLS SCHOOL. S.25.d.65.10.	X.19.c.2.9.
C/211.	F.5.c.6.3. (5) A.13.b.42.42. (1)	RINSE.	O.E.17.	HEYTESBURY HOUSE A.3.c.75.75.	W.24.c.5.C.
D/211.	A.1.b.0.2. (1)	RIB.	O.E.26.	'V' HOUSE O.P. A.3.c.92.35.	W.30.b.3.2.
C/210. (attached)	F.11.d.25.45. (4) F.7.d.7.7. (2)	RIDDLE.	O.D.20.	SAPPERS HOUSE A.9.c.70.25.	F.13.a.3.2.
84th Army Bde. R.F.A. Lieut-Col. CORNES. D.S.O.					
Headquarters.	X.17.b.1.4. (Not in action)				X.17.c.6.5.
A/84.	X.23.a.7.2. (6) att'd LEFT GROUP.				E.18.c.0.9.
B/84.	X.22.d.7.8. (6) -do-			GUN HOUSE S.20.d.15.15.	F.13.b.95.20.
C/84.	F.10.d.95.35. (6) -do-			FENTONS FOLLY A.9.c.90.46.	E.20.b.3.8.
D/84.	F.11.b.2.7. (Not in action)			GUN HOUSE S.20.d.15.15.	E.17.b.9.6. E.10.a.2.6.
84th B.A.C.					

App x VI

- 2 -

UNIT	POSITION	CODE NAME	REMARKS
42nd DIV. AMN. COLUMN. Lieut-Col.A.E.JOLLIFFE., V.D.		RIPPLE	
Headquarters.	W.29.a.8.3.		
No.1 Section.	W.13.c.1.6.		
No.2. "	W.13.d.5.4.		
S.A.A. "	F.3.b.9.7.		
A.R.F.			
(ROBEY DUMP)	W.13.b.6.1.		
T.M.Amnn.Dump.	F.13.b.2.2.		
S.A.A. Dump.	F.2.c.9.2.		
42nd TRENCH MORTAR BRIGADE. D.T.M.O. Capt.H.L.LEVITT.			
Headquarters.	F.10.b.5.2.	RAVE	Bde Rest Billets
V/42 T.M.Bty.	A.14.d.35.75.	RUSSET	BEUVRY. F.20.b.19.45.
X/42 " "	A.14.d.35.75.	RACE	
Y/42 " "	A.9.c.10.75.	RUNG.	
Z/42 " "	A.14.d.35.75.	RUCK	

LIST OF T.Ms. In Position.

RIGHT GROUP

GUINCHY 2 6" Newtons.		A.21.a.7.4.
BRAILEILL CUT. 2 6" Newtons.		A.21.c.55.50.
ESPERANTO. 1 6" "		A.15.d.20.35.
CABBAGE PATCH. 2 2" M.T.Ms.		A.15.d.6.1.
LOVERS REDOUBT. 1 2" "		A.15.d.30.25.
IKEY. 1 Short Heavy (9.45")		A.15.d.5.5.
No BON. 1 ditto.		A.21.a.9.5.
MOSES. 1 Long Heavy (9.45")		A.14.b.7.4.
PEUEK 1 ditto.		A.15.c.5C.44.

LEFT GROUP.

PIPE CAGE. 1 6" Newton.		A.9.c.2.4.
WARE ROAD. 1 6" "		A.9.c.5.9.
UPPER CUT. 1 6" "		A.9.a.3.1.
AVENUE 1 6" "		A.9.c.3.8.
ELEPHANT. 1 2" M.T.M.		A.9.d.1.5.
NEW CUT. 1 2" " "		A.9.c.75.60.
SOLLY. 1 Long Heavy 9.45"		A.2.c.25.65.

J.E.Morgan.

A/Brigade Major., 42nd Divisional Artillery.

Captain R.F.A.

24th January 1918.

App VII

Appx VII.

SECRET.

42nd DIVISIONAL ARTILLERY.
DISPOSITION REPORT.

Unit	Position	Code Name	Position Call	O.P.	Wagon Lines.
Headquarters R.A.	LES CAUDRONS W.6.d.5.5.	RIVET	C.K.6.		W.6.d.5.5.
GROUP. (CANAL) Lieut-Col. D.J.MASON. D.S.O.					
Headquarters.	F.10.b.5.2.	RING	C.E.15.		F.10.b.5.2.
/10.	F.21.a.36.84. (5)	RIBAND.	C.B.15.	BRADWELL CASTLE. A.20.d.9.7.	E.13.b.3.2.
	F.24.c.78.30. (1)				
/10.	F.17.a.1.2. (4)	RIVAL.	C.C.35.	SPOIL BANK. A.15.c.97.93.	F.14.b.8.1.
	F.16.a.2.1. (2)				
/10.	F.11.d.25.45. (4)	RIDDLE.	C.D.20.	SAPPERS HOUSE A.9.c.70.25.	F.13.a.8.2.
	A.7.d.7.1. (2)				
/10.	F.23.b.30.65. (4)	HISSCLF.	C.B.17.	KINGSCLERE A.15.c.3.3.	F.14.b.7.3.
	A.20.c.32.71. (2)				
GROUP (GIVENCHY) Lieut-Col. CORVES. D.S.O.	X.23.a.7.3.	KINGSWAY.			X.7.c.6.5.
/211	F.4.1.2.6. (4)	RIFT.	C.E.10.	'V' HOUSE O.P. A.3.a.92.35.	X.25.a.9.7.
	X.24.a.9.6. (2)				
/211.	F.5.b.5.3. (3)	RIOT.	C.E.22.	GIRLS SCHOOL S.25.d.65.10.	X.19.c.2.9.
/211.	F.5.c.6.3. (5)	RINSE.	C.E.17.	HEYTESBURY HO. A.3.a.75.75.	W.24.c.5.0.
	A.13.b.42.42. (1)				
D/211.	A.1.b.0.2. (1)	RIB.	C.E.26.	'V' HOUSE O.P. A.8.a.92.35.	W.30.b.6.2.
	F.5.c.3.8. (5)				
A/34.	X.23.b.0.3. (6)	PUSS.	C.G.21.	GIRLS SCHOOL S.25.d.65.10.	E.13.a.0.9.
B/34.	X.22.d.5.6. (6)	MADGE.	C.F.10.	GUN HOUSE S.20.d.15.15.	F.3.b.95.20.
C/34.	F.10.1.9.3. (6)	OLIVE.	C.E.35.	HEYTESBURY HO. A.3.a.75.75.	F.20.b.8.8.
D/34.	F.11.b.27. (4)	IVY.	C.E.34.	GUN HOUSE S.20.d.15.15.	E.17.b.9.0.
84th B.A.C.		POLICEMAN.			RIFLE RANGE BETHUNE.
211th Bde H.Q.	X.7.b.1.4. (LOGON)	RIDGE.	C.F.2.		X.19.c.2.9.

UNIT.	POSITION.	CODE NAME.	REMARKS.

LIST OF T.Ms. in Position.

42nd DIV. AMM. COLUMN. Lieut-Col. A.E. JOLLIFFE V.D. — RIPPLE.

Headquarters.	W.29.a.8.8.
No.1 Section.	W.19.a.2.6.
No.2 "	W.13.d.5.7.
S.A.A. "	F.8.b.9.7.
A.R.P.	W.13.b.8.1.
(ROBEY DUMP).	F.13.b.2.2.
T.M.Amm.Dump.	F.2.c.8.2.
S.A.A. Dump.	

42nd TRENCH MORTAR BRIGADE. I.T.M.O. Capt. H.L.LEVITT.

Headquarters.	F.10.b.5.2.	RAVE.
V/42 T.M.Bty.	A.14.d.35.75.	RUSSET. Bde Rest Billets EEUVRY. F.20.b.10.45.
X/42 "	A.14.d.35.75.	RACE
Y/42 "	A.3.c.10.75.	RUNG
Z/42 "	A.14.d.35.75.	RUCK

RIGHT GROUP.

CUINCHY	2 6" Newtons.	A.21.a.7.4.
BRADDELL CUT.	2 6" Newtons.	A.21.c.55.50.
ESPERANTO.	1 6" "	A.15.d.20.35.
	1 6" "	A.21.a.02.70.
	1 6" "	A.21.a.30.70.
CABBAGE PATCH.	2 2" M.T.Ms.	A.15.d.6.1.
LOVERS REDOUBT.	1 2" "	A.15.d.20.25.
IKEY.	1 Short Heavy (9.45")	A.15.d.5.5.
NO BON.	1 —do—	A.21.a.3.5.
REUBEN.	1 Long Heavy (9.45")	A.15.c.50.44.
MOSES.	1 —do—	A.14.b.7.6.

LEFT GROUP.

BIRD CAGE.	1 6" Newton.	A.3.c.2.4.
WARE ROAD.	1 6" "	A.9.c.5.9.
UPPER CUT.	1 6" "	A.9.a.8.1.
AVENUE	1 6" "	A.9.c.8.8.
HILDERS No.1.	1 6" "	A.9.c.3.2.
HILDERS No.2.	1 6" "	A.9.c.35.30.
ELEPHANT.	1 2" M.T.M.	A.9.d.1.5.
NEW CUT.	1 2" "	A.9.c.75.90.
SCILY.	1 Long Heavy (9.45")	A.2.25.65.

signature
Captain.R.F.A.
for Brigade Major., 42nd Divisional Artillery.

31/1/18.

CONFIDENTIAL.

WAR. DIARY

OF.

H.Q., R.A., 42ⁿᵈ DIVISION

FROM. 1-2-18.   TO. 28-2-18

VOLUME. XII.

42 A.A. H.Q.

WAR DIARY

(Erase heading not required.)

Army Form C. 2118.

Vol XII Sheet I

Place	Date	Hour	Summary of Events and Information	Remarks and references to Appendices
LOCON	1st		Capt E.P. BRASIER-CREAGH R.F.A. to 42 D.A. from 84 Army Bde R.F.A. as Staff Learner	
	7th		Disposition Report	App × I
	11th		Raid by 126 Inf Bde. 42 D.A. + 84 Army Bde. co-operating. Successful 7 prisoners + 1 machine gun captured.	
			Brig. Gen. F.W.H. WALSHE DSO relinquishes temp. command 42 Div. & returns command 42 D.A.	
	14th		Disposition Report	App × II
	15th		Brig. Gen. F.W.H. WALSHE DSO proceeded to ENGLAND on Private Officers Course M.G. School GRANTHAM + leave.	
			2r MALCOLM R.O. 42 D.A. proceeded to ENGLAND on leave.	
			HQ 42 D.A. moved from LOCON to HINGES.	
			42 D.A. in the line being relieved by 55 D.A. — 2 Batteries relieved at night. No exchange of equipment (temp).	
	16th		Lt Col A.J. HANSON D.S.O. 210th Bde R.F.A. assumes command 42 D.A. Remainder of Batteries in line relieved. 42 Div in GHQ reserve	
	17th		Disposition report	App × III

WAR DIARY
or
INTELLIGENCE SUMMARY

Army Form C. 2118.

Vol XII Sheet 2.

Place	Date	Hour	Summary of Events and Information	Remarks and references to Appendices
	9-16		Capt R. Blewitt L.S.O. R.F.A. posted to C/63 Bde R.F.A — Lewis guns (2 per Battery) authorised	
	22nd			

B Morgan Capt
for B.M. 42nd D.A.

13/18

SECRET.   Copy* I   7/2/18

42nd DIVISIONAL ARTILLERY.
DISPOSITION REPORT.

UNIT.	POSITION.	CODE NAME.	POSITION CALL.	O.P.	WAGON LINES.
Headquarters.R.A.	LES CAUDRONS. W.6.d.5.5.	RIVET.	C.K.6.		W.6.d.5.5.
RIGHT GROUP. (CANAL) Lieut-Col.D.J.MASON. D.S.O.					
Headquarters.	F.10.b.47.20. (5)	RING.	C.D.15.		F.10.b.33.30.
A/210	F.24.a.40.93. (1) F.24.c.80.32. (4)	RIBAND.	C.B.15.	BRADDELL CASTLE. A.20.d.9.7.	E.18.b.6.2.
B/210	F.17.a.12.16. (2) F.18.a.35.20. (4)	RIVAL.	C.C.35.	SPOIL BANK. (A.15.c.97.93.)	F.14.b.8.1.
C/210	F.11.d.25.45. (2) A.7.d.7.1. (4)	RIDDLE.	C.D.20.	SAPPERS HOUSE. (A.9.c.70.25)	F.13.a.8.2.
D/210	F.23.b.35.65. (4) A.20.c.32.71. (2)	RISSOLE.	C.B.17.	KINGSCLERE (A.15.c.6.3.)	F.14.b.7.3.
LEFT GROUP.(GIVENCHY) Lieut-Col.CORNES., D.S.O.					
Headquarters.	X.28.a.7.8. (4) F.4.d.33.87. (2)	KINGSWAY.	C.F.2.		X.7.c.6.5.
A/211	X.24.a.9.6. (3) F.5.b.45.25. (2)	RIFT.	C.E.10.	'V'HOUSE,A.8.a.92.35.	X.25.a.9.7.
B/211	F.5.b.1.1. (1) A.8.a.1.1. (5)	RIOT.	C.E.22.	GIRLS SCHOOL. (S25.d-65.22.)	X.19.c.2.9.
C/211	F.5.c.6.3. (1) A.13.b.42.42 (5)	RINSE.	C.E.17.	HEYTESBURY HOUSE (A.8.a-77.73)	W.24.c.5.0.
D/211	F.5.c.1.9. (1) F.6.a.9.2. (6)	RIB.	C.E.26.	'V' HOUSE, A.8.a.92.35.	W.30.b.8.2.
A/84	X.23.b.0.3. (6)	PUSS.	C.G.21.	GIRLS SCHOOL.S.25.d.65.10.	E.18.a.0.9.
B/84	X.22.d.6.6. (6)	MADGE.	C.F.18.	GUN HOUSE. S.20.d.12.12.	F.18.b.95.20.
C/84	F.10.d.9.3. (6)	OLIVE.	C.D.35.	HEYTESBURY HO.A.8.a.77.73.	F.20.b.8.8.
D/84	F.11.b.2.7. (4)	IVY.	C.D.34.	GUN HOUSE.S.20.d.12.12	E.17.b.9.8.
84th B.A.C.		POLICEMAN.			RIFLE RANGE.BETHUNE
211th Bde.H.Q.	X.7.b.1.4. (LOCON)	RIDGE.			X.19.c.2.9.

-2-

UNIT.	POSITION.	CODE NAME.	REMARKS.

42nd DIV. AMM. COLUMN. Lieut.Col. A.E.JOLLIFFE V.D.   RIPPLE.

Headquarters.	W.29.a.8.8.	
No.1.Section.	W.18.a.2.6.	
No.2.Section.	W.18.d.5.7.	
S.A.A.Section.	F.8.b.9.7.	
A.I.P.		
(MOBEY DUMP)	W.18.b.8.1.	
T.M. AMM DUMP.	F.13.b.2.2.	
S.A.A.Dump.	F.2.c.9.2.	

42nd TRENCH MORTAR BRIGADE D.T.M.O. Capt.H.L.LEVITT.   Brigade Rest Billets.
BEUVRY F.20.b.10.45.

Headquarters.	F.10.b.5.2.	RAVE.
X/42 T.M.B.	A.14.d.35.75.	RACE.
Z/42 T.M.B.	A.14.d.35.75.	RUCK.

LIST of T.M's in Position.

RIGHT GROUP.

CUINCHY.	2 6" Newtons.	A.21.a.7.4.
BRADDELL CUT.	2 6" Newtons.	A.21.c.55.50.
ESPERANTO.	1 6" "	A.15.d.20.35.
CHURCH FARM.	2 6" "	A.21.d.8.7.

LEFT GROUP.

BIRD CAGE.	1 6" Newton	A.9.c.2.4.
WARE ROAD.	1 6" "	A.9.c.5.9.
UPPER CUT.	1 6" "	A.9.a.8.1.
AVENUE	1 6" "	A.9.c.8.8.
HILDERS No.1.	1 6" "	A.9.c.3.2.
" No.2.	1 6" "	A.9.c.35.20.

/signature/
Captain., R.F.A.
for Brigade Major., 42nd Divisional Artillery.

SECRET.   42nd DIVISIONAL ARTILLERY.   App* II

DISPOSITION REPORT.   14th February, 1918.

UNIT.	POSITION.	CODE NAME.	POSITION CALL	O.P.	WAGON LINES.
Headquarters.R.A. LES CAUDRONS W.6.d.5.5.		RIVET.	C.K.6.		W.6.d.5.5.
RIGHT GROUP (CANAL) Lieut-Col.D.J.MASON.D.S.O.					
Headquarters.	F.10.b.47.20.	RING	C.D.15.		F.10.b.33.3.
A/210	F.24.a.40.93. (5)	RIBAND.	C.B.15.	BRADDELL CASTLE. (A.20.d.9.7.)	E.18.b.6.2.
	F.24.c.80.32. (1)				
B/210	F.17.a.12.15. (4)	RIVAL	C.C.35	SPOIL BANK. (A.15.c.97.93)	F.14.b.8.1.
	F.18.a.35.20. (2)				
C/210	F.11.d.25.45 (4)	RIDDLE	C.D.20.	SAPPERS HOUSE. A.9.c.70.25)	F.13.a.8.2.
	A.7.d.7.1. (2)				
D/210	F.23.b.35.65 (4)	RISSOLE	C.B.17.	KINGSCLERE. (A.15.c.6.3.)	F.14.b.7.3.
	A.20.c.32.71 (2)				
LEFT GROUP. (GIVENCHY) Lieut.Col.CORKES.,D.S.O.					
Headquarters.	X.28.a.7.8	KINGSWAY.	C.F.2.		X.7.c.6.5.
A/211	F.4.d.33.87. (4)	RIFT.	C.E.10.	'V'HOUSE A.8.a.92.35.	X.25.a.9.7.
	X.24.a.9.6. (2)				
B/211	F.5.b.45.25 (3)	RIOT.	C.E.22.	GIRLS SCHOOL.S.25.d.65.22.X.19.c.2.9.	
	F.5.b.1.1. (2)				
	A.8.a.4.1. (1)				
C/211	F.5.c.63. (5)	RINSE.	C.E.17	HEYTESBURY HOUSE. (A.8.a.77.73.)	W.24.c.5.0.
	A.13.b.42.42. (1)				
D/211	F.5.c.19. (5)	RIB.	C.E.26.	'V' HOUSE. A.8.a.92.35	W.30.b.8.2.
	F.6.a.9.2. (1)				
A/84.	X.23.b.0.3. (4)	PUSS	C.G.21.	GIRLS SCHOOL. (S.25.d.65.22)	E.18.a.0.9.
	X.24.c.3.5. (2)				
B/84	X.22.d.6.6. (5)	MADGE	C.F.18.	GUN HOUSE.S.20.d.12.12.	F.8.b.35.20.
	X.24.a.42.16. (1)				
C/84	F.10.d.9.3. (5)	OLIVE	C.D.35	HEYTESBURY HOUSE. (A.8.a.77.73)	F.20.b.8.6.
	A.14.a.08.92. (1)				
D/84.	F.11.b.2.7. (4)	IVY	C.D.34	GUN HOUSE S.20.d.12.12.	E.17.b.9.8.

- 2 -

UNIT.	POSITION.	CODE NAME	WAGON LINES.	LIST OF T.M's IN POSITION.

211th Bde. H.Q. X.7.b.1.4.(100ON) RIDGE.   X.19.c.2.9.

42nd DIV. AMN. COLUMN. Lieut.Col.A.E.JCLIFFE V.D. RIPPLE
```
Headquarters.    W.29.a.8.8.
No.1.Section     W.18.a.2.6.
No.2.Section     W.18.d.5.7.
No.3..Section.   F.8.b.9.7.
```

RIGHT GROUP.
```
CUINCHY       2 6"Newton.        A.21.a.7.4.
BRADDELL CUT  2 6" Newton.       A.21.c.55.50. - 1 out of
CHURCH FARM   2 6"   "           A.21.a.8.7.     action.
IKEY.         1 6"   "           A.15.d.5.5.
```

LEFT GROUP.
```
BIRD CAGE     1 6" Newton.       A.9.c.2.4.
WARE ROAD.    1 6"   "           A.9.c.5.9.
UPPER CUT     1 6"   "           A.9.a.8.1.
AVENUE        1 6"   "           A.9.c.8.8.
HILDERS No.1. 1 6"   "           A.9.c.3.2.
"       No.2. 1 6"   "           A.9.c.35.20.
```

```
       R.P.
(ICBEY DUMP)     W.18.b.8.1.
T.M.AMN.DUMP.    F.13.b.2.2.
S.A.A.DUMP.      F.2.c.9.2.
```

42nd TRENCH MORTAR BRIGADE. D.T.M.O. Capt.H.L.LEVITT.
```
                             RAVE.       Bde Rest Billets
                             RACE        BEUVRY F.20.b.10.45.
                             RUCK.
```

```
Headquarters.    F.10.b.5.2.
X/42 T.M.Bty.    A.14.d.35.75.
Y/42 T.M.Bty.    A.14.d.35.75
```

14th February.1918.

Ralph Blewitt

for Brigade Major., 42nd Divisional Artillery.

Captain.,R.F.A.

-2-

UNIT.	POSITION.	CODE NAME	WAGON LINES.

211th Bde. H.Q.   X.7.b.1.4. (LOCON)   RIDGE.

42nd DIV. AMN. COLUMN. Lieut.Col.A.E.JOLIFFE V.D.   RIPPLE.   X.19.c.2.9.
Headquarters.   W.29.a.8.8.
No.1 Section   W.18.a.2.5.
No.2 Section.   W.18.d.5.7.
No.3 Section.   F.8.b.9.7.

R.R.P.
(ICERY DUMP)   W.18.b.8.1.
T.M.AMN.DUMP.   F.13.b.2.2.
S.A.A.DUMP.   F.2.c.9.2.

42nd TRENCH MORTAR BRIGADE. D.T.M.O. Capt.H.L.LEVITT.
Headquarters.   F.10.b.5.2.   RAVE.   Bde Rest Billets
X/42 T.M. Bty.   A.14.d.35.75.   RACE.   BEUVRY F.20.b.10.45.
Y/42 T.M. Bty.   A.14.d.35.75   RUCK.

LIST OF T.M's IN POSITION.

RIGHT GROUP.

CUINCHY 2 6"Newton.   A.21.a.7.4.
BRADDELL CUT 2 6" Newton.   A.21.c.55.50. - 1 out of action.
CHURCH FARM 2 6"   "   A.21.a.8.7.
IKEY   1 6"   "   A.15.d.5.5.

LEFT GROUP.

BIRD CAGE   1 6" Newton.   A.9.c.2.4.
WARE ROAD.   1 6"   "   A.9.c.5.9.
UPPER CUT   1 6"   "   A.9.a.8.1.
AVENUE   1 6"   "   A.9.c.8.8.
HILDERS No.1 1 6"   "   A.9.c.3.2.
    "   No.2. 1 6"   "   A.9.c.35.20.

Ralph Blewitt

Captain.,R.F.A.
for Brigade Major., 42nd Divisional Artillery.

14th February, 1918.

SECRET.

62nd DIVISION. R. ARTILLERY.

DISPOSITION REPORT.

14th February, 1918.

UNIT.	POSITION.	CODE NAME.	POSITION CALL	O.P.	WAGON LINES.
Headquarters.R.A.	LES CAUDRONS W.6.d.5.5.	RIVET.	C.K.6.		W.6.d.5.5.
RIGHT GROUP (CANAL) Lieut-Col.D.J.MASON. D.S.O.					
Headquarters.	F.10.b.47.20.	RING	C.D.15.		F.10.b.33.30
A/210.	F.24.a.40.93. (5) F.24.c.80.32. (1)	RIBAND.	C.B.15.	BRADDELL CASTLE. (A.20.d.9.7.)	E.18.b.6.2.
B/210	F.17.a.12.16. (4) F.18.a.35.20. (2)	RIVAL	C.C.35	SPOIL BANK (A.15.c.97.93)	F.14.b.8.1.
C/210	F.11.d.25.45 (4) A.7.d.7.1. (2)	RIDDLE	C.D.20.	SAPPERS HOUSE. A.9.c.70.25)	F.13.a.8.2.
D/210	F.23.b.35.65 (4) A.20.c.32.71 (2)	RISSOLE	C.B.17.	KINGSCLERE. (A.15.c.6.3.)	F.14.b.7.3.
LEFT GROUP. (GIVENCHY) Lieut.Col.CORNES.,D.S.O.					
Headquarters.	X.28.a.7.8.	KINGSWAY.	C.F.2.		X.7.c.6.5.
A/211	F.4.d.33.87. (4) X.24.a.9.6. (2)	RIFT.	C.E.10.	'V' HOUSE A.8.a.92.35	X.25.a.9.7.
B/211	F.5.b.45.25 (3) F.5.b.11. (2) A.8.a.1.1. (1)	RIOT.	C.E.22.	GIRLS SCHOOL.S.25.d.65.22 X.19.c.2.9.	
C/211	F.5.c.6.3. (5) A.13.b.42.42. (1)	RINSE.	C.E.17	HEYTESBURY HOUSE. (A.8.a.77.73.)	W.24.c.5.0.
D/211	F.5.c.1.9. (5) F.6.a.9.2. (1)	RIB.	C.E.26.	'V' HOUSE. A.8.a.92.35	W.30.b.8.2.
A/84.	X.23.b.0.3. (4) X.24.c.3.6. (2)	PUSS	C.G.21.	GIRLS SCHOOL. (S.25.d.65.22)	E.18.a.0.9.
B/84	X.22.d.6.6. (5) X.24.a.42.16. (1)	MADGE	C.F.18.	GUN HOUSE.S.20.d.12.12.	F.8.b.95.20.
C/84.	F.10.d.9.3. (5) A.14.d.08.92. (1)	OLIVE	C.D.35	HEYTESBURY HOUSE. (A.8.a.77.73)	F.20.b.8.6.
D/84.	F.11.b.2.7. (4)	IVY	C.D.34	GUN HOUSE S.20.d.12.12.	E.17.b.9.8.

App x III

42nd DIVISIONAL ARTILLERY.

LOCATION OF UNITS

Reference BETHUNE Combined Sheet 1/40,000   17th February, 1918.

UNIT.	POSITION.
HEADQUARTERS., R.A.	HINGES.
210th Brigade R.F.A. O.C.,Lieut.Col.D.J.MASON.,D.S.O.	
Headquarters.	E.21.a.40.35.
A/210	D.30.d.6.0.
B/210	E.21.a.35.35.
C/210	E.25.d.4.4.
D/210	E.25.c.0.4.
211th Brigade R.F.A. O.C.,Lieut.Col.E.J.INCHES.,D.S.O.	
Headquarters.	E.9.b.2.9.
A/211	W.27.c.00.50.
B/211	W.26.d.60.50.
C/211	E.10.a.10.80.
D/211	E.10.a.10.70.
42nd Div.Ammn.Column. O.C.,Lieut.Col.A.E.JOLLIFFE. V.D.	
Headquarters.	V.17.d.7.7.
No.1.Section.	V.23.b.6.8.
No.2.Section.	V.18.c.95.90
S.A.A.Section.	W.26.d.3.3.
42nd Trench Mortar Brigade. D.T.M.O. Captain.H.L.LEVITT.	
D.T.M.O. H.Q.	VERDIN-les-BETHUNE
	E.4.a.4.4.
X/42 T.M.Bty.	E.4.a.4.4.
V/42 T.M.Bty.	W.27.d.6.9.

J.E.Morgan
Captain., R.F.A.
17-2-18.   for Brigade Major, R.A. 42nd Division.

42nd Divisional Artillery.

C. R. A.

42nd DIVISION

MARCH 1918

Attached:-

Appendices I to VI.

Confidential

WAR DIARY
OF
H.Q., R.A., 42nd Division

VOLUME XIII

FROM 1/3/1918.   TO. 31/3/18.

MARCH 1918 VOL XIII Sheet I

Reference Maps
Bethune 1/40000 Contoured Sheet
Lens 11 1/10000
1/20000 57D NE

WAR DIARY
or
INTELLIGENCE SUMMARY

Army Form C. 2118.

(Erase heading not required.)

Place	Date	Hour	Summary of Events and Information	Remarks and references to Appendices
HINGES	3		42"DA 700 HQRA moved from HESDIGNEUL-VENDIN area to HAM-EN-ARTOIS area in GHQ reserve Disposition report	Dkl. Appx I BW 1/1
LA BEUVRIERE	5		HQ RA moved from HINGES to LA BEUVRIERE	DW " BW 1/1
LA BEUVRIERE	7		Major RR MITCHELL BMRA 42nd Div. rejoined from attachment to 1st Corps RA	BW
	8		Brig. Gen. D.W.H. WALSHE DSO RA returned from leave Capt. J.E. WALTON HS.O. Bde RFA attached HQ.RA Disposition report	BW BW Appx III BW
	9		Lt-Col. DJ MACON relinquished Command of 42 DA — Brig. Gen. D.W.H. WALSHE DSO.RA resumes Command	BW
	10 to 20th		TRAINING CARRIED OUT	BW
	21		Disposition report amendment	RA Appx IV BW
	23		42 DA received orders to move to MONCHY-BRETON area	RA
	24		42 DA received orders to move to BAVINCOURT - LAHERLIERS area	RA
			Orders received en route for DA to proceed night through to ADINFER (8 miles S of ARRAS) — HQ. RA established at MONCHY-AU-BOIS	RA
MONCHY-AU-BOIS	25	1am	42 DA in action at dawn on ABRAINZEVELLE - COURCELLES Ridge supporting 40 Div	BW
		Noon	211 Bde took up forward position S of LOGEAST Wood	BW
		6pm	211 " removed to former position behind COURCELLES	BW
		11"	211 " position S of ABRAINZEVELLE	BW
			HQRA 42 relieved HQRA 40 at BUCQUOY	BW

Army Form C. 2118.

VOL XIII Sheet II WAR DIARY
or
INTELLIGENCE SUMMARY.

(Erase heading not required.)

Place	Date	Hour	Summary of Events and Information	Remarks and references to Appendices
	25		42 DA removed to positions SE of ESSARTS	GU
			HQ RA removed to FONQUEVILLERS	DW
FONQUEVILLER	26		ARTILLERY covering 42nd Div front reorganised into 3 groups	XH
			Right Group 42 DA under Lt. Col. E.J. INCHES DSO	JH
			Centre " 40 " " Lt. Col. W.F. PARSONS	TH
			Left " 59 " " Brig. Gen. STIRLING CB CMG	KH
			+ 26 AFA Bde	
	27		40 DA withdrawn from line - leaving RIGHT & LEFT groups as above on 42 Div/front-DA	XH
	28		HQ RA moved from FONQUEVILLERS to St AMAND.	XH
St AMAND	28/29		293 AFA Bde came into action RIGHT GROUP	XH
	30		Disposition Report	RN App V
	31		Disposition Report	" " VI

D Walcotty Lt.
for BM 42 DA.
1.4.18.

APPENDICES

I to VI.

War Diary 28 appx I
Copy No:......

SECRET.

42nd DIVISIONAL ARTILLERY ORDER No. 60.

1st March, 1918.

Reference Maps BETHUNE Combined Sheet 1/40,000
Sheet 36A 1/40,000.

1. Consequent on the re-adjustment of the I Corps Front the 42nd Divisional Artillery will evacuate the HESDIGNEUL - VENDIN Area on March 3rd.

2. 210th and 211th Brigades will march on March 3rd from their present billets to the HAM en ARTOIS Area.

3. Route via CHOCQUES and LILLERS.

4. Starting Point level crossing on CHOCQUES-BETHUNE Road D.6.a.8.8.

5. Time and Order of March:-
    (a) Head of 210th Bde to pass S.P. 9.0 am.
    (b) Head of 211th Bde to pass S.P. 10.15 am.

    Approximate time of march 3½ hours.
    Watches will be synchronised with H.Q., R.A. by telephone at 10.0 pm on March 2nd.

6. Distances to be observed:-

    Between Batteries - 500 yards.
    Between Sections - 25 yards
    Between Battery & Transport - 25 yards.

    The Transport of each battery will march in rear of the battery in each case.

7. Each Brigade will halt for 10 minutes when the head of the column reaches cross roads BAS-RIEUX U.24.b.2.6.

8. The S.A.A. Section, 42nd D.A.C. will move on March 3rd from VENDIN to GONNEHEM, clearing present lines by noon.
    Any route may be used except the main CHOCQUES-BETHUNE Road.
    The accomodation of this section at GONNEHEM will be arranged by O.C., D.A.C.

9. On arrival in HAM area Brigades will be billeted as follows:-

    210th Bde in HAM en ARTOIS.
    211th Bde in MANQUEVILLE.

    Billeting parties will proceed on 2nd instant. There is a Billet Warden in each village. S.A.C. is at BUSNES

10. Supply Refilling point will remain at GONNEHEM.

11. O.C., D.A.C. will arrange for 10 G.S. wagons to be at the disposal of each of 210th and 211th Bdes from March 2nd until further orders

cont/d

cont/d.
-2-

12. H.Q., 42nd Div.Arty. closes at 12 noon March 5th, at HINGES and re-opens at same hour at LABEUVRIERE.

13. 210th, 211th Bdes and D.A.C. to acknowledge.

                              F.E.Morgan
                              Captain., R.A.
            for Brigade Major., R.A. 42nd Division.

Issued at... 9 p.m.
By D.R.L.S.
Copies to :- Nos. 1 to 5   210th Bde.
             6 to 10   211th Bde.
            11 to 14   42nd D.A.C.
            15   D.T.M.O.
            16   42nd Div. 'G'
            17   42nd Div. 'Q'
            18 & 19   42nd Div. Train.
            20   R.A., I Corps.
            21   S.A.C. BUSNES.
            22   S.A.C. ANNEZIN.
            23   A.C. CHOCQUES.
            24   S.A.C. HESDIGNEUL
            25   42nd Div. Signals.
            26   Postal Supervisor, 42nd Div.
            27   I.O.M. No.1.O.M.W.L.

appx I.

SECRET.

Amendment No. 1. to 42nd D.A. Order No. 60.

Reference Map HAZEBROUCK Sheet 5.A. 1/100,000.

1. Cancel para 5 (a) and (b) and substitute:-

    (a) Head of 211th Bde. to pass S.P. 9.0 a.m.

    (b) Head of 210th Bde to pass S.P. 10.15 a.m.

2. Cancel those portions of paras 2 and 9 relating to 211th Bde R.F.A.

3. 211th Bde.R.F.A. will march to billets in AMES and AMETTES, 4 miles S.W. of LILLERS.

4. Fresh billeting parties will be sent in advance of the Brigade on the morning of the 3rd inst. These parties should report for billets to S.A.C. LIGNY-les-AIRE, 6 miles W of LILLERS..

5. Route to be followed by 211th Bde - as already ordered up to LILLERS thence via HURIONVILLE.

6. O.C.211th Bde will arrange for billeting parties now at MANQUEVILLE to rejoin their unit.

7. 210th Bde and 211th Bde will acknowledge by wire.

F.E.Morgan.

Captain., R.A.

Issued at 11.50 p.m.   for Brigade Major.,R.A. 42nd Divn.Artillery.
By D.R.L.S.
On. 2-3-18.
Copies to:- All recipients of 42nd D.A. No.60, less S.A.C. ANNEZIN and S.A.C. HESDIGNEUL and PLUS S.A.C. LIGNY-les-AIRE.

Appx II

42nd DIVISIONAL ARTILLERY.

LOCATION STATEMENT.

Reference Map HAZEBROUCK 5.A. 1/100,000.

3rd March.1918.

H.Q.,R.A.   -   -   -   HINGES.

210th Bde.R.F.A. - - - HAM-en-ARTOIS.

211th Bde.R.F.A. - - - AMES and BELLERY.

42nd D.A.C. - - - GONNEHEM.

42nd Div.Medium.T.M.Btys. Attached 11th Division.

3-3-18.

[signature]

for Brigade Major., R.A. 42nd Division.
Captain., R.A.

SECRET.
3-3-18.

LOCATION OF UNITS OF 42nd DIVISIONAL ARTILLERY.

Reference Maps. Sheets 36.A & B.& BETHUNE Combined Sheet 1/40,000.

UNIT.	LOCALITY.	MAP REFERENCE.
H.Q.,R.A.	LA BEUVRIERE.	D.11.d.2.2.

210th Bde. R.F.A. Lieut.Col.D.J.MASON.,D.S.O.

H.Q.	HAM-en-ARTOIS.	O.27.c.45.40.
A/210.	" " "	O.33.a.9.5.
B/210.	" " "	O.27.c.1.4.
C/210	" " "	O.27.d.3.5.
D/210	" " "	O.28.c.5.3.

211th Bde. R.F.A. Lieut.Col.E.J.INCHES.,D.S.O.

H.Q.	AMES.	T.29.b.8.1.
A/211	"	T.30.a.2.9.
B/211	"	T.28.d.0.8.
C/211	"	T.29.d.2.1.
D/211	BELLERY	

42nd Div.Ammn.Col. Lieut.Col.A.E.JOLLIFFE.,V.D.

H.Q.	GONNEHEM	V.17.d.7.7.
No.1.Section.	"	V.23.b.6.8.
No.2.Section.	"	V.18.c.25.90.
S.A.A.Section.	"	V.18.central.

42nd D.v.T.M.s. Captain.H.L.LEVITT.

School of Mortars, FIRST ARMY.

P.R. Mitchell
Brigade Major., R.A. 42nd Division.

appx IV.

AMENDMENT TO 42nd Divisional Artillery

LOCATION STATEMENT dated 8-3-18.

D.T.M.O.   CONNEREM   V.18.c.8.4.

X.&.Y/42 T.M.Btys.   V.11.b.2.7.

                              P.R. Mitchell
                                    Major., R.A.
21-3-18.   Brigade Major., R.A. 42nd Division.

42nd Divisional Artillery.

Location of H.Qs vide G.13/A.   30.3.18.

H.Q. 42nd Div.Arty.   ST.AMAND.   D.15.b.7.7.

210th Bde H.Q.   ESSARTS.   F.19.c.2.4.
211th Bde R.F.A.   "   E.24.d.5.5.
42nd D.A.C. H.Q.   GAUDIEMPRE.
Nos.1 & 2 Sects.
S.A.A.Section.   BIENVILLERS.
42nd T.M.Bs.   GAUDIEMPRE.

Attached Artillery Units.

59th D.A.,H.Q.   ESSARTS.   F.19.a.3.0.
59th D.A.C.,H.Q.   GAUDIEMPRE.

26th A.F.A.Bde.   ESSARTS.
293rd A.F.A.Bde.   "

In Liaison with 42nd Division.

48th H.A.Bde R.G.A.   SOUASTRE.   D.22.b.5.4.
    H.Q.
87th H.A.Bde R.G.A.
    H.Q.   FONQUEVILLERS.E.27.a.4.3.

                                    Major.,R.A.
30.3.18.   Brigade Major.,R.A. 42nd Division.

SECRET.

41st Divisional Artillery Group.

(Covering LEFT Division, IV Corps.)

LOCATION   REPORT.   31-3-18.

H.Q., 22nd Div.Arty.   ST.AMAND.   D.15.b.7.7.

RIGHT GROUP.

RIGHT GROUP.H.Q.		E.24.c.5.6.
210th Bde R.F.A., H.Q.		E.24.d.6.9.
A/210. " "		F.19.b.65.20.
B/210 " "		E.24.d.85.10.
C/210. " "		E.24.b.3.1.
D/210. " "		E.24.b.5.2.
A/211. " "		E.13.a.10.05.
B/211. " "		F.19.b.1.6.
C/211. " "		F.25.a.1.7.
D/211. " "		F.19.b.2.8.
A/293. A.F.A.Bde		E.18.d.3.2.
B/293. " "		E.18.d.2.5.
C/293. " "		
D/293. " "		E.18.d.7.2.

LEFT GROUP.

LEFT GROUP.H.Q.		
(59th D.A.)	ISSARTS.	F.19.c.2.4.
295th Bde R.F.A.,H.Q.		F.9.a.8.8.
A/295th " "		No guns.
B/295th Bde R.F.A.		F.8.d.4.6.
C/295th Bde R.F.A.		F.9.c.8.6.
D/295th Bde R.F.A.		F.3.c.3.1.
296th Bde R.F.A. H.Q.		F.13.b.9.7.
A/296th Bde R.F.A.		No guns.
B/296th " "		F.13.c.5.4.
C/296th " "		F.13.a.3.9.
D/296th " "		F.7.a.6.4.

cont/d.

cont/d.

26th A.F.A.Bde. H.Q.	F.8.d.7.8.
A/26th " "	F.7.d.8.6.
116th Bty.	F.7.d.9.7.
117th Bty.	No guns.
42nd D.A.C. H.Q.	GAUDIEMPRE.
Nos.1.&.2.Sections.	
S.A.A.Section.	BIENVILLERS.
42nd T.M.Bs.	GAUDIEMPRE.
59th D.A.C.	GAUDIEMPRE.

IN LIAISON WITH 41st Div.Arty.

48th Bde R.G.A.		SOUASTRE.	D.22.b.5.4.
133rd Heavy Bty.	60-pdrs.		E.16.b.50.85.
147th " "	60-pdrs.		E.16.b.45.50.
59th Siege "	6" Hows.		E.10.c.95.50
81st " "	6" "		E.16.a.75.20.
87th Bde R.G.A.		SOUASTRE.	E.15.c.9.3.
154th Heavy Bty.	60-pdrs.		E.15.c.9.3.
156th " "	60-pdrs.		E.20.d.9.2.
219th Siege "	6" Hows.		E.21.a.7.5.
194th " "	6" "		E.21.a.9.8.

H.H.Pilcher

Major.,R.A.
Brigade Major.,R.A.42nd Division.
A/B.M.,R.A., 41st Division.

31-3-18.

NOTE:- Any correction to the above will be sent to this Office as early as possible.

IV.Corps.
Third Army.

Headquarters.

42nd DIVISIONAL ARTILLERY.

A P R I L

1 9 1 8

Attached:

Appendices I to VII.

WA 15

CONFIDENTIAL.

WAR. DIARY.
OF
H.Q., R.A., 42ND DIVISION.

FROM. 1ST. APRIL. 1918.   TO. 30TH. APRIL. 1918.

XIX. 101

Reference Maps
1/20,000 57D NE Sheet I
1/40,000 57D NE Sheet XIV
1/100,000 HENS II

April 1918

WAR DIARY or INTELLIGENCE SUMMARY

Army Form C. 2118

Place	Date	Hour	Summary of Events and Information	Remarks and references to Appendices
HENU	1/2nd		42nd Div. (less artillery) relieved 41st Div (less arty) on left Sector IV Corps front.	S/D app x I S/D
	3		Disposition Report	S/D
	5	5am	Heavy enemy shelled HE Bombardment of Support line ESSARTS ovicoing N&S of ESSARTS	S/D
		10am	All telephone communication broken, visual impossible owing to mist. In response to message received by visual that enemy was attacking centre of 42 Div. front in BUCQUOY. The artillery put down an SOS barrage	S/D
		5.30am	Right group 42 DA supported attack on ROSSIGNOL Wood by 37 Div	S/D
	7	7.30am	Enemy advanced towards centre of BUCQUOY. Barrage put down in response to SOS - caught enemy waiting to advance. Attack was stopped.	S/D app x II S/D
			Disposition Report	S/D
	8/9		42nd Div (less Cavalry) relieved by 62 Div (less arty) on left Sectn IV Corps front.	S/D
PAS	10		Disposition Report HQRA 42 DA moved to Pas	app III S/D
COUIN	16		HQ RA 42 DA relieved HQRA 37 Div at COUIN	S/D
	15/16 16/17		42 Div (less arty) relieved 37th Div (less arty) on Centre Sector IV Corps front.	S/D
	18		Disposition Report	app x IV S/D V S/D
	21		"	
	23/24		Various changes in Divisional Boundaries - Composition of Div Arty on IV Corps front	S/D
	24/25		as follows :-	S/D

Reference maps
1/20,000 57 D NE
1/10,000 Lens 11

Sheet 1
WAR DIARY
or
INTELLIGENCE SUMMARY.
Army Form C. 2118.
(Erase heading not required.)

Place	Date	Hour	Summary of Events and Information	Remarks and references to Appendices
COUIN	Night Apl. 23/24		42nd Divl. took over from 62nd Divl a/o to L2 c 9.1. (Sheet 57 DNE)	
			187 Bde RFA transferred to CENTRE Division and drawn into Corps Reserve	
	Night 24/25		N.Z. Divl took over from 4th Australian Bde & 42 Divl. up to R10 d 4.0. (Sheet 57 DNE)	(SLY)
			Right group 235 & 236 Bdes RFA transferred in situ to N.Z. Divl.	
			On completion of above relief The ARTY covering the 42nd (Centre) Divn. Front was regrouped as follows	
			Right Group 37th DA (123 + 124 Bdes RFA) covering Right Inf Bde	Appx VI BM
	24		LEFT " 42" DA (210 + 211 " ") " Left " "	BM
	25/26 Night		Personnel of 37 DA (R.ght Gp. 42 Divl) changed over with personnel of 62nd DA.	BM
	26	4pm	Command of RIGHT Group 42 DA passed to Lt. Col. EDEN, 312 Bde RFA	BM
	28		Disposition Report	Appx VII BM
	30		187 Bde RFA relieved 190 Bde RFA in the LEFT Group 42 DA	BM
	"	7pm	Lt. Col. Lyon DSO. RA. 187 Bde. assumed Command of LEFT Group 42 DTA	BM

D.W. Walcester Lt.
for BM 42 DA
1.5.18.

A P P E N D I C E S

I to VII.

Appx T.

42nd DIVISIONAL ARTILLERY.

LOCATION STATEMENT. 3rd April.1918.

6.0 p.m.

UNIT.	LOCATION.	MAP.	APPROXIMATE FRONT COVERED.

H.Q. 42nd Div.Arty.

RIGHT GROUP.
RIGHT GROUP.H.Q. E.24.c.5.3.
210th Bde R.F.A. H.Q. E.24.d.6.8.
A/210.   E.18.b.3.5.)
B/210.   E.24.d.85.10)   E.9.b.9.9.
C/210.   E.24.b.3.1.)   to
D/210.   E.24.b.5.2.)   L.4.a.1.1.

A/211.   F.13.a.10.05.)
B/211.   E.18.b.85.45) E.4.c.1.1.
C/211.   F.25.a.1.7.   ) to
D/211.   At Wagon Lines) F.23.c.5.1.

A/925rd A.F.A.Bde E.18.d.3.2.)
B/295.   E.18.c.2.5.) E.23.c.5.1.
C/295.   E.18.c.9.0) to
D/295.   E.18.d.7.2.) E.28.b.1.5.

LEFT GROUP.
LEFT GROUP H.Q. 236.MTS. F.19.c.20.40.
295th Bde R.F.A.H.Q. E.9.a.60.80.)
A/295.   F.9.c.30.60.)   F.23.b.1.5.
B/295.   (2) F.3.d.40.60)
)   to
C/295.   F.7.d.70.60)
D/295.   Resting.   )   F.29.a.2.8.
             (2) F.3.d.25.25)
             (4) F.2.c.40.05.)

236th Bde R.F.A. H.Q. F.15.b.90.70.
A/296.   E.15.a.10.30)   F.29.a.2.8.
B/296.   Resting.   )   to
C/296.   F.3.c.3.3.   )
D/296.   F.7.a.50.20.)   F.22.d.8.7.

26th A.F.A.Bde H.Q. F.13.a.35.55
A/26   F.15.b.10.70)   F.22.d.8.7.
117th Bty.   F.7.b.60.20)   to
116th Bty.   Resting.   )   F.22.b.9.9.

(2)

UNIT.	LOCATION.
42nd.Div.Ammn.Column.	SOUASTRE.
No.1.&.2.Sections.	SOUASTRE.
S.A.A.Section	BIENVILLERS.
A.R.P.	SOUASTRE.
42nd.Div.T.Mc.	SOUASTRE.
59th.D.A.C.	D.21.b.8.8.

IN LIAISON WITH 42nd Div.Artillery.

48th Bde R.G.A.		SOUASTRE.	D.22.b.5.4.
133rd Heavy Bty.	60-pdrs.		E.16.b.50.85.
147th " "	60-pdrs.		E.16.b.45.50
59th Siege "	6" Hows.		E.10.c.95.50
81st " "	6" "		E.16.a.75.20

87th Bde R.G.A.		SOUASTRE.	
154th Heavy Bty.	60-pdrs.		E.15.c.9.3.
156th " "	60-pdrs.		E.20.d.9.2.
219th Siege "	6" Hows.		E.21.a.7.8.
194th " "	6" "		E.21.a.9.8.

for Major., R...
3rd APRIL.1918.   Brigade Major., R... 42nd Division.

App X II

42nd DIVISIONAL ARTILLERY.

LOCATION STATEMENT. 7th April.1918.

UNIT.	LOCATION.	WAGON LINES.	APPROXIMATE FRONT COVERED.
H.Q.,42nd Div.Arty. H.QU.			
RIGHT GROUP.			
RIGHT GROUP. H.Q.	E.24.c.5.8.)		
210th Bde R.F.A.H.Q.	E.24.c.6.8.)	E.2.d.	L.3.c.5.5.
A/210	E.18.b.8.5.)	&	to
B/210	E.24.d.85.10)	E.3.c.	L.4.a.7.7.
C/210	E.22.b.5.1)		
D/210	E.22.b.5.2.)		
A/211.	F.13.c.10.05)	E.1.d.	L.4.a.7.7.
B/211.	E.13.b.85.45)	&&	to
C/211.	F.25.a.1.7.)	&	F.28.d.9.7.
D/211.	At Wagon lines	E.2.c.	
LEFT GROUP.			
LEFT GROUP. H.Q.	F.15.c.20.20)		
295th Bde R.F.A.H.Q.	F.9.d.60.30)	E.1.b.,	F.28.d.9.7.
A/295. (1)	F.9.b.90.80)	E.2.c.,	to
(1)	F.9.c.30.80)	E.7.b.	
(4)	F.9.c.80.60)	C.d.	F.29.a.8.3
B/295.	F.7.d.80.60)		
C/295. (2)	In Rest.)		
D/295. (4)	F.2.d.25.25)		
	F.2.c.40.05)		
296th Bde R.F.A.H.Q.	F.13.b.90.70)		F.29.a.8.8
A/296.	F.13.a.10.80)	E.2.b.,	to
B/296.	F.8.c.8.8.)	c.c.d.	F.23.c.5.7.
C/296.	E.18.d.3.2)	D.2.c.	
D/296.	F.7.c.50.20)		
26th A.F.A.Bde H.Q	F.13.a.85.55)		F.23.c.5.7
A/26	In Rest.)	L.2.b.	to
117th Bty.	F.7.b.60.20)		F.23.a.5.9
116th Bty.	F.13.b.10.70)		

(2)

UNIT.	LOCATION.
42nd Div.Amm.Column. H.Q.)	D.15.d. &
No.1.&No.2.Sections.)	D.16.c.
3.A.A.SECTION.	C.24.b.5.2.
A.R.P.	D.21.b.9.9.
42nd Div.T.Hs. D.A.D.M.O.)	E.10.b.9.8.
A.S.Y/42.)	
59th D.A.C.	D.21.b.8.8.

IN LIAISON WITH 42nd Div.Arty.

48th Bde R.G.A.	D.22.b.5.4.
133rd Heavy Bty. 60-pdrs.	E.16.b.50.85
147th " " 60-pdrs	E.16.b.45.50
59th Siege " 6" Hows	E.10.c.95.50
81st " " 6" "	E.16.a.75.20
87th Bde R.G.A.	SOUASTRE.
154th Heavy Bty. 60-pdrs.	E.15.c.9.3.
156th " " 60-pdrs.	E.20.d.9.2.
219th Siege " 6" Hows	E.21.a.7.5.
194th " " 6" Hows	E.21.a.9.8.

D.M. Malcolm Lt.
for Major., R.A.
Brigade Major., R.A., 42nd Division.

7th April, 1918.

Appx III

SECRET.

42nd DIVISIONAL ARTILLERY.

LOCATION STATEMENT.   10th April.1918.

U.IT.	LOCATION.	WAGON LINES.	APPROXIMATE FRONT COVERED.

H.Q.,42nd Div.Arty.   PERNU.

RIGHT GROUP.

RIGHT GROUP H.Q.	E.25.d.7.9		
210th Bde R.F.A.	H.Q.E.24.d.6.8.		
A/210	E.18.b.6.5.	M.2.d.	L.3.c.5.5.
B/210	F.13.a.10.55.	&	to
C/210	E.24.b.5.1.	M.3.c.	L.4.a.7.7.
D/210	E.22.b.5.2.		
A/211	F.13.a.4.2.		
B/211	E.18.d.9.5.	E.1.d.	L.4.a.7.7.
C/211	E.18.d.2.5.	&	to
D/211	E.18.d.2.6.	E.2.c.	F.28.c.9.7.
A/26 A.F.A.Bde.	E.13.d.0.0.		
116th Bty.A Sect.	E.18.d.3.8.		

LEFT GROUP.

LEFT GROUP.H.Q.	F.13.b.90.50.		
Left Sub-Group R.Q.	F.9.a.80.90.		
A/295.	F.9.b.2.2.		
	(3)		
D/295.	F.9.c.8.6.	E.1.b.	F.28.c.9.7.
B/296.	F.7.d.5.7	E.2.c.	to
C/296.	F.7.b.3.4.	F.7.b	F.29.a.8.8.
D/295. (2)	F.7.d.90.55.	& d.	
(4)	F.2.d.25.25.		
	F.2.c.40.05.		

Right Sub-Group.H.Q. F.13.a.8.6.

116th Bty.	F.13.b.1.9.	L.2.b.	F.29.a.8.8.
117th Bty.	F.7.b.6.2.	c.d.d.	to
A/296.	F.13.a.4.3.	D.2.c.	F.25.a.5.9.
D/296.	F.7.a.5.0.	M.2.b.	

26th A.F.A.Bde H.Q. F.13.a.85.55.

(2)

UNIT.		LOCATION.
42nd Div.Amm.Column.		D.15.d & D.16.c.
42nd D.T.M.O.		L.10.b.2.8.
59th D.A.C.		D.21.b.8.8.

IN LIAISON WITH 42nd DIV.ARTY.

28th Bde.R.G.A.	SOUASTRE.	D.22.b.6.3.
59th Siege Bty. 5 – 6" Hows.		L.10.c.7.3.
81st " " 2 – 6" "		E.16.a.7.3.
133rd Heavy.Bty. 2 – 60 pdrs.		E.9.d.45.27.
147th " "		At Rest.
503rd Siege Bty. 3 – 6"Hr.		
XIX Guns.		E.1.a.94.36.
87th Bde.R.G.A.	SOUASTRE.	D.22.d.2.9.
154th Heavy Bty. 3 – 60 pdr.		E.15.c.9.3.
156th " " 3 – 60 pdrs.		E.20.d.90.85.
194th Siege Bty. 3 – 6" Hows.		E.21.a.97.67.
219th " " 4 – 6" Hows.		E.21.a.8.7.

10th April,1918.

P.R. Mitchell
Major.,R.A.
Brigade Major.,R.A. 42nd Division.

Ap/b × IV

M.f.1/40,000   42nd Divisional Artillery.   Hqurs. rd. COUL..
Sh..t 57.D.   13th April.1918.

LOCATION STATEMENT.

UNIT.	POSITION.	Approx. Front Cov rd	Advance LI.
RIGHT GROUP.			
Lt.Col.Bowring.R.F.A.	CHATEAU D L AIF.		
235 Bd. R.F.A. H.Q.	HENU		
A/235 Bd R.F.A. (6)	J.6.b.6.8.		
B/235 " " " (6)	E.26.c.85.90)	A.23.c.0.8.	D.17.c.6.1.
C/235 " " " (6)	K.2.c.15.20)	to	to
	K.2.c.20.80)	K.22.a.1.1	D.17.c.8.4.
D/235 (How) " (2)	J.6.d.70.50)		
	J.12.b.80.70)		
236 Bd. R.F.A. H.Q.	CHATEAU D L..M.IE		
	GROUP H.Q.		
A/236 Bd. R.F.A. (6)	E.21.c.10.75)	K.22.a.1.1.	D.23.c.3.5.
B/236 " " " (6)	E.20.b.60.00)	t	
C/236 " " " (6)	E.20.d.10.20)	K.16.d.0.3.	D.17.c.5.1. COUIN.
D/236 " " " (6)	E.21.c.50.40)		D.23.c.4.9
CENTRE GROUP.			
Lt.Col...P...R.F.A.	CHATEAU D L..M.IE		
A/123 Bd. R.F.A. (6)	A.7.d.55.55)	K.16.c.0.0.	J.7.b.6.1.
B/123 " " " (6)	K.2.c.15.35)	to	
C/123 " " " (6)	J.12.d.65.45)	K.11.d.2.6.	J.12.c.25.45	J.8.b.4.7.
D/123 " " " (6)	K.7.d.5.4)	K.16.c.0.0.	J.18.b.2.6.	J.8.b.2.7.
		to	J.18.c.0.8.	J.8.c.4.5.
		K.17.c.18.15.	J.18.c.9.8.	J.7.b.7.4.
124 Bd. H.Q.				
A/124 Bd. R.F.A. (6)	K.3.c.20.25)	K.17.c.18.15	J.16.a.10.90	J.7.b.5.7.
B/124 " " " (6)	K.7.a.40.80.)	to	D.28.c.2.2.	J.7.c.6.7.
C/124 " " " (6)	K.12.b.80.15)	K.11.d.20.60.	J.16.a.10.90	J.7.d.1.5.
D/124 " " " (4)	J.12.b.99.15)		D.28.d.20.20	K.12.b.8.4.
	A.2.c.99.42)			

appx V

42nd DIVISIONAL ARTILLERY
LOCATION STATEMENT. 21-4-18

UNIT.	POSITION.	Approximate Front Covered.	Wagon Lines Advanced.	Rear.

Headquarters. R.A. COUIN. (Chateau)

RIGHT GROUP. Lt.Col.Bowring.R.F.A.
235 Bde R.F.A. Headquarters. J.18.c.95.90
A/235 " " H.Q. (6) J.6.b.6.8.)
B/235 " " (6) E.26.a.85.90)
C/235 " " (4) K.2.c.15.20)   K.28.a.0.7.   HENU.
            (2) K.2.c.20.80)
D/235 " " (2) J.6.d.70.50)   to
            (2) J.12.b.80.90.) K.22.c.0.9.

236 Bde R.F.A.. H.Q. J.18.c.95.90)
A/236 " " (6) E.21.c.10.75)
B/236 " " (6) E.20.b.60.00)   K.16.d.0.3.   D.23.a.7.8.   J.1.a.7.8.
C/236 " " (6) E.20.d.10.20)
D/236 " " (6) E.21.c.50.40)

CENTRE GROUP. Lt.Col.N.E.PEAL.R.F.A.
Headquarters. Chateau de la Haie.
A/123 Bde R.F.A.. (2) K.7.d.55.55)
                  (4) K.7.c.65.55)
B/123 " " (6) K.2.c.15.35)
C/123 " " (6) J.12.d.65.45)   M.16.c.95.05   J.12.c.25.45   J.8.b.4.7.
D/123 " " (6) K.7.d.5.4.)   J.11.a.4.8.   J.8.b.2.7.
                                                              J.18.a.0.8.   J.8.a.4.5.
                                to   J.18.a.9.8.   J.7.b.7.4.

A/124 " " (6) K.3.a.20.25)   K.16.d.80.55   J.16.a.10.90   J.7.b.5.7.
B/124 " " (6) K.7.a.40.80)   D.28.d.2.2.   J.7.a.6.7.
C/124 " " (6) K.2.b.50.15)   to   J.16.a.10.90   J.7.a.1.5.
D/124 " " (4) J.12.b.99.15)   D.28.d.20.20   I.12.b.8.4.?
            (2) K.2.c.99.42)   K.11.d.2.6.

Hqrs. 37th D.A.C. I.12.a.1.3. Wagon lines. I.11.d.5.6.
No.1. Sect. I.11.d.2.0.   No.2.Sect. I.11.c.0.6.   No.3.Sect. J.7.b.3.0.

(2)

UNIT.	POSITION.	APPROXIMATE FRONT COVERED.	WAGON LINES ADVANCED
			REAP.

LEFT GROUP. Lt.Col.CARDEW. R.F.A.

Headquarters: J.6.b.1.8.

A/190 Bde R.F.A.	(6)	E.15.d.0.5.	K.11.a.20.45	
B/190 " "	(6)	E.22.b.55.10	to	
C/190 " "	(6)	E.23.d.1.8.	K.11.b.45.25	D.18.central. COUIN.
D/190 " "	(2)	E.29.c.25.95	to	
	(4)	E.20.d.55.10	K.12.a.20.50	
210 Bde R.F.A. H.Q.		E.11.a.2.1	to	
A/210 " "	(6)	E.15.d.70.45	K.12.b.50.30	
B/210 " "	(6)	E.17.b.0.5	to	SOUASTRE
C/210 " "	(6)	E.17.d.5.5	L.7.c.30.60	
D/210 " "	(6)	E.18.c.75.70	to	
210 " " H.Q.		E.10.d.7.9.	L.4.c.0.4.	
A/211 " "	(6)	E.18.a.4.7		
B/211 " "	(4)	E.17.b.8.0.	Superimposed	D.22.a.8.5.
	(2)	E.22.a.4.5	K.12.b.10.35	
C/211 " "	(6)	E.15.d.8.7	to	
D/211 " "	(6)	E.12.d.3.7	L.4.c.0.4.	

Hqrs. 41st D.A.C. D.21.d.8.8. No.2 Section. D.21.b.5.0.
Hqrs. 42nd D.A.C. J.1.d.9.0. No.1 Sect. J.2.c.2.2. No.2 Section. J.2.c.7.7.
Hqrs. 47th D.A.C. S.A.A. Section. J.1.b.5.7.
 J.1.d.7.3. No.1 Sect. J.1.a.8.5. No.2 Sect. J.7.b.7.4.

42nd D.T.M.O. Hqrs. COUIN.

X/42 T.M.B. H.Q. E.27.c.85.10		Y/42 T.M.B. H.Q. K.4.b.45.60	
(1) K.16.a.25.50		(1) K.10.b.95.90	
(2) K.16.a.28.50	In action.	(2) K.10.b.95.90	In action.
(3) K.10.c.95.70		(3) K.6.c.95.95	
(4) K.10.c.95.70		(4) K.6.c.95.95	
(5) K.9.a.55.25	Under construction.	(5) GOMMECOURT	
(6) K.9.a.55.25		(6) "	

21-4-18.

P.R.Mitchell Maj
for Lieut.R.H.A.
Reconnaissance Officer, 42nd Divisional Artillery.

Appx VI

42nd DIVISIONAL ARTILLERY.

LOCATION ST.LEGER. 7 p.m. 24-4-18.

UNIT.	POSITION.	APPROXIMATE FRONT COVERED.	WAGON LINES. ADVANCED.	REAR.

HEADQUARTERS. R.A. COUIN (CHATEAU)

RIGHT GROUP. Lt.Col.T.E.PEAL.R.F.A.
Headquarters.	CHATEAU de la HIE.			
A/123.	(2) K.7.d.55.55.			J.12.c.25.45. J.8.b.5.9.
	(4) K.7.c.65.35.			
B/123.	(6) K.2.c.15.35.	K.10.c.4.0.		J.11.a.4.8. J.8.b.2.7.
C/163.	(6) J.12.d.65.45.			J.13.a.0.8. J.8.c.4.5.
D/123.	(6) K.7.d.5.4.	to		J.13.c.9.8. J.7.b.4.8.
A/124.	(6) K.3.a.20.25.			J.16.a.10.90. J.7.b.5.7.
B/124.	(6) K.7.c.40.80.			D.28.d.2.2. J.7.d.6.7.
C/124.	(6) K.2.b.50.15.	K.12.b.0.8.		J.16.a.10.90. J.7.a.1.5.
D/124.	(4) J.12.b.99.15			D.28.d.2.2. I.12.b.8.4.
	(2) K.2.c.99.42			

LEFT GROUP. Lt.Col.CARDEN.R.F.A.
Headquarters.	J.6.b.1.8.			
A/190.	(6) E.15.d.0.5.			
B/190.	(6) E.22.b.55.10		D.18.Central. COUIN.	
C/190.	(6) E.23.d.1.8.			
D/190.	(2) E.29.c.75.95.			
	(4) E.20.d.35.10			

210th Bde R.F.A. H.Q. E.11.a.2.1.
A/210	(6) E.15.c.6.8.			
B/210	(c) E.17.b.0.5.	K.12.b.0.8.		SOUASTRE.
C/210	(6) E.17.d.5.5.	to		
D/210	(6) E.18.c.75.70			

App x VII.

2nd DIVISIONAL ARTILLERY.

LOCATION STATEMENT. 8-4-18.

UNIT.	POSITION.	APPROXIMATE FRONT COVERED.	WAGON LINES.

HEADQUARTERS.R.A. COUIN (CHATEAU)

RIGHT GROUP. Lt.Col.EDEN.R.F.A.
Headquarters. Chateau d L.L.B. J.6.a.6.5.
A/310.   (2)   K.7.c.7.3.   J.1.a.Central.
            (2)   K.7.d.55.55.
B/310.   (6)   L.2.c.15.35.   K.17.a.0.0.
C/310.   (6)   J.12.d.65.45.   to
D/310.   (6)   K.7.d.5..

A/312.   (6)   K.3.a.20.25.   J.1.c.central.
B/312.   (6)   K.7.a.4.8.
C/312   (6)   K.2.b.50.45.   K.12.a.75.40
D/312   (4)   J.12.b.99.15.
            (2)   K.2.c.99.42.

LEFT GROUP. Lt.Col.CARDEW.R.F.A.
Headquarters.   J.6.b.1.8.
A/190.   (6)   E.15.d.0.5.
B/190   (6)   E.22.b.55.10.   D.18.central.& COUIN.
C/190   (6)   E.23.d.1.8.
D/190   (2)   E.29.c.75.95.
            (4)   E.20.d.35.10.

210th Bde R.F.A. H.Q. E.11.a.2.1.
A/210   (6)   E.15.c.6.2.   K.12.a.75.40
B/210   (6)   E.21.c.13.
C/210   (6)   E.22.c.0.5.   to   SOUASTRE.
D/210   (6)   E.18.c.75.70.

-2-

UNIT.	POSITION.	APPROXIMATE ROUTE COVERED.		WAGON LINES.
211th Bde R.F.A. H.Q.	E.8.c.7.1.			
A/211	(6) E.22.c.6.8.)			
B/211	(6) E.22.a.4.5.)		to	L.8.b.7.6.
C/211	(6) E.15.d.7.8.)			
D/211	(4) E.22.a.0.1.)			D.22.a.8.5.
	(2) E.28.b.15.15.)			

42nd D.T.M.O. Headquarters. COUIN. J.1.d.55.35.

X/42 T.M.B. H.Q. E.27.c.85.10. Y/42 T.M.B. H.Q. K.4.b.45.60.

	3.O.S.POINTS.			S.O.S.POINTS.
X.1. K.16.a.25.50.	K.17.c.10.15.	Y.1. K.10.b.95.90.	K.11.d.10.50.
X.2. K.16.a.28.50.	K.17.c.52.90.	Y.2. K.10.b.95.90.	K.11.b.90.30.
X.3. K.10.c.95.70.	K.17.b.00.50.	Y.3. K.6.c.95.95.	K.12.b.20.50.
X.4. K.10.c.95.70.	K.11.d.10.10	Y.4. K.6.c.95.95.	K.12.d.65.90
X.5. K.9.a.55.25.) Under construction		Y.5. E.28.c.60.10) under construction
X.6. K.9.a.55.25.) to cover PURPLE LINE		Y.6. E.28.c.75.30.) to cover PURPLE LINE

H.Q. 42nd D.A.C. J.1.d.9.0.   No.1.Sect. J.2.c.2.2.   No.2.Sect. J.2.c.7.7.

H.Q. 41st D.A.C. D.21.d.8.8.   S.A.A.Sect. J.1.b.5.7.   No.2.Sect. D.21.b.5.0.

H.Q. 62nd D.A.C. D.19.d.3.8.   No.1.&.2.Sects. D.15.d.   S.A.A.Sect. AUTHIE.

28-4-18.

P.R.Mitchell Maj. for
Lieut., R.A.
Reconnaissance Officer, 42nd Div.Artillery.

Vol 16

Confidential
War Diary
of
Ha. Qrs. R.A. 42nd Division

From 1st May 1918. To 31st May 1918

Volume XV

May 1918 Vol XV. Sheet I. Reference Maps 1/20,000 57D NE

Army Form C. 2118.

WAR DIARY
or
INTELLIGENCE SUMMARY.
(Erase heading not required.)

Place	Date	Hour	Summary of Events and Information	Remarks and references to Appendices
	1st		Location Statement	See App. I.
	5th		187 Bde. RFA withdrawn from line on 42nd Divisional front - to relieve Certain Batteries of 47 DA on the NZ Div. front.	See App. II
			Location Statement	See
	6th		42nd Div. (less Arty) relieved by 57 Div. (less Arty)	See
			HQ. 42 DA. established at PAS.	See
	6th to 31st		During this period the 42 Division being the Division in Army Reserve the CRA 42 Division was responsible for the Artillery arrangements for defence of the "Red Line".	See App. III

J. Malcolm Lt.
for Bn. 42 DA
1.6.18

UNIT.	POSITION.	APPROXIMATE FRONT COVERED.	WAGON LINES.
211th Bde R.F.A. H.Q.	E.8.c.7.1.		
A/211 (6)	E.22.c.6.8.	)	
B/211 (6)	E.22.a.4.5.	) L.8.b.7.6. to	D.22.a.8.5.
C/211 (6)	E.15.d.7.8.	)	
D/211 (5)	E.22.a.0.1.	)	
(1)	E.29.a.5.5.		

42nd.D.T.M.O. Headquarters. COURN. J.1.d.55.35.

X/42 T.M.B. H.Q.	D.27.c.85.10			Y/42 T.M.B. H.Q.	K.4.b.45.60	
		S.O.S.POINTS.				S.O.S.POINTS.
X.1.	K.16.a.25.50.	K.17.c.10.15.		Y.1.	K.10.b.95.90	K.11.d.10.50
X.2.	K.16.a.28.50.	K.17.c.52.90.		Y.2.	K.10.b.95.90	K.11.b.90.30
X.3.	K.10.c.95.70	K.17.b.00.50		Y.3.	K.6.c.95.95	K.12.b.20.50
X.4.	K.10.c.95.70	K.11.d.10.10.		Y.4.	K.6.c.95.95	K.12.d.65.90
X.5.	K.9.a.55.25) Under construction to			Y.5.	K.28.c.60.10) Under construction	
X.6.	K.9.a.55.25) cover PURPLE Line			Y.6.	K.28.c.75.30) to cover PURPLE Line	

H.Q. 42nd.D.A.C. J.1.d.9.0. No.1.Sect. J.2.c.2.2. No.2.Sect. J.2.c.7.7.
S.A.A.Sect. J.1.b.5.7. 42nd A.R.P. D.26.central.
H.Q. 41st D.A.C. D.21.d.8.8. No.2.Sect. D.21.b.5.0.
H.Q. 62nd D.A.C. D.19.c.3.8. No.1.&.2.Sects. D.15.d. S.A.A.Sect. AUTHIE.

IN LIAISON WITH 42nd Div.Arty.

54th Bde R.G.A. H.Q. ROSSIGNOL FARM J.3.c.
56th Bde R.G.A. H.Q. J.9.a.5.2.

1st May.1918.

P.R. Mitchell
Maj. for Lieut.,R.A.,
Reconnaissance Officer, 42nd Divisional Artillery.

APPENDIX I

Reference Map.
Sheet 57.D.
1/40.000

42nd DIVISIONAL ARTILLERY.

LOCATION ST. E ENT. 1st May.1918.

UNIT.	POSITION.	APPROXIMATE FRONT COVERED.	WAGON LINES.
HEADQUARTERS.R.A. . . COUIN (CHATEAU)			
RIGHT GROUP. Lt.Col. EDEN.R.F.A.			
Headquarters. Chateau de la Haie. J.6.a.6.3.			
A/310. . . . (4)	K.7.c.7.3.)		
B/310. . . . (8)	K.7.d.55.55)		
C/310. . . . (6)	K.2.c.15.35)	K.17.a.0.0.	J.l.a.Central.
D/310. . . . (6)	J.12.d.65.55)		
	K.7.d.5.4.)	to	
A/312. . . . (6)	K.3.a.20.25)		
B/312. . . . (6)	K.7.a.4.8.)		
C/312. . . . (6)	K.2.b.50.15)	K.12.a.75.40	J.l.c.Central.
D/312. . . . (6)	J.12.b.99.15)		
	K.3.c.99.42)		
LEFT GROUP. Lt.Col.C.D.G.LYON.D.S.O.,R.F.A.			
Headquarters.	J.6.b.1.8.		
A/187. . . . (6)	E.15.d.0.5.)		
B/187. . . . (6)	E.22.b.55.10)		
C/187. . . . (6)	E.23.c.1.8.)	D.18.central & COUIN.	
D/187. . . . (2)	E.29.c.75.95)		
	E.20.d.35.10)		
210th Bde R.F.A. H.Q.	E.11.a.2.1.		
A/210. . . . (6)	E.15.c.70.45)	K.13.a.75.40	
B/210. . . . (4)	E.21.c.1.3.)		
	E.23.c.4.1.)	to	SOUASTRE.
C/210. . . . (6)	E.29.a.99.51.)		
D/210. . . . (6)	E.18.c.75.70)		

SECRET.

APP. II

42nd DIVISIONAL ARTILLERY.

LOCATION STATEMENT. 7 p.m. 5-5-18.

Reference Map Sheet 57.D. 1/40,000.

UNIT.	POSITION.	APPROXIMATE FRONT COVERED.	WAGON LINES.
Headquarters.R.A.	COUIN (CHATEAU)		

RIGHT GROUP. Lt.Col.EDEN.R.F.A.
Headquarters. Chateau de la Haie. J.6.a.6.3.

A/310 Bde R.F.A.	(4)	K.7.c.54.20	)		
	(2)	K.7.d.73.70	)		
B/310 " "	(6)	K.2.c.27.32	) K.17.a.0.0.	J.1.a.Central.
C/310 " "	(6)	J.12.d.70.63	)		
D/310 " "	(6)	K.7.d.31.29	)		
			to		
A/312 " "	(6)	K.3.a.22.25	)		
B/312 " "	(6)	K.7.a.14.45	) K.12.a.75.40	J.1.c.Central.
C/312 " "	(6)	K.2.d.22.60	)		
D/312 " "	(6)	K.2.c.84.27	)		

LEFT GROUP. Lt.Col.E.J.INCHES,D.S.O,R.F.A.
Headquarters. E.8.c.7.2.
210th Bde R.F.A. H.Q. E.11.a.2.1.

A/210th Bde R.F.A.	(6)	L.15.c.70.45	)		
B/210 " "	(4)	E.21.c.1.3.	)		
	(2)	E.23.c.4.1.	) K.12.a.75.40	SOUASTRE.
C/210 " "	(6)	E.22.a.99.51	)		
D/210 " "	(6)	E.18.c.75.70	)		
			to		
A/211 " "	(6)	E.22.c.6.8.	)		
B/211 " "	(6)	E.22.a.4.5.	)		
C/211 " "	(6)	E.15.d.7.8.	) L.8.b.7.6.	D.22.a.8.5.
D/211 " "	(5)	E.22.a.0.1.	)		
	(1)	E.29.c.95.95	)		

42nd D.T.M.O. Headquarters. COUIN.J.1.d.55.35.
X/42 T.M.B. H.Q. E.27.c.85.10

S.O.S.POINTS.			S.O.S.POINTS.
X.1. K.16.a.25.50.	K.17.c.10.15.	Y.1. K.10.b.95.90.	K.11.d.10.50.
X.2. K.16.a.28.50.	K.17.c.52.90.	Y.2. K.10.b.95.90.	K.11.b.90.30.
X.3. K.10.c.95.70.	K.17.b.00.50.	Y.3. K.6.c.95.95.	K.12.d.27.95.
X.4. K.10.c.95.70.	K.11.d.10.10.	Y.4. K.6.c.95.95.	K.12.d.65.90.
X.5. K.9.a.55.25)	To cover	Y.5. E.28.c.60.10)	To cover
X.6. K.9.a.55.25)	PURPLE LINE.	Y.6. E.28.c.75.30)	PURPLE LINE.

H.Q. 42nd D.A.C. J.1.d.9.0. No.1.Section. J.2.c.2.2.
No.2.Section. J.2.c.7.7. S.A.A.Section. J.1.b.5.7.
42nd A.R.P. D.26.central.

H.Q. 41st D.A.C. D.20.a.0.2. No.1.Sect. D.20.a.5.5. No.2.Sect. D.21.b.5.0.

H.Q. 62nd D.A.C. I.12.a.1.2. No.1.&.2.Sects. I.11.d.5.8.
S.A.A.Sect. AUTHIE.
IN LIAISON WITH 42nd Div.Arty.

54th Bde R.G.A. H.Q. ROSSIGNOL FARM J.3.c.
56th Bde R.G.A. H.Q. J.9.a.5.2.

P.R. Mitchell
Maj. for Lieut.R.H.A.
Reconnaissance Officer, 42nd Divnl.Artillery.

5-5-18.

APP. III

42nd D.A., No. B.M.495.

<u>URGENT & SECRET.</u>

123rd Brigade R.F.A.	285th Brigade R.F.A.
124th Brigade R.F.A.	210th Brigade R.F.A.
36th A.F.A.Bde.	211th Brigade R.F.A.
295th Brigade R.F.A.	312th Brigade R.F.A.
296th Brigade R.F.A.	

Please cause all positions selected by you to cover the CHATEAU de la HAIE Switch and the RED LINE (LEFT Sector) to be marked similarly to the PURPLE LINE Positions, i.e., :-

A small cross trench will be dug at the position for each pivot gun -

like this

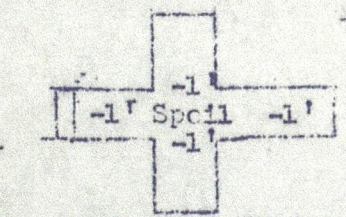

The number board should be erected in the centre of this trench.

This should be completed by the evening of June 2nd and a certificate rendered to this office that this has been done.

The re-secting of the positions will be undertaken by the Field Survey Coy as soon as the positions have been marked in the above manner.

P.R. Mitchell
Major., R.A.
Brigade Major., R.A., 42nd Division.

31st May 1918.

Copies to :- R.A., IV Corps.
            37th D.A.
            57th D.A.
            62nd D.A.

SECRET.   Copy No. 15

42nd Divisional Artillery Instruction No.1.

FIELD ARTILLERY DEFENCE OF RETIRED LINES
(LEFT SECTOR - IV CORPS)

1. All previous orders on this subject are cancelled.

2. **REARWARD LINES OF DEFENCE.**

   The Field Artillery Brigades covering the LEFT & CENTRE Divisions in the line will - in the event of a retirement from their PURPLE LINE Positions - be employed successively to cover -

   (a) The CHATEAU de la HAIE Switch from K.13.c.5.0. to E.13.c.8.4.

   (b) The LEFT Sector of the RED LINE from J.9.d.5.0. to E.13.c.8.4.

   (c) The PAS Switch from I.11.d.0.9. to C.12.c.0.0.

   For (a) & (b) they will come under the orders of the Division in Army Reserve - at present the 42nd Division.

3. **NUMBER OF BDES. R.F.A. AVAILABLE.**

   The number of Brigades covering the LEFT & CENTRE Divisions for the defence of the PURPLE Line, and therefore available for the defence of the CHATEAU de la HAIE Switch and RED LINE (LEFT Sector), is **8**.

   In addition, the Brigade R.F.A. in Corps Mobile Reserve may be allotted to the defence of the LEFT SECTOR of the Rearward Lines of Defence.
   For the defence of the RED LINE (LEFT Sector) -
   1 D.A. will be placed in Corps Reserve.

   Brigade Areas have therefore been reconnoitred for the maximum number of Brigades available for each line, viz,

CHATEAU de la HAIE Switch	-	9 Bdes. R.F.A.
RED LINE (LEFT Sector)	-	7 Bdes. R.F.A.
PAS Switch.	-	7 Bdes. R.F.A.

4. **RECONNAISSANCE OF POSITIONS.**

   Reconnaissances have been carried out for the maximum number of Bdes. R.F.A. in each case.

   The locations of Batteries, Bde. H.Qrs., and O.Ps. to cover the various lines are shewn in Appendices 'A', 'B', & 'C'.

   Brigade Areas are numbered -

   For the CHATEAU de la HAIE Switch - 7A,8A,9A,10,11,12,13A,14A & 15A
   "   "   RED LINE (LEFT Sector)   - 7 to 13.
   "   "   PAS Switch.   - 7B to 13B.

   NOTE. Areas 10,11 & 12 cover both the CHATEAU de la HAIE Switch and the RED LINE (LEFT Sector).

                                                                    T.T.O.

5. ALLOTMENT OF BRIGADES TO AREAS.

Owing to the constant change of Brigades R.F.A. in the line it is impossible to allot Brigades R.F.A. permanently to Brigade Areas.

Appendix 'D', which will be re-issued from time to time, shows the allotment of Brigade Areas to Brigades R.F.A.

Brigades R.F.A. are responsible that the necessary reconnaissances to enable positions to be occupied at short notice are carried out.

6. GROUPING OF ARTILLERY.

Brigades will be formed into a RIGHT & LEFT Group as shown in Appendices 'A', 'B' & 'C'.

The Senior Brigade Commander in each Group will be Group Commander.

Groups will be divided into Sub-Groups as required.

7. ARTILLERY GROUP H.QRS.

These will be with the Infantry Brigade H.Qrs.

For the CHATEAU de la HAIE Switch these are located as follows :-

RIGHT INFANTRY BRIGADE H.Q. - D.28.c.2.3.
LEFT INFANTRY BRIGADE H.Q. - D.17.c.6.3.

Artillery accommodation for 4 Officers and 25 O.Rs. is being provided by the R.E.

Artillery Group H.Qrs. for the RED LINE (Left Sector) and PAS Switch will be notified later.

8. LIMITS OF GROUP ZONES.

The dividing line between Artillery Groups may be taken to be as follows:

CHATEAU de la HAIE Switch - An E. & W. Line through J.6.Central.
RED LINE (LEFT Sector)   - An E. & W. Line through D.28.c.0.0.
PAS Switch   - An E. & W. Line through C.29.Central.

9. ORDERS FOR WITHDRAWAL FROM THE PURPLE LINE.

Orders for the withdrawal of the Artillery from the PURPLE LINE to the CHATEAU de la HAIE Switch will be issued by the Divisions in the line. Brigades pass under the orders of the Division in Army Reserve on vacating their PURPLE LINE Positions in order to take up their CHATEAU de la HAIE Switch Positions.

10. POSITION OF D.A. BATTLE H.Q.

D.A. Battle H.Q. for the defence of the CHATEAU de la HAIE Switch is in the Sunken Road at D.13.d.6.3.

Immediately a Brigade vacates its PURPLE LINE positions it will send an officer to report to D.A. Battle H.Q. for instructions and to give information bearing on fighting efficiency of Brigade, such as number of casualties, number of guns in action, &c.

As soon as the Brigade is in action in its CHATEAU de la HAIE Switch positions that fact is to be reported to D.A., H.Q.

10. (cont/d).

A mounted or cyclist orderly per Brigade will be detailed to remain at D.A.,H.Q. This orderly will be relieved daily.

D.T.MOs. will report at D.A.,H.Q. immediately on receipt of orders to fall back from the PURPLE LINE.

The same procedure will be adopted if a retirement is ordered to the RED LINE or the PAS Switch. The position of D.A.,H.Q. for those Lines will be notified later.

11. NUMBERING OF POSITIONS.

Battery positions will be numbered as shewn in Appendices 'A', 'B', and 'C'.

Brigades to whom areas are allotted will erect numbered boards at each battery position, checking them from time to time.

12. ROUTES OF WITHDRAWAL.

The following emergency routes have been made in order that shelled areas may be avoided as far as possible :-

CAHTEAU de la HAIE TRACK: J.6.b.0.4. - D.29.c.7.4. - D.28.c.0.3. - D.27.d.7.0. - D.27.b.2.1. - C.30.b.7.7.

WILLOW PATCH TRACK: E.13.c.9.8. - D.18.b.1.2. - D.17.c.3.0. - D.16.c.9.1. - D.15.d.8.6. - D.15.c.6.3.

The following gaps exist in wire and trenches :-

(a) In HAIE Switch. (1) About J.6.d.8.8.; (2) About D.30.d.5.8.
                     (3) At SOUASTRE-FONQUEVILLERS Road.

(b) In RED LINE. (1) At ROSSIGNOL FARM-BAYENCOURT Road.
               (2) About J.4.c.9.3.; (3) At track about D.28.d.2.2.
               (4) At SOUASTRE-BAYENCOURT Road.
               (5) At SOUASTRE-SAILLY Road.
               (6) At SOUASTRE-Ch.de la.HAIE Road.
               (7) At SOUASTRE-FONQUEVILLERS Road.

13. COMMUNICATIONS.

Group Headquarters for the CHATEAU de la HAIE Switch will be situated with the Advanced Infantry Brigades, to which lines from Division now exist.

Group Signal Officers will connect their exchange by a junction to the Infantry Brigade exchange.

For the initial stages of the occupation of the CHATEAU de la HAIE Switch a visual station has been established at D.19.d.7.0. From this point good communication can be established with -

(1) Visual station anywhere on high ground between BAYENCOURT and CHATEAU de la HAIE, which might be used as an O.P. from which reports as to the progress of withdrawal of our troops and advance of enemy could be sent.
(2) High ground about ROSSIGNOL FARM.
(3) Ground in C.23.
(4) GAUDIEMPRE CHURCH, and Ground in D.2.cd.
(5) Ridge S. of ST AMAND D.15.cd.
(6) Vicinity of Windmill (W. of SOUASTRE) D.21.b.7.2.
(7) Ground in D.14.a. & c.
(8) Ground in D.3.d.

13. (cont/d).

This main visual station will be manned and will have instructions to got in communication with any station showing a light with a view to –

(a) Establishing communication with D.A.
(b) Helping Groups or Brigades by transmitting messages.

This station will also be used for Infantry purposes and will have visual communication to Infantry Brigades.

It is connected to Divisional Exchange by telephone and also to the H.Q. of the Infantry Brigade in Reserve at D.26.d.2.4.

14. CONCRETE O.PS.

With regard to the defence of the ARMY RED LINE, a certain number of sites suitable for Observation Posts have been reconnoitred under Army arrangements.

On these sites it is proposed to sink concrete O.Ps. of standard design, under arrangements made by C.E., Third Army who has now the matter in hand and if possible short lengths of buried cable (about 500 yds to 800 yds) will be laid to these posts under arrangements being made by D.D. Signals Third Army.

The approximate co-ordinates of these O.P. sites as far as the LEFT Sector is concerned are –

D.21.a.8.1.   J.2.b.7.5.   J.3.d.8.6.   J.9.b.6.9. (Sheet
J.9.c.9.3.   J.15.a.0.0.   J.14.c.7.3.   J.13.b.0.5.)   57 d.

It is not known which of the above O.Ps. will be available for Field Artillery use or when they will be completed. Brigades will therefore reconnoitre for O.Ps. independently of the above.

15. SURVEY PICKETS.

The 3rd Field Survey Coy. is arranging to attach labels to the Survey Pickets near Rear Line positions on which will be recorded the square position of the picket and the grid bearing from the picket to two prominent objects.

16. WAGON LINES, AMMUNITION DUMPS &c.   SEE Appendix 'E.

17. ACKNOWLEDGE.

P.R. Mitchell
Major. R.A.
24th May 1918.   Brigade Major., 42nd Divisional Artillery.

Copy No. 1   R.A., IV Corps.
       2   42nd Division 'G'.
      3 - 8   62nd D.A.
      9 - 12   57th D.A.
       13   50th D.A.
       14   37th D.A.
       15   S.C., R.A., 42nd Division.
       16   R.O., R.A., 42nd Division.
       17   Signal Officer, 42nd D.A.
       18   War Diary.
       19   File.
       20   295 Bde R.F.A.
       21   42 Bde
       22   42 DT MO

APPENDIX 'A' - (Issued with 42nd D.A. Instruction No.1.)

FIELD ARTILLERY POSITIONS TO COVER THE CHATEAU DE LA HAIE SWITCH

AREA	Battery	Location	Position No.	Suggested O.Ps.
RIGHT GROUP.				
7A.	Bde. H.Q.	D.26.c.2.5.		J.5.d.5.5.
	'A'	J.2.a.9.9.	C.111.	
	'B'	D.26.d.7.6.	C.112.	
	'C'	D.26.c.2.1.	C.113.	
	'D'	D.26.d.4.4.	C.114.	
8A	Bde. H.Q.	J.2.d.2.2.		J.5.d.7.0.
	'A'	J.2.b.70.05.	C.101.	
	'B'	J.2.d.8.4.	C.102.	
	'C'	J.2.b.3.0.	C.103.	
	'D'	J.2.b.05.00.	C.104.	
9A.	Bde. H.Q.	D.26.c.2.5.		J.5.d.45.50. and
	'A'	D.27.a.0.0.	C.121.	J.12.a.3.1.
	'B'	D.27.a.2.4.	C.122.	
	'C'	D.27.a.5.6.	C.123.	
	'D'	D.26.d.6.7.	C.124.	
15A.	Bde. H.Q.	D.27.b.7.8.		J.6.c.
	'A'	D.21.d.5.7.	C.181.	
	'B'	D.21.d.4.4.	C.182.	
	'C'	D.21.d.2.1.	C.183.	
	'D'	D.21.d.5.0.	C.184.	
LEFT GROUP.				
∅ 10.	Bde. H.Q.	D.14.a.30.80.		D.24.a. & D.24.b.
	'A'	D.14.a.30.60.	R.131.	
	'B'	D.14.a.50.70.	R.132.	
	'C'	D.14.a.70.90.	R.133.	
	'D'	D.14.a.10.50.	R.134.	
∅ 11.	Bde. H.Q.	D.8.d.50.20.		D.21.a.8.1. and
	'A'	D.14.b.30.90.	R.151.	D.24.a.7.3.
	'B'	D.8.d.70.00.	R.152.	
	'C'	D.9.c.00.10.	R.153.	
	'D'	D.9.c.30.30.	R.154.	
∅ 12	Bde. H.Q.	D.13.b.10.80.		D.24.c.3.7.
	'A'	D.9.a.95.05.	R.141.	
	'B'	D.9.b.50.40.	R.142.	
	'C'	D.9.b.80.90.	R.143.	
	'D'	D.9.b.10.30.	R.144.	
13A	Bde. H.Q.	D.13.b.4.2.		D.24.a.7.0.
	'A'	D.16.a.25.65.	C.161.	
	'B'	D.16.a.50.75.	C.162.	
	'C'	D.16.a.65.85.	C.163.	
	'D'	D.15.d.95.80.	C.164.	
14A.	Bde. H.Q.	D.20.b.4.6.		D.24.a. & D.24.b.
	'A'	D.21.a.0.7.	C.171.	
	'B'	D.21.a.4.7.	C.172.	
	'C'	D.15.c.5.6.	C.173.	
	'D'	D.15.d.85.65.	C.174.	

NOTE. ∅ These Areas also cover the RED LINE.

24/5/18

APPENDIX 'B' - (Issued with 42nd D.A. Instruction No.1.)

FIELD ARTILLERY POSITIONS TO COVER RED LINE (LEFT SECTOR)

AREA	Battery	Location.	Position No.	Suggested O.Ps.
RIGHT GROUP.				
7	Bde. H.Q.	C.29.a.7.4.	R.111.	J.3.d.9.6.
	A	C.30.b.6.6.	R.111.	
	B	C.30.b.4.4.	R.112.	
	C	C.30.b.2.1.	R.113.	
	D	C.30.a.1.5.	R.114.	
8	Bde. H.Q.	C.29.a.7.4.		J.9.b.20.60.
	A	C.30.a.00.37.	R.101.	
	B	C.29.b.15.30.	R.102.	
	C	C.29.b.52.34.	R.103.	
	D	C.29.b.70.52.	R.104.	
9	Bde. H.Q.	C.23.c.10.65.		J.9.b.6.9.
	A	C.23.d.85.65.	R.121.	
	B	C.23.d.48.10.	R.122.	
	C	C.23.d.00.00.	R.123.	
	D	C.23.b.5.5.	R.124.	
LEFT GROUP.				
∅ 10.	Bde. H.Q.	D.14.a.30.80.		D.21.a.8.1.
	A	D.14.a.30.60.	R.131.	
	B	D.14.a.50.70.	R.132	
	C	D.14.a.70.90.	R.133.	
	D	D.14.a.10.50.	R.134.	
∅ 11.	Bde. H.Q.	D.8.d.50.20.		D.27.c.31.75.
	A	D.14.b.30.90.	R.151.	
	B	D.8.d.70.00.	R.152.	
	C	D.9.c.00.10.	R.153.	
	D	D.9.c.30.30.	R.154.	
∅ 12.	Bde. H.Q.	D.13.b.10.80.		Front Line E.13.c.
	A	D.9.a.95.05.	R.141.	
	B	D.9.b.50.40.	R.142.	
	C	D.9.b.80.90.	R.143.	
	D	D.9.b.10.30.	R.144.	
13	Bde. H.Q.	D.13.b.10.70.		Front Line E.24.b.
	A	D.2.c.90.80.	R.161.	
	B	D.2.b.10.90.	R.162.	
	C	D.2.b.30.45.	R.163.	
	D	D.2.c.60.20.	R.164.	

NOTE. ∅. These Areas also cover the CHATEAU de la HAIE Switch.

24th May 1918.

APPENDIX 'O'.   Issued with 42nd D.A. Instruction No.1.

FIELD ARTILLERY POSITIONS TO COVER THE PAS SWITCH.

Area.	Battery.	Location.	Position No.	Suggested O.Ps.
RIGHT GROUP.				
7 B.	Bde. H.Q.	C.25.c.4.6.		I.5.a.0.5.
	'A'	I.1.a.05.85.	P.111	
	'B'	B.30.d.90.30.	P.112	
	'C'	B.30.d.85.05.	P.113	
	'D'	B.30.b.15.15.	P.114.	
8 B.	Bde. H.Q.	I.1.c.80.15.		I.5.a.0.6.
	'A'	I.1.c.55.50.	P.101.	
	'B'	I.1.c.85.75.	P.102.	
	'C'	I.1.c.7.2.	P.103.	
	'D'	I.1.d.25.25.	P.104.	
9 B.	Bde. H.Q.	B.24.d.6.3.		I.5.b.0.6.
	'A'	C.25.a.5.8.	P.121.	
	'B'	C.19.c.6.0.	P.122.	
	'C'	C.25.a.4.4.	P.123.	
	'D'	C.25.a.4.6.	P.124.	
LEFT GROUP.				
10.B.	Bde. H.Q.	C.14.c.4.5.		In Front Line about C.23.Central.
	'A'	C.20.a.4.8.	P.131.	
	'B'	C.20.a.7.9.	P.132.	
	'C'	C.14.c.2.3.	P.133.	
	'D'	C.20.b.15.25.	P.134.	
11.B.	Bde. H.Q.	C.14.c.6.5.		C.20.c.4.4.
	'A'	C.13.d.70.90.	P.151.	
	'B'	C.13.b.50.10.	P.152.	
	'C'	C.13.b.20.20.	P.153.	
	'D'	C.14.c.10.85.	P.154.	
12.B.	Bde. H.Q.	C.13.c.9.5.		C.12.b.0.8.
	'A'	C.14.a.2.5.	P.141.	
	'B'	C.8.c.0.2.	P.142.	
	'C'	C.7.d.8.6.	P.143.	
	'D'	C.14.d.1.9.	P.144.	
13.B.	Bde. H.Q.	B.18.c.8.3.		In BOIS DE St. PIERRE about C.22.
	'A'	C.19.a.7.4.	P.161.	
	'B'	C.19.a.8.1.	P.162.	
	'C'	*C.29.c.9.7.	P.163.	
	'D'	C.19.c.5.3.	P.164.	

* C.19.c.9.7.

6th June 1918.

APPENDIX 'D' - Issued with 42nd D.A. Instruction No.1.

(This replaces APPENDIX 'D' dated 24-5-18 which should be destroyed.)

Allotment of Brigades R.F.A. to Brigade Areas to cover -

    (A) CHATEAU de la HAIE Switch.
    (B) RED LINE (LEFT Sector).
    (C) PAS Switch.

(vide Appendices 'A', 'B' & 'C')

Brigade R.F.A.	CHATEAU de la HAIE Area No.	RED LINE (LEFT Sector) Area No.	PAS Switch Area No.
RIGHT GROUP.			
210th Bde R.F.A.	8 A	8	8 B
211th Bde R.F.A.	7 A	7	7 B
26th A.F.A.Bde.	9 A	9	9 B
LEFT GROUP.			
@ 123rd Bde R.F.A.	10	10	-
@ 124th Bde R.F.A.	11	11	11 B
296th Bde R.F.A.	12	12	12 B
285th Bde.R.F.A.	14 A	14 A	13 B
295th Bde R.F.A.	13 A	13	10 B.

@ Brigade R.F.A. in Reserve.

NOTE 1. 123rd & 124th Bdes.R.F.A., at present in Reserve, will have the above areas reserved for them in the event of their being allotted to the defence of the LEFT Sector of the Corps Front.

3rd June 1918.

APPENDIX 'E' - (Issued with 42nd D.A. Instruction No.1.)

ALLOTMENT OF WAGON LINE AREAS TO BRIGADES TO COVER BOTH
CHATEAU DE LAAHAIE SWITCH AND RED LINE.

Serial Number of Wagon Line Area.	Allotted to Brigade which occupies Area.	Map Location.
W.L.7.	7 & 7 A.	C.17.a.
W.L.8.	8 & 8 A.	C.16.b.
W.L.9.	9 & 9 A.	C.27.a.
W.L.10.	10.	C.16.a.
W.L.11.	11.	C.15.d.
W.L.12.	12.	C.15.a.
W.L.13.	13.	C.15.b.

2. D.A.C. areas are allotted as follows :-

   37th D.A.C. .... H.2.b.&.d.

   42nd D.A.C. to whom is affiliated 26th ARMY BDE. Amm. Col.
   H.1.b. & H.2.a.

   59th D.A.C. .... H.1.a. & b.

3. AMMUNITION SUPPLY. As soon as Batteries occupy positions to cover the CHATEAU de la HAIE Switch Battery Wagon Lines will draw ammunition direct from any dump, either Corps Reserve or Divisional A.R.P. in the neighbourhood. Divisional Dumps are in existence at present at D.26.d., C.30.d., & D.20.b. Corps Dumps are at I.20.a. and C.23.b. Railhead Dumps are at ST LEGER, I.12.b. & MONDICOURT C.1.b.

   On receiving the order to retire from the PURPLE LINE positions all D.A.Cs. will at once dump what ammunition is in their vehicles at Brigade Wagon Line Areas given above and will then proceed to their RED LINE positions. As soon as D.A.Cs. arrive at RED LINE positions ammunition supply will be by normal method, i.e., by M.T. from Railhead to D.A.C. and thence by horse transport.

   NOTE. Permission has been asked to move Wagon Lines from W.L.7. & W.L.8. to C.16.c. and C.15.c. respectively, but has not yet been granted. Arrangements are in train for the sinking of Wells and the construction of large Water-Points in the HALLOY-GRENAS Area. As soon as these are completed this area will become the D.A.C. area in place of that allotted above.

42nd D.A.No.B.M.404.

Reference 42nd D.A.No.B.M.395 dated 14th May.1918.

1. Areas allotted to Brigades R.F.A. to cover the CHATEAU de la HAIE Switch are as shewn on the attached tracing. @.
It will be seen that the areas for the 124th and 296th Bdes R.F.A. are the same as are allotted to these Bdes for the purpose of covering the RED Line.

2. The areas shewn are only to be taken as rough indications and a liberal interpretation may be placed upon them provided –

   (a) Bdes R.F.A. do not clash with one another
   (b) Positions already marked by the Corps Heavy Artillery are not interferred with.

3. Brigades R.F.A. will be formed into a RIGHT and LEFT Group in the same manner as for the RED Line.

4. Battery positions, positions for Brigade H.Qrs. and O.Ps. will be reconnoitred <u>at once</u> and results forwarded to C.R.A. 42nd Division.

5. The LEFT Group will cover from –

   Willow Patch "A" to the grid line through E.25.c.0.0.

   The RIGHT Group will cover from –

   E.25.c.0.0. to grid line through K.7.c.0.0.

6. It is important that these reconnaissances should be carried out <u>at once</u>.

7. ACKNOWLEDGE.

P.R. Mitchell
Major., R.A.

16th May.1918.   Brigade Major., R.A., 42nd Division.

Copies to all recipients of 42nd D.A.No.B.M. 395.

@. Copies of tracing only attached for the following:-

   1 copy to each Brigade. *R.F.A. concerned.*
   1 copy to R.A. IV Corps.
   1 copy to 42nd Division 'G'.

SECRET.

42nd D.A., No. B.M.395.

Reference 42nd D.A., No.B.M.368 dated 10th May 1918, and 41st D.A. Instructions No.6 dated 5th May 1918.

The Field Artillery that comes under the command of the C.R.A. of the Division in Army Reserve for the defence of the RED LINE will be under the same command for the defence of the CHATEAU de la HAIE Switch.

Where necessary Bdes. R.F.A. now in the line are reconnoitring for positions to cover the CHATEAU de la HAIE Switch under orders of the Divisions in the line.

Further orders as to the grouping of this Artillery for the defence of the CHATEAU de la HAIE Switch will be issued later.

P.R. Mitchell
Major, R.A.

14th May 1918. Brigade Major., 42nd Divisional Artillery
Copies to all recipients of 42nd D.A., No.B.M.368.

42nd D.A.No.B.M.374.

Reference 42nd D.A.No.B.M.368 of 10th May.1918, para 6,

line 3. For RIGHT read LEFT

line 5. For LEFT read RIGHT

ACKNOWLEDGE.

P.R. Mitchell
Major, R...,
Brigade Major, R..., 42nd Division.

11th May.1918.

Copies to all recipients of 42nd D.A.No.B.M.368.

Copy N° 27

42nd D.A.No.B.M.368.

Reference 41st Div.Arty.Instructions No.6. dated 5th May.

FIELD ARTILLERY DEFENCE OF THE RED LINE.

1. These instructions hold good during the period that 42nd Division are in Army Reserve and are hereby ratified by C.R.A., 42nd Division.

   Wherever the word "41st" occurs the word "42nd" will be substituted.

2. Brigade areas for the RED Line will be known by <u>numbers</u> instead of <u>letters</u> in order to distinguish them from Brigade areas for defence of the PURPLE Line.

Area	"S"	becomes	Area	"7"
"	"L"	"	"	"8"
"	"T"	"	"	"9"
"	"O"	"	"	"10"
"	"V"	"	"	"11"
"	"U"	"	"	"12"
"	"Q"	"	"	"13"

   Paras 3, 4, 6 and 10 will be amended accordingly.

3. <u>Para 5,(b)</u> - Gaps in RED Line wire & trenches.

   Amend J.4.c.7.5. to read J.4.c.9.3.

4. With regard to the Defence of Army RED LINE, a certain number of sites suitable for observation Posts have been reconnoitred under Army arrangements.

   On these sites it is proposed to sink concrete O.Ps. of standard design, under arrangements made by C.E., Third Army who now has the matter in hand and if possible short lengths of buried cable (about 500 yds to 800 yds) will be laid to these posts under arrangements being made by D.D.Signals, Third Army.

   The approximate co-ordinates of the O.P sites as far as the Left Sector is concerned are -

   D.21.d.8.1. J.2.b.7.5. J.3.d.9.6. J.9.b.6.9.,) Sheet
   J.9.c.9.3. J.15.a.0.0. J.14.c.7.3. J.13.b.0.5.) 57 d.

   It is not known which of the above O.Ps. will be available for Field Artillery use or when they will be completed. Brigades will therefore reconnoitre for O.Ps. independently of the above and on the lines indicated in para 10, of 41st D.A.Instruction No.6.

5. Communications. Lines will be laid from Divisional Headquarters, HENU, to Headquarters RIGHT & LEFT Groups as soon as these are fixed.

   For the initial stages of the occupation of the RED LINE a Visual Station has been established at D.19.d.7.0. (vide para,9. 41st D.A. Instruction No.6.). From this point good communication can be established with -

Para 5.cont/d.

    (1) Visual Station anywhere on high ground between BAYENCOURT and CHATEAU de la HAIE, which might be used as an O.P. from which reports as to the progress of withdrawal of our troops and advance of enemy could be sent.
    (2) High ground about ROSSIGNOL FARM.
    (3) Ground in C.23.
    (4) GAUDIEMPRE CHURCH and ground in D.2.cd.
    (5) Ridge S. of ST AMAND. D.15.cd.
    (6) Vicinity of Windmill (W.of SOUASTRE) D.21.b.7.2.
    (7) Ground in D.14.a.&.c.
    (8) Ground in D.3.d.

This main visual station will be manned and will have instructions to get into communication with any station showing a light with a view to -
    (a) Establishing communication with D.A.
    (b) Helping Groups or Brigades by transmitting messages.

This station will also be used for Infantry purposes and will have visual communication to Infantry Brigades.
It is connected to Divisional Exchange by telephone and also to 126th Inf.Brigade.

6.   GROUP H.Q. 59th D.A. and the Senior Brigade Commander of 37th D.A. will each forward early to this office their suggestions as to a suitable position for the RIGHT Group H.Q. → LEFT
    Lieut.Col.E.J.INCHES,D.S.O. Cmdg. 211th Bde R.F.A. will similarly forward suggestions for the LEFT Group H.Q. → RIGHT.
    When the above positions have been finally decided upon the R.E. will be asked to provide shell proof accommodation.
    Reports should therefore state roughly what work is required.

7.   The results of reconnaissances mentioned in para.6. (41st D.A. Instruction No.6.) will be forwarded <u>at once</u> to this office.

8.   ACKNOWLEDGE.

                                          D.P. Mitchell
                                                    Major.,R.A.
10th May.1918.   Brigade Major.,R.A.,42nd Division.

Copy No.		
1 - 2		IV Corps.
3		IV Corps R.A.
4 - 5		42nd Division.
6 - 15		37th Div.Arty.
16 - 20		41st " "
21 - 22		59th " "
23 - 24		62nd " "
25		S.C.R.A. 42nd Division.
26		Sig.Officer,42nd D.A.
27		War Diary.
28		File.

Vol 17

Confidential

War Diary

of

H.Q., R.A. 42nd Divn.

From 1st June 1918 – To 30th June 1918.

Vol. XVI.

June 1918 · Vol XVI Sheet T. Reference Map 1/20,000 57 D NE

Army Form C. 2118.

WAR DIARY
or
INTELLIGENCE SUMMARY.
(Erase heading not required.)

Place	Date	Hour	Summary of Events and Information	Remarks and references to Appendices
PAS-EN ARTOIS	1st		42nd Division (less Arty) in Army Reserve	DW
"	2		42nd Division (less Arty) in Corps Reserve	DW
"	3		Brigades of 42 Div arty stay in line CENTRE Sector - IV Corps under	DW
"	4		Tactical Command of 57th Division	DW
"	5			
"	6		42nd Div (less arty) relieved NZ Div (less arty) in the line. Right sector IV Corps	DW
			on the nights 6/7 + 7/8 June	
BUS-EN-ARTOIS	7		HQ RA, 42 Div moved from PAS-EN-ARTOIS to BUS-EN-ARTOIS on right sector IV Corps	"
			at 12 midnight June 7th	
			Disposition Report	App x I, DW
"	9			DW
"	10/11		2nd Army Bde NZFA withdrew into Corps Reserve	"
"	13		Disposition Report	" II, DW
			The FA covering 42nd Div, formed into 2 groups for Tactical purposes	III DW
	16		Disposition Report	IV DW
	17		Lt. Col. Main DSO, RFA. assumed command of right Group RA	
	19		Disposition report	V "

Army Form C. 2118.

Sheet II.
WAR DIARY
or
INTELLIGENCE SUMMARY.
(Erase heading not required.)

Instructions regarding War Diaries and Intelligence Summaries are contained in F. S. Regs., Part II. and the Staff Manual respectively. Title pages will be prepared in manuscript.

Place	Date	Hour	Summary of Events and Information	Remarks and references to Appendices
BUS-EN-ARTOIS	23		Disposition Report	App X 14 BDE " VII " " VIII " " IX "
	26		Disposition Report	
	29		Various change of Tm personnel	
	30		Disposition Report	
			Relief of 293 Army Bde RFA by 2nd Army Bde NZFA Caucused - tractors issued for 2nd Army Bde NZFA from Corps Reserve to relieve 174 Bde in the line - Relie	
			Scots TV Corps - on the nights June 30 - July 1st & July 1st & 2nd	TM
			Lt. Col. McQuarrie MC, Comdg 3 Bde NZFA assumed command of Left Group RA.	TM TM
			During this period the artillery covering the 42 Division carried out daily - during the night early morning on railway tracks roads trenches - trench junctions - main centres of activity	
			The FA cooperated with infantry for raids on our own front and	
			Rej(Crus) fronts on 8th 15/16" 18/19 20/21"	TM

D Malcolm Lt.
for BM 42 D.A.
1.7.18.

SECRET.

APP. I WD

42nd DIVISIONAL ARTILLERY. LOCATION LIST.

Reference 1/40,000 Sheet 57 D. 6 p.m. 9th June 1918.

Unit.	Position.		Approximate Front covered	Wagon Lines.
42nd D.A., H.Qrs.	(CHATEAU (BUS LES ARTOIS.	—		J.26.a.50.50.
1st Bde. NZFA. H.Q.	J.34.d.60.80.			J.26.c.80.80.
1st Battery.	J.35.c.28.32.	6 Guns 'A'	Q.4.a.80.40.	J.26.a.40.00.
3rd Battery.	J.35.c.30.81.	6 Guns 'A'	to	J.26.d.00.60.
7th Battery.	J.36.d.95.26.	6 Guns 'S'	K.33.b.65.85.	J.26.c.50.50.
15th Battery.	(J.35.a.20.20.	2 Hows 'A'		
	(J.28.d.60.00.	4 Hows 'A'		J.25.d.80.80.
293rd Army Bde RFA.	H.Q. J.23.a.70.20.			J.25.a.70.40.
'A' Battery.	(J.28.d.50.90.	5 Guns 'A'		
	(J.28.d.56.79.	1 Gun 'A'	K.33.b.65.85.	J.19.a.50.80.
'B' Battery	K.19.a.30.70.	6 Guns 'S'	to	
'C' Battery	(J.23.a.12.41.	4 Guns 'A'	K.21.d.00.00.	J.25.c.80.90.
	(J.23.a.84.65.	2 Guns 'A'		
'D' Battery.	J.29.a.80.24.	6 Hows 'A'		J.25.a.00.60.
2nd Army Bde. NZFA.	H.Q. J.20.c.Central.			J.20.c.50.00.
2nd Battery.	J.22.c.55.68.	4 Guns 'S'	Fires on	J.20.b., J.25.d.
5th Battery.	J.22.a.3080.	6 Guns 'S'	S.O.S. and	
9th Battery.	(J.16.d.20.50.	6 Guns 'S'	Counter-	Mobile
	(K.32.b.70.05.	2 Guns AT	Preparation.	Section
6th Battery.	J.23.d.95.42.	6 Hows 'S'	only.	J.15.b.7.2.
286th Bde R.F.A.H.Q.	J.18.b.10.60.			J.7.b.50.50.
'A' Battery.	J.5.a.95.65.	6 Guns 'SS'		
'B' Battery.	(J.12.c.89.12.	4 Guns 'S'	K.21.d.00.00.	Advanced
	(J.12.b.74.87.	2 Guns 'S'	to	D.28.a., D.22.c.
'C' Battery.	(K.2.c.14.16.	4 Guns 'A'	K.16.c.20.60.	
	(K.2.a.53.22.	2 Guns 'A'		
'D' Battery.	(J.6.d.75.50.	4 Hows 'S'		Rear J.7.b.,
	(J.6.b.80.34.	2 Hows 'S'		J.1.c. & d.
3rd Bde. NZFA. H.Q.	J.18.c.80.80.			
11th Battery.	(J.24.b.30.60.	4 Guns 'S'		
	(K.19.b.40.10.	2 Guns 'A'		Rear P.1.a.
12th Battery.	(J.18.a.40.12.	3 Guns 'A'	K.16.c.20.60.	& O.6.b.
	(J.18.c.12.82.	3 Guns 'A'	to	Advanced
13th Battery.	(J.11.d.65.35.	4 Guns 'S'	K.10.d.40.00.	J.10.a.& b.
	(J.17.c.55.83.	2 Guns 'A'		J.21.a.& c.
4th Battery.	(K.13.a.12.20.	85 Hows. 'A'		
	(K.13.a.05.30.	1 How. 'A'		
N.Z., D.T.M.C.	BUS LES ARTOIS.			
X/N.Z.Battery.	(K.25.d.30.65.	2 -6" 'C'		
	(K.31.a.50.40.	3 -6" 'S'		
	(K.33.c.70.10.	1 -6" 'A'		
	(Q.3.c.70.70.	1 -6" 'A'		
Y/N.Z.Battery.	(K.27.c.32.58.	1 -6" 'A'		
	(K.27.a.60.50.	1 -6" 'A'		
	(K.26.d.15.85.	5 -6" 'S'		
X/57 Battery.	(K.9.a.60.50.	2 -6" 'A'		
	(K.16.a.20.60.	2 -6" 'A'		
X/62 Battery.	K.21.a.45.35.	2 -6" 'A'		
N.Z. D.A.C.	LOUVENCOURT			I.35.a.80.30.
57th D.A.C.(1 Sect.)	HENU.			D.19.
2nd N.Z. B.A.C.	LOUVENCOURT			I.35.a.40.60.
293rd B.A.C.	BUS LES ARTOIS			J.25.a.50.00.

P.R. Mitchell
Major., R.A.
Brigade Major., 42nd Divnl. Artillery.

SECRET.

42nd DIVISIONAL ARTILLERY - LOCATION LIST.

Reference 1/40,000 Sheet 57 D.　　　　　6 p.m. June 1918.

War Diary APP II

Unit.	Position		Approximate Front covered	Wagon Lines
42nd D.A., H.Q.	(CHATEAU (BUS LES ARTOIS.			J.26.a.50.50.
(RIGHT GROUP R.A. Lt. Col. SYMON C.M.G.,D.S.O.,N.Z.F.A.(1st Bde.N.Z.F.A.).				
(H.Q.	J.34.d.60.60.			J.26.c.80.80.
(1st Battery.	J.35.c.28.32.	'6 Guns 'A'	Q.4.a.80.40.	J.26.a.40.00.
(3rd "	J.35.c.30.81.	'6 Guns 'A'	to	J.26.d.00.60.
(7th "	J.36.d.95.26.	'6 Guns 'S'	K.33.b.65.85.	J.26.c.50.50.
(15th "	(J.35.a.20.20.	'2 Hows 'A'		
(	(J.28.d.60.00.	'4 Hows.'A'		J.25.d.80.80.
(293rd Army Bde.R.F.A., H.Q. J.23.a.70.20.				J.25.a.70.40.
('A' Battery	(J.28.d.50.90.	'5 Guns 'A'		
(	(J.28.d.56.79.	'1 Gun 'A'	K.33.b.65.85.	J.19.a.50.80.
('B' "	K.19.a.30.70.	'6 Guns 'S'	to	
('C' Battery.	(J.23.a.12.41.	'4 Guns 'A'	K.21.d.00.00.	J.25.c.80.90.
(	(J.23.a.84.65.	'2 Guns 'A'		
('D' "	J.29.a.80.24.	'6 Hows 'A'		J.25.a.00.60.
(LEFT GROUP.R.A. Lt. Col. COTTER D.S.O., R.A.(286th Brigade R.F.A.)				
(H.Q.	J.18.b.10.60.			J.7.b.50.50.
('A' Battery.	J.5.a.95.65.	'6 Guns 'S'		
('B' "	(J.12.c.89.12.	'4 Guns 'S'	K.21.d.00.00.	Advanced
(	(J.12.b.74.87.	'2 Guns 'S'	to	D.28.a. and
('C' "	(K.2.c.14.16.	'4 Guns 'A'	K.16.c.20.60.	D.22.c.
(	(K.2.a.53.22.	'2 Guns 'A'		
('D' "	(J.6.d.75.50.	'4 Hows 'S'		Rear J.7.b.
(	(J.6.b.80.34.	'2 Hows 'S'		J.1.c. & d.
(3rd Bde. N.Z.F.A., H.Q. J.18.c.80.80.				
(11th Battery.	(J.24.b.30.60.	'4 Guns 'S'		
(	(K.19.b.40.10.	'2 Guns 'A'		Rear P.1.a.
(12th "	(J.18.a.40.12.	'3 Guns 'A'	K.16.c.20.60.	& O.6.b.
(	(J.18.c.12.82.	'3 Guns 'A'	to	Advanced
(13th "	(J.11.d.65.35.	'4 Guns 'S'	K.10.d.40.00.	J.10.a.& b.
(	(J.17.c.55.83.	'2 Guns 'A'		J.21.a.& c.
(4th "	(K.13.a.12.20.	'2 Hows 'A'		
(	(J.24.b.90.65.	'4 Hows.'S'		

2 - 15 pdrs.(A.T) (K.32.b.50.50. 8) manned by personnel of 5th N.Z.Battery
　　　　　　　　　(K.32.b.30.10.) 2nd Army Brigade N.Z.F.A.

2nd Army Bde N.Z.F.A. H.Q. J.20.c.Central in Corps Mobile Reserve.

N.Z.,D.T.M.C.	BUS LES ARTOIS			
X/N.Z. Bty.	(K.25.d.30.65.	'2 - 6" 'S'		
	(K.31.a.50.40.	'3 - 6" 'S'		
	(K.33.c.70.10.	'1 ∂ 6" 'A'		
	(Q.3.c.70.70.	'1 - 6" 'A'		
Y/N.Z. Bty.	(K.27.c.32.58.	'1 - 6" 'A'		
	(K.27.a.00.00.	'1 - 6" 'A'		
	(K.25.d.15.85.	'5 - 6" 'S'		
X/57. Bty.	(K.9.a.60.50.	'2 - 6" 'A'		
X/62. Bty.	(K.21.a.45.35.	'2 - 6" 'A'		
N.Z.,D.A.C.	LOUVENCOURT.			I.35.a.80.30.
57th D.A.C.(1 Sect)	HENU.			D.19.
2nd N.Z. B.A.C.	LOUVENCOURT.			I.35.a.40.60.
293rd B.A.C.	BUS LES ARTOIS			J.25.a.50.00.

H.A. affiliated to 42nd D.A.

| 29th Bde R.G.A. | BERTRANCOURT | | | |

13th June 1918.　　　　　　　　　　　　P. ?. M. ?????? Major., R.A.
　　　　　　　　　　　　　　　　　　　B.M., R.A., 42nd Division.

APPENDIX III

SECRET.   42nd D.A., No. B.M.1/21.

1st Brigade N.Z.F.A.
2nd Army Brigade N.Z.F.A.
3rd Brigade N.Z.F.A.
283th Brigade R.F.A.
293rd Army Brigade R.F.A.

1. The Field Artillery covering 42nd Division will be formed into 2 Groups, for tactical purposes, from 10.0 a.m., 13th June, 1918, as follows :-

   RIGHT GROUP.   -   covering RIGHT Infantry Brigade.

   293rd Army Bde. R.F.A.)   Commander
   1st Brigade N.Z.F.A.   )   Lt. Col. SYMON C.M.G., D.S.O.,
                                                        N.Z.F.A.

   LEFT GROUP.   -   covering LEFT Infantry Brigade.

   3rd Brigade N.Z.F.A.   )   Commander
   283th Brigade R.F.A.   )   Lt. Col. COTTER D.S.O., R.A.

2. The Group Commanders will act in the closest liaison with the G.O.C. Inf. Bdes. they support.

3. O.C., R.A., Signals will arrange for good lateral communication between Brigades R.F.A. where this does not already exist.

4. Intelligence Summaries, Harassing Fire targets, Evening Situation Wires etc. etc., will be sent in to this Office by "Groups", and not by "Brigades", from 10.0 a.m. June 13th.

   Correspondence of a tactical nature will be sent from this office addressed to "Groups" from the same hour.

5. RIGHT GROUP will provide a Senior Liaison Officer, not below the rank of Captain, to line at RIGHT Infantry Brigade H.Q.

   This officer will have direct telephone communication with 1st Brigade N.Z.F.A., H.Q., by a buried cable. Visual and a service of mounted orderlies will also be arranged.

                                                    Major R.A.
                                                    Brigade Major., R.A.
11th June 1918.   42nd Division.

Copies to :- R.A., IV Corps.
              42nd Divn. 'G'.
              125th Inf. Bde.
              126th Inf. Bde.
              127th Inf. Bde.
              42nd Divn. Signals.
              R.A. Signals.
              File.

SECRET.   42nd DIVISIONAL ARTILLERY - LOCATION LIST.

Reference 1/40,000. Sheet 57 D.   6 p.m. June 16th 1918.

Unit.	Position	No. of Guns or Hows.	Approximate Front covered.	Wagon Lines.
42nd D.A., H.Q.	CHATEAU BUS LES ARTOIS.			J.26.a.50.50.
(RIGHT GROUP R.A. Lt. Col. SYMON.C.M.G.,D.S.O.(1st Bde. N.Z.F.A.)				
H.Q.	J.34.d.80.60.			J.26.c.80.80.
1st Battery.	J.35.c.28.32.	6 G. 'A'	Q.4.a.80.40.	J.26.a.40.00.
3rd "	J.35.c.30.81.	6 G. 'A'	to	J.26.d.00.60.
7th "	J.36.d.95.26.	6 G. 'S'	K.33.b.65.85.	J.26.c.50.50.
15th "	(J.35.a.20.20.	2 H. 'A'		
	(J.28.d.60.00.	4 H. 'A'		J.25.d.80.80.
(293rd Army Bde.R.F.A. H.Q. J.23.a.70.20.				J.25.a.70.40.
'A' Battery.	(J.28.d.50.90.	5 G. 'A'		
	(J.28.d.56.79.	1 G. 'A'	K.33.b.65.85.	J.19.a.50.80.
'B' "	K.19.a.30.70.	6 G. 'S'	to	
'C' "	(J.23.a.18.41.	4 G. 'A'	K.21.d.00.00.	J.25.c.80.90.
	(J.23.a.04.65.	2 G. 'A'		
'D' Battery.	J.29.a.80.24.	6 H. 'A'		J.25.c.00.60.
(LEFT GROUP R.A. Lt.Col. COTTER.D.S.O.,R.A.(286th Bde R.F.A.)				
H.Q.	J.18.b.10.60.			J.7.b.50.50.
'A' Battery.	H.5.a.95.65.	6 G. 'S'	K.21.d.00.00.	Advanced
'B' "	(J.12.c.89.12.	4 G. 'S'	to	D.28.a. &
	(J.12.b.74.87.	2 G. 'S'	K.16.c.20.60.	D.22.c.
'C' "	(K.2.c.14.16.	4 G. 'A'		
	(K.2.a.53.22.	2 G. 'A'		Rear J.7.b.
'D' "	(J.6.d.75.50.	4 H. 'S'		J.1.c. & d.
	(J.6.b.80.34.	2 H. 'S'		
(3rd Bde. N.Z.F.A.H.Q. J.18.c.80.80.				
11th Battery.	(J.24.b.30.60.	4 G. 'S'		Rear P.1.a.
	(K.19.b.40.10.	2 G. 'A'	K.16.c.20.60.	& O.6.b.
12th "	(J.18.a.40.12.	3 G. 'A'	to	Advanced
	(J.18.c.12.82.	3 G. 'A'	K.10.d.40.00.	H.10.a&b.
13th "	(J.11.d.65.35.	4 G. 'S'		J.21.a.& c.
	(J.17.c.55.83.	2 G. 'A'		
4th "	(K.13.a.12.20.	2 H. 'A'		
	(J.24.b.90.65.	4 H. 'S'		

2 - 15 pdrs.(A.T.)(K.32.b.50.50.) Manned by personnel of 5th N.Z.Bty.
            (K.32.b.30.10.) 2nd Army Brigade N.Z.F.A.

2nd Army Bde. N.Z.F.A.(H.Q. J.20.c.Central) in Corps Mobile Reserve.

N.Z.,D.T.M.O.	BUS LES ARTOIS.	6" T.Ms.		
X/N.Z.Bty.	(K.25.d.30.65.	2 - 'S'		
	(K.31.a.50.40.	3 - 'S'		
	(K.33.c.70.10.	1 - 'A'		
	(Q.3.c.70.70.	1 - 'A'		
Y/N.Z.Bty.	(K.27.c.32.58.	1 - 'A'		
	(K.27.a.00.00.	1 - 'A'		
	(K.25.d.15.85.	5 - 'S'		
X/57 Bty.	K.9.a.60.50.	2 - 'A'		
X/62 Bty.	K.21.a.45.35.	2 - 'A'		
N.Z.,D.A.C.	LOUVENCOURT.			I.35.a.80.30.
57 D.A.C.(1 Sect)	HENU.			D.19.
2nd N.Z.B.A.C.	LOUVENCOURT.			I.35.a.40.60.
293rd B.A.C.	BUS LES ARTOIS.			J.25.a.50.00.

H.A. affiliated to 42nd D.A. - 29th Bde. R.G.A., H.Q. BERTRANCOURT.

P.D. Mitchell
Major., R.A.
Brigade Major., 42nd Divisional Artillery.

16th June 1918.

SECRET.   42nd DIVISIONAL ARTILLERY - LOCATION LIST.

Reference 1/40,000. Sheet 57 D.   6 p.m. 19th June 1918.

Unit.	Position.	No. of Guns or Hows.	Approximate Front covered.	Wagon Lines.
42nd D.A., H.Q.	CHATEAU BUS LES ARTOIS.			J.26.a.50.50.
(RIGHT GROUP R.A.(Lt.Col.MAIN D.S.O. 293rd Army Bde.R.F.A.)				
H.Q.	J.23.a.70.20.			J.25.a.70.40.
(H.Q. 1st Bde.N.Z.F.A.	J.34.d.60.60.			J.26.c.80.80.
1st Battery.	J.35.c.28.32.	6 G. 'A'	Q.4.a.80.40.	J.26.a.40.60.
3rd "	J.35.c.30.81.	6 G. 'A'	to	J.26.d.00.60.
7th "	J.36.d.95.26.	6 G. 'S'	K.33.b.65.65.	J.26.c.50.50.
15th "	(J.35.a.20.20.	2 H. 'A'		
	(J.28.d.60.00.	4 H. 'A'		J.25.d.80.80.
(A/293 Battery	(J.28.d.50.90.	5 G. 'A'		
(	(J.28.d.50.79.	1 G. 'A'	K.35.b.65.85.	J.19.a.50.30.
(B/293 "	K.19.a.30.70.	6 G. 'S'	to	
(C/293 "	(J.23.a.12.41.	4 G. 'A'	K.21.d.00.00.	J.25.c.80.90.
(	(J.23.a.84.65.	2 G. 'A'		
(D/293 "	J.29.a.80.24.	6 H. 'A'		J.25.c.00.30.
(LEFT GROUP R.A.(Lt.Col.COTTER D.S.O., 286th Bde.R.F.A.)				
H.Q.	J.18.b.10.00.			J.7.b.50.50.
('A' Battery.	J.5.a.95.65.	6 G. 'S'		
('B' "	(J.12.c.69.12.	4 G. 'S'	K.21.d.00.00.	Advanced
(	(J.12.b.74.87.	2 G. 'S'	to	D.28.a. &
('C' "	(K.2.c.14.16.	4 G. 'A'	K.16.c.20.60.	D.22.c.
(	(K.2.a.53.22.	2 G. 'A'		
('D' "	(J.6.d.75.50.	4 H. 'S'		Rear J.7.b.
(	(J.6.b.80.34.	2 H. 'S'		J.1.c. & d.
3rd Bde. N.Z.F.A.H.Q.	J.18.c.60.00.			
(11th Battery.	(J.24.b.30.60.	4 G. 'S'		
(	(K.19.b.40.10.	2 G. 'A'		Rear P.1.a.
(12th "	(J.18.a.40.12.	3 G. 'A'	K.16.c.20.60.	& O.6.b.
(	(J.18.c.12.82.	3 G. 'A'	to	Advanced
(13th "	(J.11.d.65.35.	4 G. 'S'	K.10.d.40.00.	J.10.a.&.b.
(	(J.17.c.55.03.	2 G. 'A'		J.21.a.&.c.
(4th "	(K.13.a.12.20.	2 H. 'A'		
(	(J.24.b.90.65.	4 H. 'S'		

2-15pdrs.(A.T.) (K.32.b.50.50.) manned by personnel of 5th N.Z.Bty
                (K.32.b.30.10.) 2nd Army Bde.N.Z.F.A.

2nd Army Bde.N.Z.F.A. (H.Q. J.20.c.central) in Corps Mobile Reserve.

T.M.,D.T...O.	BUS LES ARTOIS	6"T.Ms		
X/N.Z. Bty.	(K.25.d.30.65.	2 -'S'		
	(K.31.a.50.40.	3 -'S'		
	(K.33.c.70.10.	1 -'A'		
	(Q.3.c.70.70.	1 -'A'		
Y/N.Z.Bty.	(K.27.c.32.58.	1 -'A'		
	(K.27.a.00.00.	1 -'A'		
	(K.25.d.15.35.	5 -'S'		
X/57 Bty.	(K.9.a.65.50.	2 -'A'		
	(K.16.a.20.60.	2 -'A'		
X/62 Bty.	(K.21.a.45.35.	2 -'A'		
N.Z.,D.A.C.	LOUVENCOURT			I.35.a.50.30.
57 D.A.C.(1 Sec.)	HENU			D.19.
2nd N.Z.B.A.C.	LOUVENCOURT			I.35.a.40.60.
293rd B.A.C.	BUS LES ARTOIS			J.25.a.50.00.

H.A. affiliated to 42nd D.A.-29th Bde. R.G.A. H.Q. BERTRANCOURT.

19th June 1918.   Brigade Major., 42nd Divisional Artillery.

SECRET.   42nd DIVISIONAL ARTILLERY - LOCATION LIST.   APP. VI

Reference 1/40,000 Sheet 57 D.   6 p.m. 23rd June 1918.

Unit.	Position	No. of Guns or Hows.	Approximate Front covered	Wagon Lines.
42nd D.A.H.Q.	CHATEAU BUS LES ARTOIS.			J.26.a.50.50.

(RIGHT GROUP R.A. (Lt.Col.MAIN D.S.O. 293rd Army Bde R.F.A.)

Unit	Position	Guns/Hows	Front	Wagon Lines
H.Q.	J.23.a.70.20.			J.25.a.70.40.
H.Q. 1st Bde N.Z.F.A.	J.34.d.60.60.			J.26.c.90.90.
1st Battery	J.36.d.95.26.	6 G 'S'	Q.4.a.80.40.	J.26.c.50.50.
3rd "	J.35.c.30.81.	6 G 'A'	to	J.26.d.00.60.
7th "	J.35.c.28.32.	6 G 'A'		J.26.a.40.00.
15th "	(J.35.a.20.20.	2 H 'A'	K.33.b.65.85.	
	(J.28.d.60.00.	4 H 'A'		J.25.d.50.30.
A/293rd Bty.	(J.28.d.50.90.	5 G 'A'		
	(J.28.d.56.79.	1 G 'A'	K.33.b.65.85.	J.19.a.50.90.
B/293rd "	K.19.a.30.70.	6 G 'S'	to	
C/293rd "	(J.23.a.12.41.	4 G 'A'	K.21.d.00.00.	J.25.c.80.90.
	(J.23.a.84.65.	2 G 'A'		
D/293rd "	J.29.a.80.24.	6 H 'A'		J.25.a.00.60.

(LEFT GROUP R.A.(Lt.Col.COTTER D.S.O. 286th Bde.R.F.A.)

Unit	Position	Guns/Hows	Front	Wagon Lines
H.Q.	J.18.b.10.60.			J.7.b.50.50.
A. Battery	J.5.a.95.65.	6 G 'S'		
B. "	(J.12.c.89.12.	4 G 'S'	K.21.d.00.00.	Advanced
	(J.12.b.74.87.	2 G 'S'	to	D.28.a. &
C. Battery.	(K.2.c.14.16.	4 G 'A'	K.16.c.20.60.	D.22.c.
	(K.2.a.53.22.	2 G 'A'		
D. "	(J.6.d.75.50.	4 H 'S'		Rear. J.7.b.
	(J.12.b.92.18.	2 H 'A'		J.1.c. & d.
3rd Bde NZFA H.Q.	J.18.c.80.80.			
11th Bty.	(J.24.b.30.60.	4 G 'S'		
	(K.19.b.40.10.	2 G 'A'		Rear P.1.a.
12th "	(J.18.a.40.12.	3 G 'A'	K.16.c.20.60.	and C.6.b.
	(J.18.c.12.82.	3 G 'A'	to	Advanced
13th "	(J.11.d.65.35.	4 G 'S'	K.10.d.40.00.	J.10.a.& b.
	(J.17.c.55.83.	2 G 'A'		J.21.a.& c.
4th "	(K.13.a.12.20.	2 H 'A'		
	(J.24.b.90.65.	4 H 'S'		

2 - 15 pdrs. (A.T) (K.32.b.50.50.) manned by personnel of 2nd N.Z. Battery
           (K.32.b.30.10.) 2nd Army Brigade N.Z.F.A.

2nd Army Bde.N.Z.F.A.(H.Q. J.20.c.central) in Corps Mobile Reserve.

N.Z.,D.T.M.O. - BUS LES ARTOIS. (6" T.Ms.)

X/N.Z.Bty. -(K.25.d.30.65. 2 -'S'   Y/N.Z.Bty. - (K.27.c.32.55. - 1-'A'
            (K.31.a.50.40. 3 -'S'   (K.27.a.00.00. - 1-'A'
            (K.33.c.70.10. 1 -'A'   (K.21.b.10.55. - 1-'A'
            (Q.3.c.70.70. 1 -'A'   (K.25.d.15.85. - 4-'S'

X/57 Bty. - (K.9.a.60.60. 2 -'A'   X/62 Bty. - (K.21.a.45.35. - 2-'A'
            (K.16.a.20.60. 2 -'A'

A.R.Ps. 42nd Divn. - I.24.d.3.5.   286th Bde. - D.21.a.3.4.

N.Z.,D.A.C.	LOUVENCOURT			I.35.a.90.30.
57th D.A.C.(1 Sec)	HENU			D.19.
2nd N.Z.B.A.C.	LOUVENCOURT			I.35.a.40.60.
293rd B.A.C.	BUS LES ARTOIS			J.25.a.50.00.

H.A. affiliated to 42nd D.A. - 29th Bde R.G.A. H.Q. BERTRANCOURT.

                                         P.R.Mitchell
                                              Major., R.A.
23rd June 1918.   Brigade Major., 42nd Divisional Artillery.

SECRET. 42nd DIVISIONAL ARTILLERY - LOCATION LIST.   APP. VII

Reference 1/40,000 Sheet 57 D.   6 p.m. 26th June 1918.

Unit.	Position.	No. of Guns or Hows.	Approximate Front Covered.	Wagon Lines.
42nd D.A., H.Q.	CHATEAU BUS LES ARTOIS.			J.26.a.50.50.

RIGHT GROUP R.A. (Lt-Col. MAIN D.S.O. 293rd Army Bde R.F.A.)

Unit.	Position.	No. of Guns or Hows.	Approximate Front Covered.	Wagon Lines.
H.Q.	J.23.a.70.20.			J.25.a.70.40.
H.Q.,1st Bde.N.Z.F.A.	J.34.d.60.60.			J.26.c.60.60.
1st Battery.	J.36.d.95.26.	6 G 'S'	Q.4.a.80.40.	J.26.c.50.50.
3rd "	J.35.c.30.01.	6 G 'A'	to	J.26.d.00.60.
7th "	J.35.c.28.32.	6 G 'A'	K.33.b.65.85.	J.26.a.40.00.
15th "	J.35.a.20.20.	2 H 'A'		
	J.28.d.60.00.	4 H 'A'		J.25.d.80.80.
A/293rd Bty.	(J.28.d.50.90.	5 G 'A'		
	(J.28.d.56.79.	1 G 'A'	K.33.b.65.85.	J.19.a.50.80.
B/293 "	K.19.a.30.70.	6 G 'S'	to	
C/293 "	(J.23.a.12.41.	4 G 'A'	K.21.d.00.00.	J.25.c.80.90.
	(J.23.a.84.65.	2 G 'A'		
D/293 "	J.29.a.80.24.	6 H 'A'		J.25.a.00.60.

LEFT GROUP R.A. (Lt.Col. COTTER D.S.O. 286th Bde R.F.A.)

Unit.	Position.	No. of Guns or Hows.	Approximate Front Covered.	Wagon Lines.
H.Q.	J.18.b.10.60.			J.7.b.50.50.
A.Battery.	J.5.a.95.65.	6 G 'S'		
B. "	(J.12.c.99.12.	4 G 'S'	K.21.d.00.00.	Advanced
	(J.12.b.74.87.	2 G 'S'	to	D.28.a. &
C. "	(K.2.c.14.16.	4 G 'A'	K.16.c.20.60.	D.22.c.
	(K.2.a.53.22.	2 G 'A'		
D. "	(J.6.d.75.50.	4 H 'S'		Rear J.7.b.
	(J.12.b.92.18.	2 H 'A'		J.1.c. & d.
3rd Bde. N.Z.F.A.H.Q.	J.18.c.80.80.			
11th Battery.	(J.24.b.30.60.	4 G 'S'		
	(K.19.b.40.10.	2 G 'A'		Rear P.1.a.
12th "	(J.18.a.40.12.	3 G 'A'	K.16.c.20.60.	and O.6.b.
	(J.18.c.12.82.	3 G 'A'	to	Advanced
13th "	(J.11.d.65.35.	4 G 'S'	K.10.d.20.00.	J.10.a.& b.
	(J.17.c.55.83.	2 G 'A'		J.21.a.& c.
4th "	(K.13.a.12.20.	2 H 'A'		
	(J.24.b.80.65.	4 H 'S'		

2 - 15 pdrs.(A.T)(K.32.b.50.50.) manned by personnel of 2nd N.Z.Battery
(K.32.b.30.10.) 2nd Army Brigade N.Z.F.A.

2nd Army Bde. N.Z.F.A.(H.Q. J.20.c.Central) in Corps Mobile Reserve.

N.Z., D.T.M.O. - BUS LES ARTOIS. (6" T.Ms)

X/N.Z.Bty.	- (K.25.d.30.65.	2 - 'S'	Y/N.Z. Bty.	- (K.27.c.32.58)	1 'A'
	(K.31.a.50.40.	3 - 'S'		(K.27.a.00.00.	1 'A'
	(K.33.c.70.10.	1 - 'A'		(K.21.b.10.55.	1 'A'
	(Q.3.c.70.70.	1 - 'A'		(K.25.d.15.85.	4 'S'

X/57 Bty.	- (K.9.a.80.60.	2 - 'A'	X/37 Bty.	- (K.21.a.45.35.	2 'A'
	(K.16.a.20.60.	2 - 'A'			

A.R.Ps. - 42nd Division - I.24.d.3.5.   286th Bde.- D.21.a.3.4.

N.Z.,D.A.C.	LOUVENCOURT.			I.35.a.80.30.
57th D.A.C.(1 Sec. HENU.				D.19.
3rd N.Z.,B.A.C.	LOUVENCOURT.			I.35.a.40.60.
293rd B.A.C.	BUS LES ARTOIS.			J.25.a.50.60.

R.A. affiliated to 42nd D.A. - 29th Bde,R.G.A. -H.Q. BERTRANCOURT.

P.R. Mitchell
Major., R.A.
26th June 1918.   Brigade Major, 42nd Divisional Artillery.

SECRET.   Copy No............ 15.

APP. VIII

42nd Divisional Artillery Order No.10.

1. On June 29th the following changes in the personnel manning the 6"
T.Ms. on the RIGHT Divisional Front will take place.

  (a) 42nd Division T.M.Brigade will take over the 14 T.Ms. at present
  manned by the N.Z. Division T.M. Brigade.

  (b) The personnel of 57th Division T.M. Brigade at present manning the
  2 T.Ms. at K.9.a.5.5. will take over the 2 T.Ms. at K.21.a.45.35. at
  present manned by 37th Division T.M. Brigade.

  (c) The N.Z. Division T.M. Brigade will take over the 2 T.Ms. at
  K.9.a.5.5. and, under orders of the 57th Division, 10 Mortars
  covering the CENTRE Division.

2. All details will be arranged between the D.T.M.Os. concerned.

3. Sufficient personnel must always be present with each Trench Mortar
to carry on the service of the piece.

4. Ammunition at Trench Mortar positions will be handed over and
receipts given and obtained.

5. On the night July 2nd/3rd the 2 T.Ms. at K.9.a.5.5. and the 2 T.Ms.
at K.21.a.45.35. will be transferred to the CENTRE Division, in situ,
to conform with the new Divisional Boundaries.

K.16.a.20.70

6. On the morning of July 3rd the Trench Mortar situation on the RIGHT
Division front will be as follows :-

  14 - 6" Newton T.Ms. manned by 42nd Division T.M. Brigade.
   2 - 6" Newton T.Ms.   "   " 57th   "   "   "

7. ACKNOWLEDGE.

P.R. Mitchell
Major., R.A.,
28th June 1918.   Brigade Major., 42nd Divisional Artillery.

Copies to :- R.A., IV Corps.
            42nd Division 'G'.
            D.T.M.O., 42nd Divn.
            D.T.M.O., N.Z. Division.
            D.T.M.O., 37th Division.
            D.T.M.O., 57th Division.
            RIGHT GROUP R.A.
            LEFT GROUP.R.A.
            RIGHT Inf. Bde.
            Left Inf. Bde.
            57th D.A.
            37th D A.
            S.C.R.A., 42nd Division.
            FILE.
            WAR DIARY.

SECRET   **42nd Divisional Artillery - Location List.**   APP. IX

Reference 1/40,000 Sheet 57 D.   6 p.m. 30th June 1918.

Unit.	Position	No of Guns or Hows.	Approximate Front covered	Wagon Lines.
42nd D.A., H.Q.	CHATEAU BUS LES ARTOIS			J.26.a.50.50.
(RIGHT GROUP R.A. (Lt. Col. MAIN D.S.O. 293rd Army Bde R.F.A.)				
H.Q.	J.26.d.70.20.			J.25.a.70.40.
H.Q. 1st Bde. N.Z.F.A.	J.34.d.60.60.			J.26.c.80.80.
1st Battery.	J.36.d.95.26.	6 G 'S'	Q.4.a.80.40.	J.26.c.50.50.
3rd "	J.35.c.30.81.	6 G 'A'	to	J.26.d.00.60.
7th "	J.35.c.28.32.	6 G 'A'	K.33.b.65.85.	J.26.a.40.00.
15th "	(J.35.a.20.20.	2 H 'A'		
	(J.28.d.60.00.	4 H 'A'		J.28.d.80.80.
A/293 Bty.	(J.28.d.50.90.	5 G 'A'		
	(J.28.d.56.79.	1 G 'A'	K.33.b.65.85.	J.19.a.50.80.
B/293 "	K.19.a.30.70.	6 G 'S'	to	
C/293 "	(J.23.a.12.41.	4 G 'A'	K.21.d.00.00.	J.25.c.80.90.
	(J.23.a.84.65.	2 G 'A'		
D/293 "	J.29.a.80.24.	6 H 'A'		J.25.a.00.60.
(LEFT GROUP R.A. (Lt. Col. COTTER D.S.O. 286th Bde. R.F.A.)				
H.Q.	J.18.b.10.60.			J.7.b.50.50.
'A' Bty.	J.5.a.95.65.	6 G 'S'		
'B' Bty.	J.6.b.50.40.	6 G 'A'	K.21.d.00.00.	Advanced
'C' Bty.	(K.2.c.14.16.	4 G 'A'	to	D.28.a. and
	(K.2.a.33.22.	2 G 'A'	K.16.c.20.60.	D.22.c.
'D' Bty.	(J.6.d.75.50.	4 H 'S'		Rear J.7.b.
	(J.12.b.92.18.	2 H 'A'		J.1.c. & d.
3rd Bde N.Z.F.A. H.Q.	J.18.c.80.80.			
11th Bty.	(J.24.b.30.60.	4 G 'S'		Rear P.1.a.
	(K.19.b.40.10.	2 G 'A'		and O.6.b.
12th Bty.	(J.18.a.40.12.	3 G 'A'	K.16.c.20.60.	Advanced
	(J.18.c.12.92.	3 G 'A'	to	
13th Bty.	(J.11.d.65.35.	4 G 'S'	K.10.d.40.00.	J.10.a. & b.
	(J.17.c.55.83.	2 G 'A'		J.21.a. & c.
4th Bty.	(K.13.a.12.80.	2 H 'A'		
	(J.24.b.90.65.	4 H 'S'		

2 - 15 Pdrs. (A.T)(K.32.b.50.50.) manned by personnel of 2nd N.Z. Bty. (K.32.b.30.10.) 2nd Army Bde. N.Z.F.A.

2nd Army Bde. N.Z.F.A.(H.Q. J.20.e.central) in Corps Mobile Reserve.

42nd D.T.M.O. - BUS LES ARTOIS. 6" T.Ms.).

Y/42 Bty - (K.25.d.30.65. 2 'S'   Y/42 Bty - (K.27.c.32.58. 1 'A'
          (K.31.a.50.40. 3 'S'   (K.27.c.32.58. 1 'A'
          (K.33.c.70.10. 1 'A'   (K.21.b.10.55. 1 'A'
          (Q.3.c.70.70. 1 'A'   (K.25.d.15.65. 2 'S'

        X/37 Bty   -   K.21.a.45.35. 2 'A'

A.R.Ps.   42nd Division - I.24.d.3.5.   286th Bde. - D.21.a.3.4.

N.Z. D.A.C.	LOUVENCOURT			I.35.a.80.30.
57th D.A.C. (1 Sect)	HENU			D.19.
2nd N.Z. B.A.C.	LOUVENCOURT			I.35.a.40.60.
293rd B.A.C.	BUS LES ARTOIS			J.25.a.50.00.

H.A. affiliated to 42nd D.A. - 29th Brigade R.G.A. H.Q. BERTRANCOURT.

30th June 1918.   *P.R. Mitchell*
                                      Major., R.A.
                  Brigade Major., 42nd Divisional Artillery.

HQ RA 4D
No 18

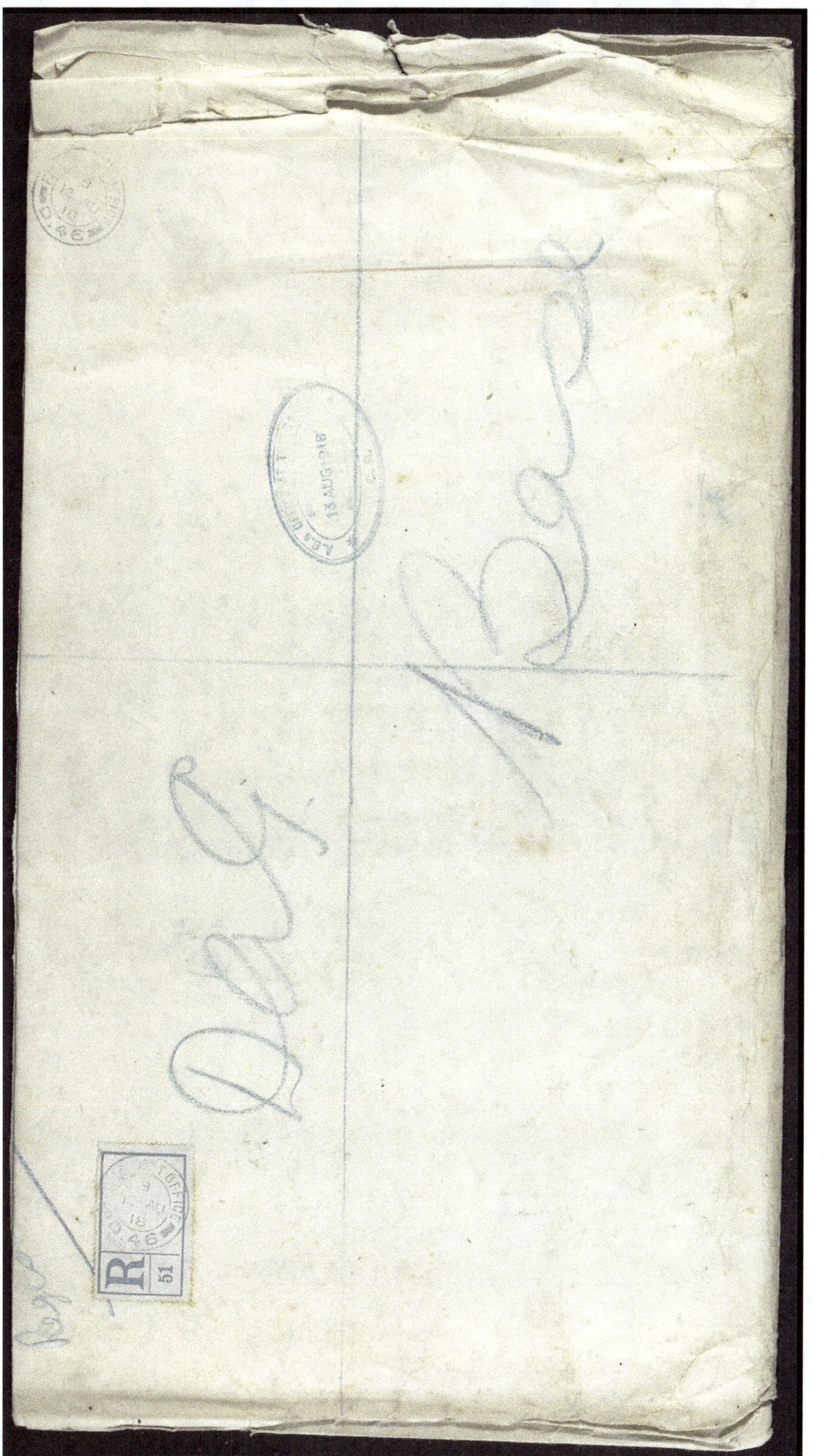

WAR DIARY or INTELLIGENCE SUMMARY

Army Form C. 2118.

July 1918   Vol. XVII.   Sheet 1.

Reference Maps 57D NE / 57D SE   1/20,000

Place	Date	Hour	Summary of Events and Information	Remarks and references to Appendices
BUS	1		Orders issued re Snowping of Arty covering 42nd Div front TOOS Carnage Line	Appx 'A' DA
			to come into force July 5th	
	3		Disposition report	Appx 'B' DA
	4/5		1st & 3rd NZ FA relieved 210 & 211 Bdes RFA in Centre Sector IV. Corps – ? Sections taken over	" C DA "
			210 & 211 Bdes RFA relieved 1st & 3rd Bdes NZ FA in Right Sector IV. Corps ? in Silu in each case	
			Lieut-Col. D.J. Mason DSO 211 Bde RFA assumed Command of Left Group – 42 DA on Completion above relief	
			3·18pdr Batteries 42 DA fired in Cooperation of 63 DA in Support of raid by 190 & 14 Bde	
	6		Orders issued re relative position to cover Purple + Red Lines	Appx D #
	7		Disposition report	" E "
1,2,3 Central	10		Disposition report	" F "
	12		Right Group fired in Support of Raid on Beaumont Hamel by 63 Div.	,
	14		Disposition report	, G "
	15		42 DA fired in cooperation with NZ DA in Support of raid by 3rd NZ (Rifle Bde)	, H "
OUTHUIS	16		42 DA cooperated with IV Corps HA in Bombardment of Pt 151 Eux	, I "
	17		Right Group RA fired in Support of infantry raid	, J "
			Disposition report	, K "

Army Form C. 2118.

Sheet 11
WAR DIARY
or
INTELLIGENCE SUMMARY.
(Erase heading not required.)

Instructions regarding War Diaries and Intelligence
Summaries are contained in F. S. Regs., Part II.
and the Staff Manual respectively. Title pages
will be prepared in manuscript.

Place	Date	Hour	Summary of Events and Information	Remarks and references to Appendices
AUTHIE	19		127 Inf Bde estabished advanced posts with assistance of 4.5 Hows	App. L
	19/20		42 DA cooperated with 62 Bde in support of raid by 188 Inf Bde	" M
	20		6" Newton Tm Gattorno of 42 DA off'd attd to group RFA	" N
	20/21		26 AB RFA relieved 293 AB RFA in the line Right Section IV Corps	
			Lieut-Col H.K. Sadler DSO. MC 26 AB RFA assumed command of Right Sp 42 BTA	
	21		HQ Right Sp RA established at J 34 d 60 60	
			HQ Left " " " J 23 a 70 20	
			Disposition report	App O
	22		125 Inf Bde occupied advanced posts	P
	23		42 DA fired in support of raid by 125 Bde	
	24		Disposition report	" Q
			IV Corps HA & 42 DA Gun General enemy Trenches in K 34	" R
	28		Disposition report	" S
	28/29		26 AB RFA withdrew from Rt Section IV Corps Xtach over guns of 285 Bde RFA (57 DA) in Sidi Left Section	" T
	30		42 DA Cooperated with V. Corps in feint attack - Smoke Groups & Arty Bombardments	" U
	31		Disposition Report	" V

D Malcolm Lt
for BM 42 DA
1.8.18

App. 'A'

SECRET.   Copy No. 26

42nd Divisional Artillery Order No. 15.

1. As soon as the relief of the 1st & 3rd Bdes. N.Z.F.A. by the 210th and 211th Bdes. R.F.A. is complete on July 5th., the following orders re -

    (a) the Grouping of Field Artillery on the 42nd Divisional Front, and

    (b) S.O.S. Barrage Lines

    will come into force.

2. **Grouping.**

    RIGHT GROUP.R.A. - (Lt. Col. A.K.MAIN D.S.O. H.Q. J.23.a.7.2.)

       293rd Army Bde.R.F.A.) covering RIGHT Infantry Brigade.
       210th Brigade R.F.A.)

    LEFT GROUP.R.A. - (Lt. Col. E.J.INCHES D.S.O. H.Q. J.34.d.6.6.)
                                                                             J.18.c.8.8.

       211th Brigade R.F.A. - covering LEFT Infantry Brigade.

3. **Liaison.**

    Each Group will maintain a Senior Liaison Officer with the H.Q. of the Infantry Brigade they cover, provision being made for the usual communications to Group H.Q's. by telephone, visual & runner.

4. **S.O.S. Barrage.**

    Until further orders the S.O.S. Barrage will remain exactly as ordered in 42nd D.A. Order No.12., paras 5 & 6, the 210th & 211th Bdes.R.F.A. taking over the tasks performed by the 1st & 3rd Bdes. N.Z.F.A.

5. ACKNOWLEDGE.

                                                P.R. Mitchell
                                                Major., R.A.,
    Issued at 4 p.m.   Brigade Major., 42nd Divisional Artillery.
    On 1-7-1918. By. D.R.

    Copy No. 1 R.A., IV Corps.   Copy No.16. 57th D.A.
            2 42nd Division 'G'.   17. 63rd D.A.
            3 H.A.,IV Corps.   18. 125th Inf. Bde.
            4 C.B.S.O. IV Corps.   19. 126th Inf. Bde.
            5 - 6 RIGHT GROUP.R.A.   20. 127th Inf. Bde.
            7 - 8 LEFT GROUP.R.A.   21. S.C.,R.A.,
            9 210th Bde. R.F.A.   22. R.O.,R.A.
           10. 211th Bde. R.F.A.   23. R.A. Sigs.
           11. D.T.M.O. 42nd Div.   24. 42nd Div. Sigs.
           12. 42nd D.A.C.   25. R.A.,R.E. Officer.
           13. 29th H.A.Bde.   26 WAR DIARY.
           14. 71st H.A.Bde.   27 FILE.
           15. N.Z.,D.A.

SECRET.

AMENDMENT NO:1 TO 42nd DIVISIONAL ARTILLERY ORDER NO:15.

Para.2. Line 4.

For J.34.d.6.6. road J.18.c.8.8.

P.R. Mitchell
Major., R.A.,
1st July 1918.   Brigade Major., 42nd Divisional Artillery.

Copies to all recipients of 42nd D.A. Order No.15.

SECRET.

42nd DIVISIONAL ARTILLERY - LOCATION LIST.

APP. 'B'

Reference 1/40,000 Sheet 57 D.   6 p.m. 3rd July 1918.

Unit.	Position	No. of Guns or Hows.	Approximate Front covered	Wagon Lines.
42nd D.A., H.Q.	CHATEAU BUS LES ARTOIS			J.26.a.50.50.

(RIGHT GROUP R.A. - Lt. Col. MAIN D.S.O., 293rd Army Brigade R.F.A.)

Unit	Position	No. of Guns or Hows.	Approximate Front covered	Wagon Lines.
H.Q.	J.23.a.70.20.			J.25.a.70.40.
H.Q., 1st Bde.N.Z.F.A.	J.34.d.60.60.			J.26.c.80.80.
1st Battery	J.36.d.95.26.	6 G 'S'	Q.4.b.55.10.	J.26.c.50.50.
3rd "	J.35.c.30.81.	6 G 'A'	to	J.26.d.00.60.
7th "	J.35.c.28.32.	6 G 'A'	K.34.c.95.60.	J.26.a.40.00.
15th "	(J.35.a.20.20.	2 H 'A'		
	(J.28.d.60.00.	4 H 'A'		J.25.d.80.80.
A/293 Battery	(J.28.d.50.90.	5 G 'A'		
	(J.28.d.56.79.	1 G 'A'	K.34.c.95.60.	J.19.a.50.80.
B/293 "	K.19.a.30.70.	6 G 'S'	to	
C/293 "	(J.25.a.12.41.	4 G 'A'	K.27.b.95.10.	J.25.c.80.90.
	(J.23.a.84.65.	2 G 'A'		
D/293 "	J.29.a.80.24.	6 H 'A'		J.25.a.00.60.

(LEFT GROUP R.A. - Lt.Col. McQUARRIE M.C. 3rd Bde. N.Z.F.A.)

Unit	Position	No. of Guns or Hows.	Approximate Front covered	Wagon Lines.
H.Q.	J.18.c.80.80.			
11th Battery	(J.24.b.30.60.	4 G 'S'		
	(K.19.b.40.10.	2 G 'A'		Rear P.1.a.
12th "	(J.18.a.40.12.	3 G 'A'	K.21.d.95.20.	and O.6.b.
	(J.18.c.12.82.	3 G 'A'	to	Advanced
13th "	(J.11.d.65.35.	4 G 'S'	K.16.c.90.20.	J.10.a. & b.
	(J.17.c.55.83.	2 G 'A'		J.21.a. & c.
4th Battery	(K.13.a.12.20.	2 H 'A'		
	(J.24.b.90.65.	4 H 'S'		

2 - 15 pdrs. (A.T.) (K.32.b.50.50.) manned by personnel of
                   (K.32.a.0.4.   ) 293rd Army Brigade R.F.A.

42nd D.T.M.O. -, BUS LES ARTOIS. - 6" T.Ms.

Y/42 Bty. - (K.25.d.30.65. 2 'S'.   Y/42 Bty. - (K.27.c.32.58. 1 'A'.
            (K.31.a.50.40. 3 'S'.   (K.27.a.32.58. 1 'A'.
            (K.33.c.70.10. 1 'A'.   (K.21.b.10.55. 1 'A'.
            (Q.3.c.70.70. 1 'A'.   (K.25.d.15.85. 2 'S'.

X/37 Bty. - K.21.a.45.35. 2 'A'.

A.R.P. 42nd Division - I.24.d.3.5.

N.Z. D.A.C - LOUVENCOURT - I.35.a.80.30.

293rd B.A.C. - BUS LES ARTOIS - J.25.a.50.00.

H.A. affiliated to 42nd D.A. - 29th H.A.Bde.R.G.A. - H.Q. BERTRANCOURT.

D. Malcolm
for
Major., R.A.,
3rd July 1918.   Brigade Major., 42nd Divisional Artillery.

SECRET. Copy No. 26

42nd Divisional Artillery Order No. 13.

1. The 1st and 3rd Bdes. N.Z.F.A. will relieve 210th and 211th Bdes. R.F.A. respectively in the CENTRE SECTOR on July 4th & 5th 1918 as follows :—

   JULY 4th.

   One Section of each Battery relieves one Section of each Battery of 210th & 211th Bdes.

   JULY 5th. Remaining sections relieve similarly.

1st Bty. N.Z.F.A. relieves	A/210. at	E.21.a.00.80.	(6 Guns).	
3rd Bty N.Z.F.A. "	B/210. at	(E.21.c.10.85.	(1 Gun).	
		(E.14.b.35.9D.	(4 Guns).	
7th Bty N.Z.F.A. "	C/210. at	(E.26.b.02.91.	(4 Guns).	
		(D.30.d.87.35.	(2 Guns).	
15th Bty N.Z.F.A. "	D/210. at	(E.21.c.65.62.	(4 Guns).	
		(E.29.c.70.90.	(2 Guns).	
11th Bty N.Z.F.A. "	A/211. at	(E.16.c.40.50.	(4 Guns).	
		(E.22.c.60.85.	(2 Guns).	
12th Bty N.Z.F.A. "	B/211. at	(E.22.a.55.63.	(3 Guns).	
		(E.21.b.80.13.	(2 Guns).	
13th Bty N.Z.F.A. "	C/211. at	E.15.c.95.45.	(6 Guns).	
4th Bty N.Z.F.A. "	D/211. at	(E.27.a.23.79.	(2 Guns).	
		(E.29.c.98.96.	(1 Gun).	
		(E.27.c.23.90.	(2 Guns).	

   All details to be arranged between the Brigade Commanders concerned.

   As each portion of the N.Z.F.A. completes relief they will come under the orders of C.R.A. New Zealand D.A.

2. 210th & 211th Bdes R.F.A. are similarly relieving the 1st & 3rd Bdes N.Z.F.A. in the RIGHT SECTOR on July 4th & 5th taking over the Battery positions of the Batteries relieving them.

3. The N.Z., D.A.C. will be relieved by the 42nd D.A.C. on July 5th. Details of relief will be arranged between Commanders concerned.

4. Guns, Aiming Posts, sights, breech & muzzle covers will be taken over in situ.

5. When exchanging guns, all Gun History Sheets, records of calibration and registration will be handed over.

6. Sufficient personnel will always be present with each gun or how. to carry on the service of the piece.

7. Ammunition at Gun Positions and at the A.R.P. at I.24.d.3.5. will be handed over and copies of receipts given and exchanged sent to this office.

8. 1st and 3rd Brigades N.Z.F.A. will detail advanced parties of at least one Officer and one linesman per Bde. H.Q. and Battery to be at new position by 10.0 a.m. July 3rd.
   Similar parties will be arriving at positions of the 1st & 3rd Bdes. N.Z.F.A.

P.T.O.

9. All Defence Schemes, plans, maps, aerial photographs, details of work in hand and proposed, material and trench stores will be handed over on relief.

10. Completion of each relief will be reported by wire to 42nd D.A., H.Q.

11. Orders re the re-grouping of the Artillery covering the 42nd Division will be issued later.

12. ACKNOWLEDGE.

P.R. Mitchell
Major., R.A.,
Issued at 7-0 pm Brigade Major., 42nd Divisional Artillery.
On 29/6/18 By D.R.

```
Copy No. 1.  - R.A. IV Corps.
         2.  - 42nd Divn 'G'.
         3.  - 42nd Divn. 'Q'.
       4 - 5. - RIGHT GROUP.R.A.
       6 - 7. - LEFT GROUP.R.A.
         8.  - 2nd Army Brigade N.Z.F.A.
         9   - 210th Brigade R.F.A.
        10.  - 211th Brigade R.F.A.
        11.  - D.T.M.O. 42nd Divn.
        12.  - 42nd D.A.C.
        13.  - N.Z., D.A.C.
        14.  - 125th Inf. Bde.
        15.  - 126th Inf. Bde.
        16.  - 127th Inf. Bde.
        17.  - N.Z., D.A.
        18.  - 57th D.A.
        19.  - 63rd D.A.
        20.  - 29th H.A. Brigade.
        21.  - D.A.D.O.S., 42nd Divn.
        22.  - 42nd Div. Signals.
        23.  - S.C.,R.A., 42nd Division.
        24.  - O.C., R.A., Sigs.
        25.  - R.A.,R.E.& Officer.
        26.  - WAR DIARY.
        27.  - FILE.
```

SECRET.   42nd D.A., No.B.M.5/59.   app.'D'

210th Brigade R.F.A.
211th Brigade R.F.A.
293rd Army Brigade R.F.A.
Bde.R.F.A. in Corps Reserve.(Right Sector).

Reference attached Maps and correspondence re retired positions to cover the PURPLE and RED Line.

1. Areas are allotted to Brigades as follows :-

Brigade R.F.A.	COLINCAMPS SWITCH	PURPLE LINE	RED LINE (When BUS LOOP is being held)	RED LINE Proper
210th Bde. R.F.A.	Area 'A'	Area 'Y'	Area I	Area I
293rd A.Bde.R.F.A.	Area 'B'	Area 'A1'	Area IIIa.	Area III
211th Bde.R.F.A.	Area 'D'	Area 'D1'	Area XIV	Area XIV
Bde. R.F.A. in) Corps Reserve,) Right Sector.)	Area 'C'	Area 'C1'	Area II	Area II

2. Area 'Y' will be selected by 210th Brigade R.F.A. in the vicinity of J.31. & 32., P.1.a. & b., P.2.a. & b. - but keeping N. of Corps Boundary.

   The approximate co-ordinates of Brigade H.Q. and Batteries will be notified to this office as soon as possible when they will be accurately resected.

3. Brigades will reconnoitre the retired positions allotted to them and, in every case where this has not already been done, a cross-cut trench will be made at the position of the pivot gun and a numbered board erected in the middle of the trench.

   Cross-cut trench thus :-

4. Brigades will report to this office by July 13th that the above has been carried out.

5. Brigades will be responsible that boards, when once erected, are inspected weekly.
   Should any be removed they will be replaced at once.

6. ACKNOWLEDGE.

                                                    Major., R.A.
6th July 1918.   Brigade Major., 42nd Divisional Artillery.

Copy to R.A., IV Corps.

SECRET.

ADDENDUM NO:1 to 42nd DIVISIONAL ARTILLERY ORDER NO:13.
----

1. Guns in workshops will be taken over as well as Guns in the line. Units will mutually arrange to relieve personnel at Ordnance Workshops immediately on completion of relief.

P.R. Mitchell
Major., R.A.

1st July 1918.   Brigade Major., 42nd Divisional Artillery.

Copies to :- R.A. IV Corps.
    42nd Division 'Q'.
    RIGHT GROUP.R.A. (2))
    LEFT GROUP.R.A. (2))   <u>Please acknowledge.</u>
    210th Brigade R.F.A.)
    211th Brigade R.F.A.)
    D.A.D.O.S., 42nd Division.
    S.C.R.A., 42nd Division.
    FILE.
    57th D.A.,
    N.Z.,D.A.

SECRET.　　　　　　　　　　　　　　　　　　Issued with 42nd D.A., No.B.1.5/59.

Positions to cover COLINCAMPS SWITCH & PURPLE LINE.

(RIGHT DIVISION, IV CORPS.).

Area	Number	Location	O.P. area.	Remarks.
A	H.Q.	J.28.b.10.70.	J.30.b.	COLINCAMPS SWITCH
	68.	J.28.d.37.23.	J.34.b.	Only.
	69.	J.28.d.10.88.	J.35.central.	
	70.	J.28.c.66.26.	K.25.d.	
	71H.	J.28.c.54.93.		
A1	H.Q.	J.20.b.70.30.		COLINCAMPS
	51.	J.21.d.20.41.	J.28.a.	Switch and
	52.	J.21.d.40.71.	J.30.b.	PURPLE LINE.
	53.	J.21.b.75.21.	J.35.central.	
	54H.	J.21.d.00.91.		
B	H.Q.	J.23.a.70.20.		For COLINCAMPS
		J.28.d.50.90.	J.18.d. - 24.b.	Switch. Present
		J.23.a.90.20.	J.24.d. - K.19.a	positions except
		J.23.a.65.25.	J.30.b.	J.23.a.90.20.
		J.23.a.84.65.		
		J.29.a.80.24.		
C.	H.Q.	J.22.a.00.50.		For COLINCAMPS
	80.	J.16.d.31.40.	J.18.d. - 24.b.	Switch or PURPLE
	81.	J.22.a.29.93.	J.30.b.	LINE. All but
	82H.	J.22.a.60.63.	J.35.central	No.82H. are pre-
	83.	J.22.c.57.65.		sent position.
D.	H.Q.	J.3.d.00.50.	J.5.b.	
	125.	J.10.a.44.91.	K.13. - 14.	For
	126.	J.19.a.28.78.	J.17.d.	PURPLE LINE.
	127.	J.4.c.50.19.	J.24.d. - K.19.a.	
	128H.	J.9.b.87.49.		
Y	H.Q.			
	55.			For
	56.			PURPLE LINE.
	57.			
	58H.			

Location of positions 55 - 58H will be notified as soon as they
have been selected.

SECRET. Issued with 42nd D.A., No.B.M.5/59.

POSITIONS TO COVER -

(a) RED LINE Proper, and (b) RED LINE & PAS SWITCH.
(Right Division, IV Corps)

Area	Number	Locations	O.P. Areas	Remarks
I	H.Q. R.1. R.2. R.3. R.4.(H).	I.32.a.2.8. I.26.c.2.7. I.26.a.6.1. I.26.a.9.4. I.26.c.9.6.		
II a.	H.Q. R.13. R.14. R.15. R.16.(H).	I.16.d.2.5. I.22.b.3.7. I.22.b.6.9. I.16.d.9.2. I.17.c.3.5.	Suggested O.Ps.	
II.	H.Q. R.5. R.6. R.7. R.8.(H).	I.25.a.5.8. I.25.b.5.9. I.19.d.7.3. I.20.c.0.5. I.19.d.0.0.	(1) FOR BUS LOOP J.31.c.4.6. J.32.a.1.3. J.20.b.1.9. J.15.c.1.9.	
III a.	H.Q. R.17. R.18. R.19. R.20.(H).	I.16.d.2.5. I.22.d.9.4. I.23.c.1.9. I.23.a.3.3. I.23.a.8.8.	(2) FOR RED LINE Proper. O.10.b.4.7. I.23.a.1.4.	
III	H.Q. R.9. R.10. R.11. R.12.(H).	I.14.b.9.0. I.15.c.3.1. I.15.c.6.4. I.15.c.9.6. I.14.d.9.5.	I.29.c.6.5. J.13.b.8.6.	
XIV	H.Q. R.37. R.38. R.39. R.40.(H).	I.26.b.8.2. I.27.c.3.9. I.27.a.1.2. I.27.a.7.7. I.27.c.1.1.		

These locations are in process of being resected accurately.

Brigades should notify D.A., H.Q. if any positions are impracticable, suggesting new positions, within their areas where necessary.

- o - o - o - o - o - o - o - o - o - o - o - o -

SECRET.

42nd DIVISIONAL ARTILLERY - LOCATION LIST.

Reference 1/40,000 Sheet 57 D.   6 p.m. 7th July 1918.

Unit.	Position	No. of Guns or Hows.	Approximate Front covered	Wagon Lines.
42nd D.A., H.Q.	CHATEAU BUS LES ARTOIS			J.26.a.50.50.

(RIGHT GROUP R.A. (Lt.Col. MAIN D.S.O. 293rd Army Bde R.F.A.)

Unit.	Position	No. of Guns or Hows.	Approximate Front covered	Wagon Lines.
H.Q.	J.23.a.70.20.			J.25.a.70.40.
H.Q., 210th Bde R.F.A.	J.34.d.60.60.			J.26.c.80.80.
'A' Battery	J.36.d.95.26.	6 G 'S'	Q.4.b.55.10.	J.26.c.50.60.
'B' Battery	J.35.c.30.81.	6 G 'A'	to	J.26.d.00.60.
'C' Battery	J.35.c.28.32.	6 G 'A'	K.34.c.95.60.	J.26.c.50.50.
'D' Battery	J.35.a.20.20.	2 H 'A'		
	J.28.d.60.00.	4 H 'A'		J.25.d.80.80.
A/293 Bty.	K.19.a.30.70.	6 G 'S'		
B/293 "	J.28.d.50.90.	5 G 'A'	K.34.c.95.60.	J.19.a.50.80.
	J.28.d.56.79.	1 G 'A'	to	
C/293 "	J.23.a.12.41.	4 G 'A'	K.27.b.95.10.	J.25.c.80.90.
	J.23.a.84.65.	2 G 'A'		
D/293 "	J.29.a.80.24.	6 H 'A'		J.25.a.00.60.

(LEFT GROUP R.A. (Lt.Col. E.J.INCHES D.S.O. 211th Bde.R.F.A.)

Unit.	Position	No. of Guns or Hows.	Approximate Front covered	Wagon Lines.
H.Q.	J.18.c.80.80.			
'A' Battery	J.24.b.30.60.	4 G 'S'		
	K.19.b.40.10.	2 G 'A'		Rear P.1.a.
'B' Battery	J.18.a.40.12.	3 G 'A'	K.21.d.95.20.	and O.6.b.
	J.18.c.12.82.	3 G 'A'	to	Advanced
'C' Battery	J.11.d.65.35.	4 G 'S'	K.16.c.90.20.	J.10.a. & b.
	J.17.c.55.83.	2 G 'A'		J.21.a. & c.
'D' Battery	K.13.a.12.20.	2 H 'A'		
	J.24.b.90.65.	4 H 'S'		

2 - 15 pdrs. (A.T.) (K.32.b.50.50.)   manned by personnel of
                  (K.32.a.0.4.   )   293rd Army Brigade R.F.A.

42nd D.T.M.O. - BUS LES ARTOIS - 6" T.Ms.

X/42 Bty. - (Q.3.a.85.67. - 1 'A'   Y/42 Bty - (K.27.c.38.85. - 1 'A'
            (Q.3.a.70.90. - 1 'A'   (K.27.a.00.00. - 1 'A'
            (Q.4.a.42.30. - 1 'A'   (K.27.c.65.35. - 1 'A'
            (K.31.a.66.23. - 1 'S'   (K.25.d.28.85. - 1 'S'
            (K.31.a.65.32. - 1 'S'   (K.25.d.25.90. - 1 'S'
            (K.25.d.33.60. - 1 'S'
            (K.25.d.38.66. - 1 'S'   X/37 Bty - (K.21.a.40.25. - 1 'A'
            (K.25.d.37.75. - 1 'S'   (K.21.a.40.25. - 1 'A'

A.R.P. 42nd Division. - I.24.d.35.

42nd D.A.C. - LOUVENCOURT - I.35.a.80.30.

293rd B.A.C. - BUS LES ARTOIS - J.25.a.50.00.

H.A. affiliated to 42nd D.A. - 29th H.A.Bde.R.G.A. - H.Q.BERTRANCOURT.

Major., R.A.
for Brigade Major., 42nd Divnl. Arty.

7th July 1918.

42nd Divisional Artillery - Location List.
----

                                              6 p.m. July 10th 1918.

42nd D.A. H.Q.   ------ I.23.a.central.

Otherwise NO CHANGE.

                                      Malcolm   Lieut.R.H.A.
10th July 1918.   R.O., 42nd Divisional Artillery.

app 'G'

SECRET.

42nd Divisional Artillery - Location List.

Reference 1/40,000 Sheet 57 D.   6 p.m. 14th July 1918.

Unit.	Position	No of Guns or Hows.	Approximate Front covered	Wagon Lines.
42nd D.A., H.Q.	I.23.central.			J.26.a.50.50.
(RIGHT GROUP R.A. (Lt.Col. MAIN D.S.O. 293rd Army Bde.R.F.A.)				
H.Q.	J.23.a.70.20.			J.25.a.70.40.
H.Q., 210 Bde.R.F.A.	J.34.d.60.60.			J.26.c.80.80.
'A' Battery.	J.36.d.95.26.	6 G 'S'	Q.4.b.55.10.	J.26.c.50.60.
'B' "	J.35.c.30.81.	6 G 'A'	to	J.26.d.00.60.
'C' "	J.35.c.28.32.	6 G 'A'	K.34.c.95.60.	J.26.c.50.50.
'D' "	(J.35.a.20.20.	2 H 'A'		
	(J.22.d.60.00.	4 H 'A'		J.25.d.80.00.
A/293 Battery	J.24.c.20.30	6 G 'S'		
(B/293 "	(J.23.d.50.90.	5 G 'A'	K.34.c.95.60.	J.19.a.50.30.
	(K.28.d.56.79.	1 G 'A'	to	
(C/293 "	(J.23.a.12.41.	4 G 'A'	K.27.b.95.10.	J.25.c.80.90.
	(J.23.a.84.65.	2 G 'A'		
(D/293 "	J.29.a.80.24.	6 H 'A'		J.25.a.00.60.
(LEFT GROUP R.A. (Lt.Col. E.J.INCHES D.S.O. 211th Bde.R.F.A.)				
H.Q.	J.18.c.80.80.			
'A' Battery	(J.24.b.30.50.	4 G 'S'		
	(K.19.b.40.10.	2 G 'A'		
('B' "	(J.12.c.10.60.	4 G 'A'	K.21.d.95.20.	P.1.a.
	(J.18.c.12.32.	2 G 'A'	to	&
('C' "	(J.11.d.65.35.	4 G 'S'	K.16.c.90.20.	O.6.b.
	(J.17.c.55.83.	2 G 'A'		
'D' "	(K.13.a.12.20.	2 H 'A'		
	(J.24.b.90.65.	4 H 'S'		

2 - 15 pdrs.(A.T.) (K.26.c.00.20) manned by personnel of
                   (K.32.a.0.4.) 293rd Army Brigade R.F.A.

42nd. D.T.M.O. - BUS LES ARTOIS - 6" T.Ms.

X/42 Bty. -	(Q.3.a.85.67. - 1 'A'	Y/42 Bty. -	(K.27.c.38.85. - 1 'A'
	(Q.3.a.70.90. - 1 'A'		(K.27.a.00.00. - 1 'A'
	(Q.4.a.42.30. - 1 'A'		(K.27.c.65.85. - 1 'A'
	(K.31.a.65.32. - 1 'S'		(K.25.d.28.85. - 1 'S'
	(K.31.a.66.23. - 1 'S'		(K.25.d.25.90. - 1 'S'
	(K.25.d.33.60. - 1 'S'		
	(K.25.d.38.66. - 1 'S'	X/37 Bty. -	K.21.a.40.25 - 2 'A'
	(K.25.d.37.75. - 1 'S'		

A.R.P. 42nd. Division. - I.24.d.35.

42nd D.A.C. - LOUVENCOURT - I.35.a.80.30.

293rd B.A.C. - BUS LES ARTOIS - J.25.a.50.00

H.A. affiliated to 42nd D.A. - 29th H.A. Bde.R.G.A. - H.Q. BERTRANCOURT.

                                              D. Malcolm Lt. Major, R.A.
14th July 1918.   For Brigade Major, 42nd Divisional Artillery.

SECRET.   Copy No...19......

42nd Divisional Artillery Order No. 18.

Reference Sheet 57 D.N.E. 1/20,000 Edition 5 d.
----

1. The 3rd New Zealand (Rifle Brigade) will carry out minor
    enterprises to advance the Line of Observation and secure
    prisoners on July 15th 1918, with objectives as under :-

    (a) Front Line K.16.d.30.20. - K.22.b.40.95. thence along
    trench to K.16.d.90.50. - K.17.c.05.75. - along LIER TRENCH
    to present Front Line at K.16.b.90.75.

    (b) From Front Line at K.11.c.60.55. - K.11.c.90.35. - K.11.d.
    05.50. - K.11.c.90.65. - K.11.d.05.85. to Front Line at K.11.a.
    75.20.

2. The operation will be carried out under an Artillery Bombard-
    ment.
        At the same time M.T.Ms. will create a diversion at ROSSIGNOL
    WOOD.

3. 42nd Divisional Artillery will co-operate as shewn in
    attached table.

4. ZERO HOUR will be 4.0 P.M. (FOUR P.M.) on 15th July 1918.

5. An officer from R.A., H.Q. will attend at each Group H.Qrs.
    between 11.0 a.m. and 12. Noon. on 15th July to synchronize
    watches.

6. In the event of the operation being postponed the Code Word
    "WET WICKET" will be wired.

7. ACKNOWLEDGE.

                                              W. ? Nisbet.
                  7 a m   Major., R.A.,
Issued at .... for Brigade Major., 42nd Divnl. Artillery.
       15/7/18.
On........... By D.R.

Copies to :-

           No.1. R.A., IV Corps.   No.11. N.Z. Division.
              2. 42nd Divn. 'G'.   12. N.Z.D.A.
              3. C.B.S.O. IV Corps.   13. 63rd D.A.
            4-5. Right Group R.A.   14. 125th Inf. Bde.
              6. Left Group R.A.   15. 126th Inf. Bde.
              7. D.T.M.O. 42nd Divn.   16. 127th Inf. Bde.
              8. 29th H.A.Bde.R.G.A.   17. S.C.,R.A.,42nd Div.
              9. 71st H.A.Bde.R.G.A.   18. R.O.R.A. 42nd Div.
             10. 19 Balloon Coy.   19. War Diary.
                                           20. File.

TABLE OF TASKS. - ISSUED WITH 42nd Div. Arty. Order No.18.

Unit.	Target	Time	Rate	Ammunition.
18-pdrs.		18-pdrs. and 4.5" Hows.		
RIGHT GROUP. 2 Batteries.	Enfilade JENA AVENUE from K.22.a.20.58. to K.22.b.50.70.	Zero minus 10 minues to Zero minus 3 mins.	"SLOW"	
LEFT GROUP. 1 Battery.	Enfilade CHASSEURS HEDGE from K.23.a.18.00. to K.23.b.00.2X	Zero minus 3 minutes to Zero	"INTENSE"	
		Zero to Zero plus 15 mins.	"RAPID".	H.E. Fuze 106.
4.5" Hows. LEFT GROUP. 1 Battery.	JAM STREET & SUNKEN ROAD about K.24.c.2.2.	Zero plus 15 minutes to Zero plus 30 minutes.	"SLOW"	

15th July 1918.

	At .... m.		From ....
copy	To .... By	(Signature of "Franking Officer")	By ....

TO	Right Group R.A.		
	Left Group R.A.		
	42 Div G.		

Sender's Number.	Day of Month.	In reply to Number.	AAA
BM 97	16		

Ref	42 DA	order	No 16
AAA	PIAVE	AAA	11.30 AM
AAA	acknowledge		

From 42 DA
Place
Time

The above may be forwarded as now corrected. (Z)

Censor.   Signature of Addressor of person authorised to telegraph in his name

This line should be erased if not required.

Order No. 1625 Wt. W3253/ P 511. 27/2. H. & K., Ltd. (E. 2634).

SECRET.   Copy No..........

APP. I

42nd Divisional Artillery Order No.16.

1. On a day and at an hour to be notified later, the Corps Heavy Artillery will carry out a bombardment of PUISIEUX in accordance with Appendix "A" attached.

2. The objects of the bombardment are :-

    (a) To discover if there is any concentration of Artillery or ammunition in the ruins of houses, cellars etc., which might escape detection on a photograph.

    (b) To try to "draw" as many hostile batteries as possible and engage them by "MQNF" Calls.

3. The bombardment be the Heavy Artillery will be divided into 3 Phases.

    Phase.1.
       Enfilade Roads and Tracks in PUISIEUX.
       During this Phase aeroplanes will watch the results of our fire noting if explosions and fires occur.
       All O.Ps. will watch for explosions reporting the time and grid bearing of any that are seen to C.B.S.O. IV Corps.

    Phase 2.
       6" and 8" Howitzers will bombard selected points with aeroplane observation.

    Phase 3.
       When Phase 2 has been completed, Phase 1 will be repeated by all batteries not engaged in Counter-Battery Work.

4. During Phases 1 & 3 of the Heavy Artillery bombardment all active 18-pdrs. and 4.5" Hows. that can bear will fire as detailed in Appendix 'A' attached.
    Os.C. Groups will allot tasks to Batteries.

5. During the bombardment aeroplanes will watch certain areas and report any active batteries. These batteries will be immediately engaged by "MQNF" Calls by Heavy Artillery Counter-Batteries.

6. Day and hour for this bombardment will be notified by using the Code Word "PIAVE", e.g.,

    "Reference 42nd Div. Arty. Order No.16 AAA"PIAVE" AAA 10.a.m.

    means - the bombardment referred to in 42nd Div. Arty. Order No.16 will take place to-day. ZERO HOUR will be 10.A.M.

7. ACKNOWLEDGE.

Issued at..9 a.m....On..14/7/18.   Major., R.A.,
By. D.R.

Copy No.1. - R.A.,IV Corps.   No.12. 126th Inf. Bde.
      2. - 42nd Divn. 'G'.   13. 127th Inf. Bde.
      3. - H.A.,IV Corps.   14. 19th Balloon Coy.
      4. - C.B.S.O.,IV Corps.   15. N.Z.,Div. Arty.
    5 -6 - RIGHT GROUP.R.A.   16. 63rd D.A.
      7 - LEFT GROUP.R.A.   17. S.C.,R.A.,42nd Divn.
      8 - D.T.M.O., 42nd Division.   18. R.O.,R.A., 42nd Divn.
      9 - 29th H.A.Bde.R.G.A.   19. WAR DIARY.
     10. - 71st H.A.,Bde.R.G.A.   20. FILE.
     11. - 125th Inf. Bde.

To accompany 42nd D.A. Order No.16.   -   "APPENDIX A".

PHASE 1. Zero to Zero plus 15 minutes.

6" Hows. and 60-pdrs. bombard Roads and Tracks in L.14.c. & d. and L.20.a. & b.

18-pdrs. and 4.5" Hows. - 42nd Division.

RIGHT GROUP.R.A.	TARGET.	RATE OF FIRE.	Ammunition.
18-pdrs.	(a) Reserve Battalion Billets in K.29.b.& d. (b) Enfilade HOME AVENUE in K.22. & 23.	RAPID	(50% H.E. (50% T.S.
4.5" Hows.	(a) H.Qrs. at K.28.d.55.41. (b) H.Qrs. at K.29.a.52.00.	-do-	(H.E. (50% 106 Fuze. (50% 101 (delay)
	(c) MARK COPSE.	-do-	H.E. 106 fuze.

LEFT GROUP.R.A.

18-pdrs.	Enfilade JEAN BART Trench in K.22. & 23.	-do-	(50% H.E. (50% T.S.
4.5" Hows.	LUKE COPSE.	-do-	H.E. 106 Fuze.

18-pdrs. and 4.5" Hows. of 37th & N.Z. Divisional Artilleries are co-operating.

Phase 2. Zero plus 15 to Zero plus 90 minutes.

8" and 6" Hows. bombard Dug-outs &c. in L.14.d. and L.20.c.& b.

Phase 3. - Zero plus 120 to Zero plus 135 minutes.

Repeat Phase 1. (Batteries engaged on Counter-Battery work will not take part in this Phase.).

SECRET.   Copy No. 18

app. 'J'

42nd Divisional Artillery Order 19.

PRELIMINARY ORDER.

Reference Map Sheet 57 D.S.E. 1/20,000

1. The following operation will be carried out on 16th July 1918 with the object of :-

    (a) Obliterating the enemy posts and Machine Gun positions about Q.4.b.central.

    (b) Obtaining an identification.

2. Trenches in Q.4.b. & d. shewn in RED on the attached tracing will be bombarded by Heavy Artillery from ZERO to ZERO plus 90 minutes. Infantry will be withdrawn from the Front Line during this bombardment.

3. On completion of Heavy Artillery bombardment and under cover of a Field Artillery Barrage 3 Sections of Infantry will leave our trenches to search Posts and trenches round Q.4.b.2.5. The Infantry will be back in our lines by ZERO plus 120.

4. Field Artillery of 42nd Division will co-operate as follows :-

(A)
ZERO to ZERO plus 15 mins.	RIGHT GROUP	Barrage Line
ZERO plus 30 mins to ZERO plus 35 mins	18 – 18pdrs.	Q.4.d.5.5. –
		Q.4.b.7.3. –
ZERO plus 50 mins to ZERO plus 55 mins	12 – 4.5" Hows.	Q.4.b.4.7.
		AMMUNITION.
ZERO plus 60 mins to ZERO plus 65 mins		18-pdrs.
		50% H.E. (Fuze 106)
ZERO plus 75 mins to ZERO plus 80 mins		50% T.S.
		4.5" Hows.
		H.E. Fuze 106.
		RATE OF FIRE "INTENSE"

(B)
ZERO plus 90 mins. to		(Barrage Line.
ZERO plus 120 mins.		Q.4.d.5.5. –
		Q.4.b.7.3. –
		Q.4.b.7.8.
		AMMUNITION.
		18-pdrs.
		50% H.E. (Fuze 106).
		50% T.S.
		4.5" Hows.
		H.E. Fuze 106.
		RATE OF FIRE, "INTENSE"

5. The 63rd (R.N.) Div. Arty. is co-operating as follows :-

P.T.O.

-2-

(A)
```
ZERO to ZERO plus 15 mins    )          18-18-pdrs.     ( Barrage Line
                             )           6 - 4.5" Hows. ( Q.4.d.1.7. to
ZERO plus 30 mins to ZERO plus 35 mins )                ( K.34.d.0.0.
                             )                                   18-pdr.
ZERO plus 50 mins to ZERO plus 55 mins )                ( AMMUNITION "T.S"
                             )                          ( 4.5" Hows. H.E(106
ZERO plus 60 mins to ZERO plus 65 mins )                (           (Fuze.
                             )                          ( RATE of FIRE.
ZERO plus 75 mins to Zero plus 80 mins )                (   "INTENSE"
```
==
(B)
```
ZERO plus 90 to ZERO plus 120 mins.  )    -do-          ( Distributed
                                                         along line
                                                         Q.4.b.7.3. -
                                                         K.34.d.6.2. -
                                                         K.34.d.0.3.
                          AMMUNITION.                   ( AMMUNITION.18-pdrs.
                          4.5" Hows.                    ( 50% H.E. Fuze 106.
                          H.E. Fuze 106                 ( 50% T.S.
                                                        ( RATE OF FIRE.
                                                        (   "INTENSE".
```

6. 42nd Division 6" T.Ms. will engage enemy T.Ms. in K.34.a. & b. with intermittent fire from ZERO to ZERO plus 120 mins.

7. ZERO HOUR will be 4 P.M. (FOUR P.M.) on 16th July 1918.

8. Arrangements for synchronization of watches will be notified later.

9. ACKNOWLEDGE.

                                                        Major., R.F.A.
Issued at 3.15 p.m. for Brigade Major., 42nd Divnl. Artillery.
On 15/7/18. By. D.R.

Copies to:- No.1. R.A., IV Corps.   No.11. N.Z.D.A.
            2. 42nd Division 'G'.   12. 63rd D.A.
            3. C.B.S.O. IV Corps.   13. 125th Inf. Bde.
          4-5. RIGHT GROUP R.A.   14. 126th Inf. Bde.
            6. LEFT GROUP.R.A.   15. 127th Inf. Bde.
            7. D.T.M.O., 42nd Division.   16. S.C.,R.A., 42nd Divn.
            8. 29th H.A.Bde. R.G.A.   17. R.O.,R.A., 42nd Divn.
            9. 71st H.A.Bde. R.G.A.   18. WAR DIARY.
           10. No.19.Balloon Coy.   19. FILW.

Operation postponed for 24 hours

SECRET.

ADDENDUM No. 2 to 42nd D.A. Order No. 19.

1. Para. 4 (b)   Co-operation of 42nd Div. Arty.

   Phase A.   Rate of fire will be "RAPID." throughout, and NOT "INTENSE".

   PHASE B.   Rate of fire.   Cancel "INTENSE" and substitute following rates of fire:-

   Zero plus 90 mins. to Zero plus 100 mins.- "INTENSE".

   Zero plus 100 mins. to Zero plus 110 mins. - "NORMAL."

   Zero plus 110 mins. to zero plus 120 mins.- "SLOW".

2. ZERO HOUR will be 4 p.m. (FOUR P.M.). 17th July, 1918.

                                            Major, R.F.A.
Issued at 11:45 AM   for Brigade Major, R.A., 42nd Div.

on 17/7/18. by D.R.

Copies to all recipients of 42nd D.A. Order No. 19.

app 'K'

42nd Divisional Artillery - Location List.

Reference Sheet (1/40,000) 57 I   6 p.m. 17th July 1918.

Unit.	Position	No. of Guns or Hows.	Approximate Front covered	Wagon Lines.
42nd D.A., H.Q.	AUTHIE I.18.a.6.5.			I.15.b.9.8

(RIGHT GROUP.R.A. (Lt.Col. MAIN D.S.O. 293rd Army Brigade R.F.A.)

Unit	Position	No. of Guns or Hows.	Approximate Front covered	Wagon Lines.
H.Q.	J.35.a.70.30.			J.25.a.70.
(H.Q., 210th Bde.R.F.A.	J.34.d.60.60.			J.26.c.80.8
'A' Battery	J.36.d.95.87.	6 G 'S'	Q.4.b.55.10.	J.26.c.50.10
'B' "	J.35.c.30.83	6 G 'A'	to	J.28.d.
'C' "	J.35.c.28.38.	6 G 'A'	K.34.c.95.60.	J.26.c.50
'D' "	(J.35.a.20.30	2 H 'A'		
	(J.5.d.60.00	4 H 'A'		J.25.d.30.50
(A/293 Battery	J.24.c.16.09.	6 G 'S'		
(B/293 "	(J.23.d.50.90.	5 G 'A'	K.34.c.95.60.	J.19.a.50.30
	(J.23.d.56.79.	1 G 'A'	to	
(C/293 "	(J.23.a.15.45.	4 G 'A'	K.27.b.95.10.	J.26.c.80
	(J.23.a.84.65.	2 G 'A'		
((D/293 "	J.29.a.80.24.	6 H 'A'		J.26.a.

(LEFT GROUP R.A. (Lt. Col. E.J.INCHES. D.S.O. 211th Bde R.F.A.

Unit	Position	No. of Guns or Hows.	Approximate Front covered	Wagon Lines.
H.Q.	J.13.c.30.30			
'A' Battery	(J.24.b.30.60	4 G 'S'		
	(K.19.b.40.10	2 G 'A'		
'B' "	(J.12.c.10.60.	4 G 'A'	K.21.d.95.20	P.1.a
	(J.18.c.12.82.	2 G 'A'	to	and
'C' "	(J.11.d.65.35.	4 G 'S'	K.16.c.90.20.	O.6.b
	(J.17.c.55.88.	2 G 'A'		
'D' "	(K.13.a.12.20.	2 H 'A'		
	(J.24.b.90.65.	4 H 'S'		

2 - 15 pdrs. (A.T) (K.26.c.00.2) manned by personnel of
              (K.32.a.0.4.) 293rd Army Brigade R.F.A.

42nd D.T.M.C. - BUS LES ARTOIS - 6" T.Ms.

X/42 T.M.Bty. (Q.3.a.86.67. 1 'A'   Y/42 T.M.Bty (K.27.c.0.85. 1 'A'
              (Q.3.a.70.90. 1 'A'   (K.28.a.00.00. 1 'A'
              (Q.4.a.42.30. 1 'A'   (K.27.c.85.85. 1 'A'
              (K.31.a.65.32.1 'S'   (K.25.d.28.85. 1 'S'
              (K.3.a.66.23. 1 'S'   (K.25.d.25.90. 1
              (K.25.d.33.60. 1 'S'
              (K.25.d.38.66. 1 'S'   X/57 T.M.Bty (K.21.a.0.25. 2
              (K.25.d.37.75. 1 'S'

A.R.P. 42nd Division - I.24.d.3.5.

42nd D.A.C. - LOUVENCOURT - I.35.a.80.30.

293rd B.A.C. - BUS LES ARTOIS - J.25.a.50.00.

H.A. affiliated to 42nd D.A. - 29th H.A.Bde.R.G.A. - H.Q.BERTRANCOURT.

                                              Malcolm Major., R.F.A
17th July 1918   for Brigade Major., 42nd Divisional Artillery

SECRET. Copy No..........

42nd Divisional Artillery Order No.21.

Ref. Map.57 D.S.E. Sheet 2. & 57 D.N.E. sheet 3 & 4.

1. The 188th Inf. Brigade., 63rd (R.N.) Division), are carrying out a raid on the enemy trenches on the night of 19th/20th July 1918.

   FIRST OBJECTIVE. LAVANT Trench from Q.10.b.0.4. to Q.10.b.8.7., including the crater.

   SECOND OBJECTIVE. Q.11.a.1.4. to Q.11.a.0.9.

2. 42nd Divisional Artillery will co-operate according to Table attached. Silent guns will take part if necessary.

3. Sufficient ammunition will be dumped beforehand at the guns so that at the end of the operation the normal amount is still on the positions.

4. Artillery Brigade Commanders will arrange that the nature & extent of hostile Artillery action is recorded and reported to these H.Qrs. as soon as possible.

5. Zero hour will be notified later.

6. Arrangements for synchronization of watches will be notified later.

7. At ZERO plus 35 minutes fire will cease. Batteries will, however, remain on the lines of their allotted tasks in case of need until receipt of instructions through these H.Qrs. to resume normal tasks.

8. No mention of this operation is to be made on the telephone.

9. ACKNOWLEDGE.

Issued at....7 pm....
On 18-7-18.
by. D.R.
for Brigade Major., 42nd Divisional Artillery.

Copies to :-

No.		No.	
1.	R.A., IV Corps.	12.	N.Z., D.A.
2.	42nd Division 'G'	13.	19th Balloon Coy.
3.	IV Corps H.A.	14.	125th Inf. Bde.
4.	C.B.,S.O.,IV Corps.	15.	126th Inf. Bde.
5-6.	Right Group.R.A.	16.	127th Inf. Bde.
7.	Left Group.R.A.	17.	S.C.,R.A.,42nd Divn.
8.	D.T.M.O.,42nd Divn.,	18.	R.O.,R.A.,42nd Divn.
9.	29th H.A.Bde.R.G.A.	19.	War Diary.
10.	71st H.A.Bde.R.G.A.	20.	File.
11.	63rd D.A.		

TABLE OF TASKS to accompany 42nd Divisional Artillery Order No.21.

Time	Unit.	Task.	Rate.	Ammunition.	Remarks.
ZERO to ZERO plus 55 minutes	**LEFT GROUP.**				After ZERO plus 5 minutes half the guns of each Bty. (a) & (b) search forward and back in irregular lifts as far as LINSEED SUPPORT Q.5.a.20.95. - Q.5.a.30.00.
	(a) 1 - 18-pdr. Bty.	Bombard Front Line from Q.4.b.70.37. - to Q.4.b.55.35.	18-pdrs. ZERO to ZERO plus 5 minutes	50 % T.S. 50 % A.X.	
	RIGHT GROUP.				
	(b) 1 - 18pdr. Bty.	From Q.4.b.55.35. - Q.4.d.56.80.	"RAPID"	50 % T.S. 50 % A.X.	
	(c) 1 - 18pdr. Bty.	Enfilade (LIVE ALLEY) from Q.4.b.55.15. - Q.5.a.49.05.	ZERO plus 5 minutes onwards.	"SMOKE SHELL"	
	(d) 1 - 18pdr. Bty.	Enfilade (LINSEED LANE) from Q.5.c.25.90. - Q.5.c.80.77.	"NORMAL"	50 % T.S. 40 % A.X.	
	RIGHT GROUP.		4.5" Hows.		
	1-4.5" How. Bty.	Bombard (LINSEED RESERVE) from Q.5.c. 55.80. - Q.5.c.50.20.	"NORMAL"	H.E. Fuze 106.	
	1-4.5" How. Bty.	Bombard from Q.5.c. 30.05. - Q.5.c.9.5.	Throughout.	H.E. Fuze 106.	

18th July 1918.

WAR DIARY

42nd D.A. No. B.M. 9/35.

RIGHT GROUP R.A.
LEFT GROUP R.A.
42nd D.T.M.O.

The 6" Newton Trench Mortar Batteries of the 42nd Division will from noon tomorrow the 20th inst. be affiliated to, and under the tactical command of, Os. C. Groups.

X/42 T.M. Battery will be attached to RIGHT GROUP.
Y/42 T.M. Battery will be attached to LEFT GROUP.

D.T.M.O. will keep in touch with Group Commanders to advise them, and a definite programme of harassing fire for the Trench Mortars will be included in the harassing fire programme of each Group.

MAJOR, R.F.A.
19th July 1918.   for Brigade Major, 42nd Divisional Artillery.

SECRET.

app 'N'

Copy No. 22.

42nd Divisional Artillery Order No. 20.

1. The 293rd Army Brigade R.F.A. (less D/293 Battery and 4.5" How. portion of Brigade Ammunition Column) will be relieved in the line Right Sector by the 26th Army Brigade R.F.A. (3 18-pdr. Batteries and B.A.C. - H.qrs. at Billet 241 PAS) from Corps Reserve Left Sector, as follows :-

   Night of July 19th/20th - One section per Battery.
   Night of July 20th/21st - Two sections per Battery.

   Guns will NOT be exchanged.

2. The 26th Army Brigade R.F.A. will take over the two Anti-Tank 15-pdr. Guns in action at K.26.c.00.20. and K.32.a.0.4. and also the gun-limbers and all ammunition for same.

3. Wagon Lines will be exchanged on 21st inst. The 4.5" How. portion of 293rd Army Brigade R.F.A. will move to Wagon Lines of D/293rd Army Brigade R.F.A..

4. All details of relief will be arranged between Brigade Commanders concerned. No movement will take place while visibility lasts.

5. All defence schemes, plans, maps, aerial photographs, details of work in hand and proposed, material and trench stores will be handed over on relief.

6. After completion of relief the 293rd Army Brigade R.F.A. (less D/293 Battery and 4.5" How. portion of B.A.C.) will be the Brigade R.F.A. in Corps Reserve Left Sector and will take over all schemes etc. dealing with the action of the Brigade R.F.A. in Corps Reserve Left Sector from the 26th Army Brigade R.F.A.
   The C.R.A. 25th Division is supervising the training of the 293rd Army Brigade R.F.A. while in reserve.

7. Command of RIGHT GROUP 42nd Division R.A. will pass to O.C. 26th Army Brigade R.F.A. on completion of relief on night 20th/21st.

8. Batteries and B.A.C. of 293rd Army Brigade R.F.A. will move out with all wagons full.
   All other ammunition on charge will be handed over to 26th Army Bde. R.F.A.
   At noon 20th inst. 293rd. Army Brigade R.F.A. will report to H.Q., 42nd D.A. amounts of ammunition taken out and 26th Army Brigade R.F.A. will report amounts of ammunition brought in.

9. Completion of each night's relief will be wired to this office on night 19th/20th by Code word 'JACK' and on night 20th/21st by Code word 'JILL'.

10. ACKNOWLEDGE.

Major, R.A.,
for Brigade Major, 42nd Divisional Artillery.

Issued at 8 AM
On 16-7-18 By D.R.

P.T.O.

D I S T R I B U T I O N.

Copies to :- No. 1. R.A. IV Corps.
2. 42nd Division 'G'.
3. 42nd Division 'Q'.
4. 293rd Army Brigade R.F.A.
5. 26th Army Brigade R.F.A.
6. 210th Brigade R.F.A.
7. 211th Brigade R.F.A.
8. D.T.M.O. 42nd Division.
9. 42nd D.A.C.
10. 125th Inf. Bde.
11. 126th Inf. Bde.
12. 127th Inf. Bde.
13. N.Z.D.A.
14. 63rd D.A.
15. 29th H.A. Bde. R.G.A.
16. D.A.D.O.S. 42nd Division.
17. S.C., R.A.
18. 42nd Division Sigs.
19. O.C., R.A. Sigs.
20. R.A., R.E. Officer.
21. No. 19t Balloon Coy.
22. WAR DIARY.
23. File.

SECRET.   Copy No. 20

ADDENDUM TO 42nd DIVISIONAL ARTILLERY ORDER NO:20.

1.   In order to conform to changes of Infantry Brigade Headquarters LEFT GROUP.R.A. H.Qrs. will vacate present at J.18.c.80.80. and take over the H.Qrs. at present occupied by RIGHT GROUP.R.A. at J.23.a. 70.20.

   RIGHT GROUP.R.A. H.Qrs. will move to H.Qrs. at present occupied by 210th Brigade R.F.A. at J.34.d.60.60.

   Adjutant, 210th Brigade R.F.A., with necessary Staff will remain at present H.Qrs. Remainder of 210th Brigade H.Qrs. will be withdrawn to Wagon Lines.

2.   R.A., Signal Officer will arrange necessary adjustments of communications.

3.   This change will be carried out on 21st inst. - completion being wired to this office by Code Word "WATER"

4.   ACKNOWLEDGE.

                                                W. ? Wright
                                                Major., R.F.A.
Issued at 12 Noon.   for Brigade Major., 42nd Divisional Artillery.
On 16th July 1918. By D.R.
Copies to all recipients of 42nd D.A. Order No.20.

SECRET.

42nd Divisional Artillery - Location List.

Reference 1/40,000 - Sheet 57 D.   6 p.m. 21st July 1918.

Unit	Position	No. of Guns or Hows.	Approximate front covered	Wagon Lines
42nd D.A., H.Q.	AUTHIE I.16.a.6.8.			I.15.b.9.8.

(RIGHT GROUP R.A. (Lt.Col. H.K.SADDLER D.S.O., M.C. 26th Army Bde.R.F.A.)

H.Q.	J.34.d.60.60.			J.25.a.70.40.
(310th Bde.H.Q.	J.34.d.60.60.			J.25.c.90.50.
'A' Battery	J.35.d.95.20.	6 G 'S'	Q.4.b.85.10.	J.25.c.50.00.
'B' "	J.35.c.30.31.	6 G 'A'	to	J.25.d.00.80.
'C' "	J.35.c.20.32.	6 G 'A'	K.34.c.95.60.	J.25.c.50.00.
'D' "	(J.35.a.20.20.	2 H 'A'		
	(J.28.d.60.00.	4 H 'A'		J.25.d.20.00.
A/26 Battery	J.24.c.15.09.	6 G 'S'		
(117th "	(J.29.c.50.00.	5 G 'A'	K.34.c.95.60	J.15.a.50.00.
	(J.29.d.56.79.	1 G 'A'	to	
(116th "	(J.28.d.15.45.	4 G 'A'	K.27.b.95.10.	J.25.c.50.00.
	(J.28.a.84.66.	2 G 'A'		
(B/293 "	J.29.a.90.24.	6 H 'A'		J.25.a.00.00.

(LEFT GROUP R.A. (Lt.Col. H.J.INCHES D.S.O. 211th Bde.R.F.A.)

H.Q.	J.23.a.70.80.			
'A' Battery	(J.24.b.30.60.	4 G 'S'		
	(K.19.b.40.10.	2 G 'A'		
'B' "	(J.12.c.10.60.	4 G 'A'	K.21.d.95.30.	F.1.a.
	(J.13.c.12.32.	2 G 'A'	to	and
'C' "	(J.11.d.65.35.	4 G 'S'	K.16.c.90.30.	C.6.b.
	(K.19.a.3.7.	2 G 'A'		
'D' "	(K.13.a.12.20.	2 H 'A'		
	(J.24.b.90.65.	4 H 'S'		

B - 15 pdrs.(A.T.)(K.26.c.00.20.) manned by personnel of
                (K.32.c.0.4.)   26th Army Brigade R.F.A.

42nd D.T.M.C. - BUS LES ARTOIS - 6" T.M.

X/42 T.M.Bty. (Q.3.a.86.67. 1 'A'   Y/42 T.M.Bty. (K.27.c.38.85. 1 'A'
              (Q.3.a.70.90. 1 'A'   (K.27.a.00.00. 1 'A'
              (Q.4.a.42.30. 1 'A'   (K.27.c.65.85. 1 'A'
              (K.31.a.65.32. 1 'S'   (K.25.d.28.85. 1 'S'
              (K.31.a.66.23. 1 'S'   (K.25.d.35.90. 1 'S'
              (K.25.d.33.60. 1 'S'
              (K.25.d.38.66. 1 'S'   X/57 T.M.Bty. (K.21.a.40.25. 2 'A'
              (K.25.d.37.75. 1 'S'.

A.R.P. 42nd Division - I.24.c.3.5.

42nd D.A.C. - LOUVENCOURT - I.35.a.80.30.

26th B.A.C. - BUS LES ARTOIS - J.25.a.50.00.

293rd B.A.C.(How.Sect) - J.25.a.00.60.

H.A. affiliated to 42nd D.A. - 20th H.A.Bde.R.G.A. - H.Q. BERTRANCOURT.

21st July 1918.   for Brigade Major., 42nd Divisional Artillery.

SECRET.   Copy No. 19

App 7

42nd Divisional Artillery Order No.22.

Ref:- Map 1/20,000 Sheets 57 D.N.E. & 57 D.S.E.

1. The 125th Inf. Bde. are advancing our line by establishing a line of posts at the following points on morning 22nd July 1918 :-

    K.28.c.20.75.
    K.28.c.30.55.
    K.28.c.15.25.
    K.34.a.30.60.
    K.34.a.30.30.
    K.34.c.20.95.
    K.34.c.40.75.
    K.34.c.60.60.
    K.34.c.80.40.

2. These posts will consist of 1 N.C.O. and 6 men each, with Officers in charge of groups of posts.

3. The troops are leaving our Front Line at 11. a.m. to occupy their new positions.

4. The 42nd Divisional Artillery will stand by ready to support the operation should their assistance be required. Tasks to be performed are set out in the attached table.

    The Code Word "BUMP" will be wired to all concerned from this office as an order to open fire upon allotted targets. Fire will be continued until orders to cease are received from this office.

5. D.T.M.O. will arrange for 6" T.Ms. to stand by during this operation and be ready to retaliate on any enemy T.Ms. which may open fire.

6. IV Corps Heavy Artillery are co-operating in the event of Artillery support being required by putting down a "Protective Barrage" along the line -

    OBSERVATION WOOD K.28.b.25.30. to STAR WOOD K.24.b.80.70. and from K.23.b.50.00. to K.35.a.0.0. (approximately).
    Counter Batteries are also standing by to neutralize the fire of hostile batteries or to retaliate in case of enemy fire on our front.

7. Group Commanders will arrange that the nature and extent of all hostile retaliation is recorded and reported immediately to this office.

8. If the operation is postponed the Code Word "BAD LUCK" will be wired.

9. ACKNOWLEDGE.

                                            Major., R.F.A.,
Issued at 11.45 p/m for Brigade Major., 42nd Divisional Artillery.
On 21/7/18. By D.R.

Copies to :- No.1. R.A., IV Corps.   No.12. 63rd D.A.
              2. 42nd Divn. 'G'.   13. N.Z.,D.A.
              3. IV Corps H.A.   14. 19 Balloon Coy.
              4. C.B.S.O., IV Corps.   15. 29th H.A.Bde.R.G.A.
            5-6. Right Group R.A.   16. 71st H.A.Bde.R.G.A.
              7. Left Group R.A.   17. S.O.,R.A.
              8. D.T.M.O.   18. R.O.,R.A.
              9. 125th Inf.Bde.   19. Wardiary.
             10. 126th Inf. Bde.   20. File.
             11. 127th Inf. Bde.

TABLE to accompany 42nd Div. Arty. Order No.22.

Unit.	Target	Rate	Ammunition	Remarks.
RIGHT GROUP.				
18-pdrs. & 4.5" Hows.	BARRAGE VALLADE TRENCH, CHEAPSIDE & SACKVILLE STREET from K.34.d.25.30 - K.34.a.80.30.- K.34.b.20. 30. - K.28.c.30.25.	"RAPID"	18-pdrs. 50% T.S. 50% H.E. 4.5" Hows. H.E. Fuze 106.	
LEFT GROUP.				
18-pdrs.	BARRAGE FROM K.28.c.90.30. to K.28.a.40.10.	"RAPID"	50% T.S. 50% H.E.	
4.5" Hows.	RED COTTAGE K.28.a.55.25.	"RAPID"	H.E. Fuze 106.	

21st July 1918.

SECRET.

app. 'Q'

42nd Divisional Artillery - Location List.

Reference Map 1/40,000 Sheet 57 D.   6 p.m. 24th July 1918.

Unit	Position	No. of Guns or Hows.	Approximate Front covered	Wagon Lines.
42nd D.A., H.Q.	AUTHIE I.10.a.6.8.			I.15.b.9.0.

RIGHT GROUP R.A. (Lt.Col. H.K.SADLER D.S.O., M.C.,26th Army Bde R.F.A.)

Unit	Position	No. of Guns or Hows.	Approximate Front covered	Wagon Lines.
H.Q.	J.34.d.50.60.			J.25.a.70.40.
210th Bde.H.Q.	J.34.d.60.60.			J.26.c.60.60.
'A' Battery	J.36.d.95.26.	6 G 'S'	Q.4.b.55.10.	J.26.c.50.60.
'B' "	J.35.c.30.81.	6 G 'A'	to	J.26.d.00.60.
'C' "	J.35.c.28.32.	6 G 'A'	K.34.c.95.60.	J.26.c.50.60.
'D' "	(J.35.a.20.20.	2 H 'A'		
	(J.28.d.60.00.	4 H 'A'		J.25.d.60.80.
A/26 Battery	J.24.d.16.00.	6 G 'S'		
117th "	(J.28.d.50.90.	5 G 'A'	K.34.c.95.60.	J.19.a.50.00.
	(J.28.d.56.79.	1 G 'A'	to	
116th "	(J.23.a.15.45.	4 G 'A'	K.27.b.95.10.	J.25.c.80.90.
	(J.23.a.84.66.	2 G 'A'		
D/293 "	J.29.a.80.24.	6 H 'A'		J.25.a.00.60.

LEFT GROUP R.A. (Lt.Col. E.J.INCHES D.S.O. 211th Bde.R.F.A.)

Unit	Position	No. of Guns or Hows.	Approximate Front covered	Wagon Lines.
H.Q.	J.23.a.70.10.			
'A' Battery.	(J.24.b.30.60.	4 G 'S'		
	(K.19.b.40.10.	2 G 'A'		
'B' "	(J.12.c.10.60.	4 G 'A'	K.21.c.95.20.	P.1.a.
	(J.18.c.12.82.	2 G 'A'	to	and
'C' "	(J.11.d.65.35.	4 G 'S'	K.16.c.90.20.	O.6.b.
	(K.19.a.45.45.	2 G 'A'		
'D' "	(K.13.a.12.20.	2 H 'A'		
	(J.24.b.90.65.	4 H 'S'		

2 - 15 pdrs.(A.T.) (K.29.c.60.20.) manned by personnel of
                   (K.32.a.0.4.   ) 20th Army Brigade R.F.A.

42nd D.T.M.C. - BUS LES ARTOIS - 6" T.Ms.

V/42 T.M.Bty. (Q.3.a.66.67. 1 'A'   X/42 T.M.Bty. (K.27.c.30.85. 1 'A'
              (Q.3.a.70.90. 1 'A'   (K.27.a.00.00. 1 'A'
              (Q.4.a.42.30. 1 'A'   (K.27.c.65.85. 1 'A'
              (K.31.a.65.32. 1 'S'   (K.25.d.28.85. 1 'S'
              (K.31.a.60.23. 1 'S'   (K.25.d.25.90. 1 'S'
              (K.25.d.33.60. 1 'S'
              (K.25.d.38.66. 1 'S'   X/57 T.M.Bty. K.21.a.40.25. 2 'A'
              (K.25.d.37.75. 1 'S'

A.R.P. - 42nd Division - I.24.d.3.5.

42nd D.A.C. - LOUVENCOURT - I.35.a.30.30.

20th B.A.C. - BUS LES ARTOIS - J.25.a.50.00.

293rd B.A.C.(How. Sect) - J.25.a.00.60.

H.A. affiliated to 42nd D.A. - 29th H.A.Bde.R.G.A. - H.Q. BERTRANCOURT.

P.R. Mitchell
Major., R.A.,
24th July 1918.   Brigade Major., 42nd Divisional Artillery.

SECRET.
Copy No....29...

42nd Divisional Artillery Order No.23.

Reference Map 1/10,000 57 D.N.E. Sheets 3 & 4.

1. On July 24th, from 12 noon (ZERO HOUR) to 2.p.m., IV Corps H.A. are bombarding enemy trenches in K.34. as follows :-

   (a) K.34.d.10.30. along WATLING STREET to K.34.a.30.00. to K.34.a.40.40.

   (b) K.34.b.00.00. to K.34.a.65.80.
       K.34.b.30.90. to K.28.d.20.40.
       K.34.d.00.30. to K.34.d.30.20.

   (c) K.34.d.60.30. to K.34.b.30.60.

   Rate of fire :-   12 noon to 1.0 p.m.   -   'NORMAL'
                     1.0 p.m. to 2.0 p.m. -   'SLOW'

2. 42nd Divisional Artillery will take part as follows :-

   18-pdrs.   From ZERO to ZERO plus 15.

   RIGHT GROUP.

   All active 18-pdrs. barrage from K.34.c.90.10. to K.34.c.30.70.

   LEFT GROUP.

   All active 18-pdrs. barrage from K.34.c.30.70. to K.34.a.00.00.

   Rate of Fire. :- ZERO to ZERO plus 5   -   'RAPID'
                    ZERO plus 5 to ZERO plus 15 - 'NORMAL'

   The above barrages will be repeated in 3 minute bursts at RAPID Rates at :-

   12.25 p.m.; 12.40 p.m.; 12.50.p.m.; 1.5.p.m.; 1.15.p.m.; 1.25. p.m. 1.35.p.m.; and 1.50.p.m.

   AMMUNITION :-   SHRAPNEL - 50% Graze.

   4.5" HOWS.

   All active 4.5" Hows. of the RIGHT Group will bombard SACKVILLE STREET from K.34.b.20.70. to K.28.a.90.30. at irregular intervals from 12 noon to 2.0 p.m.

3. 125th Infantry Brigade are clearing the troops from their Front Line between Q.4.a.60.80. and K.33.b.80.10.by ZERO minus 10 minutes.

4. At 2. p.m. 125th Inf. Bde. are sending over parties to examine WATLING STREET opposite MOUNTJOY ROAD (K.34.c.90.35) and BORDEN AVENUE (K.34.c.45.80.).

   Parties are returning at 3.0 p.m.

contd./-

-2-

5. From 2.p.m. to 3.p.m. 42nd Divisional Artillery will put down a "Protective" Box Barrage as follows :-

RIGHT GROUP.

All active 18-pdrs. and 4.5" Hows. -

K.34.d.25.15. to K.34.d.35.40. to K.34.a.70.15.

LEFT GROUP.

All active 18-pdrs. and 4.5" Hows. -

K.34.a.70.15. to K.34.a.50.35. to K.34.a.20.35.

Rate of fire.:-   2.p.m. to 2.10 p.m.   -   'RAPID'
                  2.10 p.m. to 2.30 p.m. -   'NORMAL'
                  2.30 p.m. to 3.0 p.m. -   'SLOW'

AMMUNITION.:- 18-pdrs. - 50% H.E. (106 Fuze). 50% SHRAPNEL (50% Graze)
              4.5" Hows.. - 101 Fuze (non-delay).

6. A light Signal notifying that the Infantry withdrawal is complete is being arranged by B.G.C.,125th Inf. Bde. and will be notified to Groups later.
   Should this signal be observed before 3.0 p.m. the 'Protective" Barrage mentioned in para.5. may be allowed to die down. If no signal is observed the barrage will continue till 3.0 p.m.

7. Counter Batteries are requested to be prepared to neutralize enemy Batteries that may become active.

8. D.T.M.O. will be prepared to neutralize any hostile T.Ms. that may become active.

9. RIGHT and LEFT Groups will synchronize their watches by sending an officer to the H.Q. of 29th H.A.Bde. at BERTRANCOURT near J.33.d.5.3. at 9.30 a.m. July 24th.
   RIGHT GROUP will synchronize the watches of 125th Inf. Bde.

10. ACKNOWLEDGE.

                                                     R. Mac—————
                                                    Major., R.A.,
Issued at 9.30 p.m.   Brigade Major., 42nd Divisional Artillery.
On 23rd July 1918 By D.R.
Copies to :-
   No.1. 42nd Division 'G'.   No.23. 63rd (R.N) D.A.
      2. R.A., IV Corps.   24. N.Z.,D.A.
      3. IV Corps H.A.   25. S.C.,R.A.
      4. C.B.S.O. IV Corps.   26. R.O.,R.A.
   5-14. RIGHT GROUP.R.A.   27. 29th H.A.Bde.
  15-19. LEFT GROUP.R.A.   28. No.19. Balloon Coy.
     20. D.T.M.O.   29   War Diary.
     21. 125th Inf. Bde.   30. File.
     22. 127th Inf. Bde.

SECRET.

ADDENDUM No.1. to 42nd Divisional Artillery Order No.23.

Reference Para.6 of above order.

The light signal referred to will be a SMOKE RIFLE GRENADE bursting in the air.

P.R. Mitchell
Major., R.A.,
Brigade Major., R.A.,
42nd Division.

23rd July 1918.
Copies to all recipients of 42nd D.A., Order No.23.

SECRET.

App 'S'

42nd Divisional Artillery. - Location List.

Reference 1/40,000 - Sheet 57 D.   6 p.m. July 28th 1918.

Unit.	Position	No. of Guns or Hows.	Approximate Front covered.	Wagon Lines.
42nd D.A., H.Q.	AUTHIE I.16.a.6.6.			I.15.b.9.6.

(RIGHT GROUP R.A. (Lt. Col. MASON D.S.O. 210th Bde. R.F.A.)

H.Q.	J.34.d.60.60.			
'A' Battery.	J.36.d.95.20.	6 G 'S'		J.26.c.80.60.
'B' "	J.35.c.30.91.	6 G 'A'	Q.4.b.55.10.	J.26.c.50.50.
'C' "	J.35.c.28.32.	6 G 'A'		J.26.d.00.60.
'D' "	(J.35.a.90.90.	2 H 'A'	to	J.26.c.50.60.
	(J.28.d.60.06.	4 H 'A'		J.25.d.80.80.
D/295 Battery.	J.29.a.80.24.	6 H 'A'	K.27.b.95.10.	J.25.a.60.60.

(LEFT GROUP R.A. (Lt. Col. E.J.INCHES D.S.O. 211th Brigade R.F.A.)

H.Q.	J.23.a.70.20.			
'A' Battery.	(J.24.b.30.60.	4 G 'S'		
	(K.19.b.40.10.	2 G 'A'	K.21.d.95.20.	
'B' "	(J.12.c.10.60.	4 G 'A'		P.1.a.
	(J.10.c.12.82.	2 G 'A'	to	and
'C' "	(J.11.d.05.35.	4 G 'S'		O.6.b.
	(K.19.a.45.45.	2 G 'A'	K.16.c.90.20.	
'D' "	(K.13.a.12.20.	2 H 'A'		
	(J.24.b.90.65.	4 H 'S'		

2 - 18 pdrs. (A.T.) (K.26.c.60.20.) manned by personnel of
                   (K.32.a.0.4.) 210th Brigade R.F.A.

42nd D.T.M.O. - BUS LES ARTOIS. 6" T.Ms.

X/42 T.M.Bty. (Q.3.a.36.37. 1 'A'   Y/42 T.M.Bty. (K.27.c.38.85. 1 'A'
              (Q.3.a.70.90. 1 'A'   (K.27.c.60.60. 1 'A'
              (Q.4.a.42.30. 1 'A'   (K.27.c.65.35. 1 'A'
              (K.31.a.35.32. 1 'S'   (K.25.d.28.85. 1 'S'
              (K.31.a.66.28. 1 'S'   (K.25.d.25.90. 1 'S'
              (K.25.d.35.60. 1 'S'   (K.21.a.40.25. 2 'A'
              (K.25.d.38.66. 1 'S'
              (K.25.d.37.75. 1 'S'

A.R.P. 42nd Division - I.24.d.3.5.

42nd D.A.C. - LOUVENCOURT - I.35.a.80.30.

293rd B.A.C.(How. Sect.) - J.25.a.00.60.

H.A. affiliated to 42nd D.A.(29th H.A.Bde. - H.Q., BERTRANCOURT.
                            (54th H.A.Bde. - H.Q., J.32.a.60.60.

28th July 1918.   D Walcott Lt / for Major., R.A.,
                              Brigade Major., 42nd Divisional Artillery.

SECRET.

app. 'T'

Copy No. 20.

42nd Divisional Artillery Order No.24.

1. The 57th Divisional Artillery are withdrawing from action on the IV Corps Front on July 28th and on the night July 28th/29th 1918.

2. In consequence of the above the following changes will take place in the Artillery covering the RIGHT Division :-

(a) 26th Army Brigade R.F.A. will withdraw from action in the RIGHT Division on the night July 28th/29th and will take over in situ the guns of the 3 - 18pdr. batteries of 285th Brigade R.F.A. covering the LEFT Division, IV Corps.

The 26th Army Brigade R.F.A. will hand over thier own guns to the 285th Brigade R.F.A. in the Wagon Lines of the latter at MEIGNON.

This relief will be completed by 6 a.m. 29th inst.

The Wagon Lines of 26th Army Brigade R.F.A. will move to MEIGNON on the 29th inst. taking over the lines vacated by the 285th Brigade R.F.A.

(b) The 2 Medium Trench Mortars at present manned by the 57th D.A. at E.31.a.40.25. will be taken over in situ by 42nd Division T.M. personnel on July 28th.

The personnel of the 57th D.A. at present manning these Mortars will withdraw from the line on the night July 28th/29th, taking with them 2 Medium Trench Mortars complete.

D.T.M.O., 42nd Division will arrange to hand over these 2 T.Ms.

3. On receipt of this order advance parties from 26th Army Brigade R.F.A. will be despatched to the positions of the 285th Bde. R.F.A.

4. The ammunition will be cleared away from the positions vacated by the 26th Army Bde. R.F.A. as follows :-

211th Bde. R.F.A. will clear 116th Battery Position.

210th Bde. R.F.A. will clear A/26th and 117th Battery positions.

5. The 26th Army Brigade R.F.A. will march out of the Divisional Area with echelons full, reporting to this office, prior to departure, the amount and nature of ammunition taken out of the area.

6. No movement will be made by 26th Bde. R.F.A. while visibility lasts.

7. On completion of withdrawal of 26th Army Bde. R.F.A. RIGHT Group, R.A. will be commanded by Lt. Col. ELSON D.S.O. who should take over all maps, documents, Defence Schemes, &c. on July 28th.

8. Group Commanders will re-arrange S.O.S. Lines in consultation with their Infantry Brigades.

LEFT Group R.A. will bear in mind that a Battery of the N.Z.D.A., will no longer be available to fire on 42nd Division Front for S.O.S. purposes.

Field Artillery Barrage should cover the most vulnerable points, remaining portions being defended by Machine Gun Fire.

Co-ordinates to be sent to this office as soon as possible.

Contd/-

- 2 -

9. 210th Brigade R.F.A. will complete the work of exchanging the 2 - 15pdr. Anti-Tank Guns for 2 - 18pdr. Guns and will continue to man them.

Later, arrangements will be made for each Group to man one of these guns.

10. ACKNOWLEDGE.

P.R. Mitchell

Major., R.A.,
Issued at 10.30 AM   Brigade Major.; 42nd Divisional Artillery.

By S.D.R. on 23th July 1918.

Copies to :-

No. 1.	R.A., IV Corps.	No. 12.	127th Inf. Bde.
2.	42nd Division 'G'.	13.	37th D.A.
3.	H.A., IV Corps.	14.	N.Z., D.A.
4.	C.E., S.C., IV Corps.	15.	31st D.A.
5.	Right Group R.A.	16.	29th H.A. Bde. R.G.A.
6.	210th Brigade R.F.A.	17.	54th H.A. Bde. R.G.A.
7.	Left Group R.A.	18.	S.C., R.A., 42nd Divn.
8.	D.T.M.O., 42nd Division.	19.	S.C. for Reconnaissance.
9.	42nd Div. M.G. Battn.	20.	War Diary.
10.	125th Inf. Bde.	21.	File.
11.	126th Inf. Bde.		

SECRET.

ADDENDUM No. 1. to
42nd Divisional Artillery Order Number 24.

26th Army Brigade R.F.A. Ammunition Column will take over the lines
vacated by the Section of the 57th D.A.C. at C.22.d.5.5. in the
BOIS ST. PIERRE on the morning of the 29th July.

All arrangements to be made between Commanders concerned.

                                                    Major, R.A.,

Issued at......by D.R. Brigade Major, 42nd Divisional Artillery.
on 28th July 1918.

Copies to all Recipients of 42nd. Div. Arty. Order No. 24.

SECRET.   Copy. No 7

42nd Divisional Artillery Order No.25.

1. V Corps are carrying out a feint attack on July 30th 1918 by means of a Smoke Barrage and Artillery Bombardment.

2. ZERO HOUR will be 9 a.m. (NINE A.M.).

3. 42nd Divisional Artillery will co-operate as follows:-

   (a) Smoke Barrage.   -   ZERO to ZERO plus 10 minutes.

   RIGHT GROUP.R.A.

   2 - 18pdr. Batteries and 2 - 4.5" How. Batteries. -

   Q.4.b.6.4. to K.34.d.6.0. to K.34.d.2.0.

   LEFT GROUP.R.A.

   1 - 18pdr. Battery - K.34.d.2.0. to . . . K.34.a.9.0.

   Should the wind have an Easterly tendency this barrage will be advanced 500 yds. due East.

   RATE OF FIRE :-   "RAPID"

   If the wind is favourable at ZERO plus 2 minutes all 4.5" Hows. will fire 4 rounds of GAS (N.C.) as rapidly as possible and then revert to Smoke Shell.

   (b) ARTILLERY BOMBARDMENT. - ZERO plus 10 mins. to ZERO plus 25 mins.

   18-pdrs. and 4.5" Hows. bombard areas as shewn on attached tracing.

   RATE OF FIRE :- ZERO plus 10 mins. to ZERO plus 15 mins - "RAPID"
                   ZERO plus 15 mins. to ZERO plus 25 mins - "NORMAL"

   AMMUNITION.- 18-pdrs. - SHRAPNEL (50% Graze).
                4.5" Hows. - H.E. (1.0C Fuze).

4. Three 6" Newton T.Ms. will bombard selected points in VALLADE TRENCH from ZERO plus 10 minutes to ZERO plus 25 minutes.

   RATE OF FIRE. - 4 rounds per mortar per minute.

5. Orders as to synchronization will be issued later.

6. ACKNOWLEDGE.

                                                    P.R. Mitchell
                                                       Major., R.A.
Issued at 11.30 PM   Brigade Major., 42nd Divisional Artillery.
On 29.7.18. By. D.R.
Copies to :-
   No.1. R.A., IV Corps.   No.13. 21st D.A.
      2. 42nd Division 'G'.   14. N.Z.,D.A.
    3-7. Right Group R.A.   15. S.C.,R.A.,42nd Div.
    8-9. Left Group R.A.   16. S.C.for Reconnaissance,42nd D.A.
     10. D.T.M.O.,42nd Divn.   17. War Diary.
     11. Right Inf. Bde.   18. File.
     12. Left Inf. Bde.

SECRET.

42nd Divisional Artillery – Location List.
-o-o-o-o-o-o-o-o-o-o-o-o-o-o-o-o-o-o-o-o-o-o-o-

Reference 1/40,000 – Sheet 57 D.   6 p.m. July 31st 1918.

Unit.	Position	No. of Guns or Hows.	Approximate Front covered.	Wagon Lines.
42nd D.A., H.Q.,	AUTHEUIL.16.a.6.8.			I.15.b.9.8.
(RIGHT GROUP.R.A. (Lt. Col. J.D.MASON D.S.O. 210th Bde. R.F.A.)				
H.Q.	J.34.d.60.60.			J.26.c.80.80.
'A' Battery	J.36.d.95.26.	6 G 'S'		J.26.c.50.60.
'B' "	J.35.c.30.81.	6 G 'A'	Q.4.b.55.10.	J.26.d.00.60.
'C' "	J.35.c.28.32.	6 G 'A'		J.26.c.50.50.
'D' "	(J.35.a.90.20.	2 H 'A'	to	
	(J.28.d.60.00.	4 H 'A'		J.25.d.90.90.
(D/293 Battery.	J.29.a.80.24.	6 H 'A'	K.27.b.95.10.	J.25.a.00.60.
(LEFT GROUP.R.A. (Lt. Col. E.J.INCHES D.S.O. 211th Bde. R.F.A.).)				
H.Q.	J.23.a.70.20.			
'A' Battery	(J.24.b.30.60.	4 G 'S'		
	(K.19.b.40.10.	2 G 'A'	K.21.d.95.20.	
'B' "	(J.12.c.10.60.	4 G 'A'		P.1.a.
	(J.18.c.12.82.	2 G 'A'	to	and
'C' "	(J.11.d.65.35.	4 G 'S'		C.6.b.
	(K.19.a.45.45.	2 G 'A'	K.16.c.90.20.	
'D' "	(K.13.a.12.20.	2 H 'A'		
	(J.24.b.90.65.	4 H 'S'		

2 – 18pdrs. (A.T.)(K.26.c.00.20.) manned by personnel of
             (K.32.a.0.4.   ) 210th Brigade R.F.A.

42nd D.T.M.C. – BUS LES ARTOIS – 6" T.Ms.

X/42 T.M.Bty. (Q.3.a.65.67. 1 'A'   Y/42 T.M.Bty. (K.27.a.75.28. 1 'A'
              (Q.3.a.70.90. 1 'A'   (K.27.c.65.85. 1 'A'
              (K.25.d.30.70.2 'S'   (K.25.d.25.80. 2 'S'
              (Q.4.a.42.30. 1 'A'   (K.21.a.40.25. 2 'A'
              (K.21.a.80.30.2 'S'

A.R.P. 42nd Division. – I.24.d.3.5.

42nd D.A.C. – LOUVENCOURT – I.35.a.80.30.

293rd B.A.C.(How.Sect.) – J.25.a.00.60.

H.A. affiliated to 42nd. D.A. – 54th H.A.Bde. – H.Q. J.32.a.80.90.

31st July 1918.   Brigade Major., 42nd Divisional Artillery,
                                                              Major., R.A.,

Vol 19

CONFIDENTIAL

WAR DIARY

OF

HEADQUARTERS ROYAL ARTILLERY, 42nd DIVISION.

from 1st August 1918 to 31st August 1918.

VOLUME XX.

****
****

Army Form C. 2118.

WAR DIARY
or
INTELLIGENCE SUMMARY.
(Erase heading not required.)

August 1918

Reference maps.
FRANCE 57D & 57C
1/40.000

Instructions regarding War Diaries and Intelligence Summaries are contained in F. S. Regs., Part II. and the Staff Manual respectively. Title pages will be prepared in manuscript.

Place	Date	Hour	Summary of Events and Information	Remarks and references to Appendices
AUTHIE	6th		Orders for bombardment of (a) REDAN (about K35 c 2.1) and (b) Junction of LEGEND TRENCH and FLAG AVENUE at K34 d 3.8	App I (a)
	7th		Disposition Report	(a)
	11th		Disposition Report	(a)
	12th		Disposition Report	(a)
	14th		Capt F.E. MORGAN SC RA to England on leave	(a)
	15th		Disposition Report	(a)
			RA HQ to BUS LES ARTOIS with HQ 42nd Div	App II (a)
BUS	18th		Orders for attack on trenches in K34 a, c and d for capture of VALLADE TRENCH and GREEN TRENCH.	App III (a)
			Disposition Report	App IV (a)
	21st		Disposition Report	(a)
	24th		RA HQ to Checkpoint COLIN CAMPS with HQ 42nd Div	App V (a)
BUCQUOY	27th		Instructions re Artillery action with Advance Guard.	
			RA HQ to L 10 BUCQUOY with HQ 42nd Div	
	29th		Capt F.E. MORGAN SC RA from leave in England	(a)
GREVILLERS	30th		RA HQ to GREVILLERS with HQ 42nd Div	(a)

App I.

SECRET.   42nd D.A., No.B.M.1/283.

Right Group R.A.
Left Group R.A.
D.T.M.O., 42nd Division.
IV Corps Heavy T.M.Battery.

1. **12 inch Hows.** At 4 p.m. August 7th, 12" Hows. are bombarding –

   (a) REDAN (about K.35.c.2.1.) and
   (b) Junction of LEGEND TRENCH and FLAG AVENUE at K.34.b.3.3.

   The bombardment will last about an hour.

   An officer from the 12" How. Battery will call at 210th Bde. H.Q. at J.34.d.60.60. on the morning of Aug. 7th.
   210th Bde. will arrange for an officer to conduct this H.A. Officer to an O.P. or O.Ps. from whence he can observe on the above two points.

2. **HEAVY T.M.** The Heavy T.M.(9.45") will fire from 4 p.m. to 5 p.m. August 7th on the Trench Junction at K.28.d.20.45. and along the Trench WEST of this point for 100 yards.

   D.T.M.O., 42nd Division to make all arrangements with O.C., Heavy T.M. Battery.

3. **WIRE CUTTING.** Right Group and 6" T.Ms. will cut wire in front of Trench from K.34.a.2.0. to K.34.a.3.6. making arrangements with Right Infantry Brigade for withdrawal of Infantry if necessary.
   This wire cutting to commence at 4 p.m. and to continue as long as necessary.

4. The shoots detailed in paras. 1 & 2 will not necessitate the withdrawal of any Infantry Posts.

5. ACKNOWLEDGE.

                                                PRNOTT
                                                Major., R.A.,
6th August 1918.   Brigade Major., 42nd Divisional Artillery.

Copies to :- 42nd Division 'G'.
              IV Corps H.A.
              125th Inf. Bde.
              126th Inf. Bde.
              84th H.A.Bde.

SECRET.   App II   Copy No........

42nd Divisional Artillery Order No. 27.

Reference Map 57 D.N.E. 3 & 4 S.E. 2 (Part of)(Target Map No.177.)

1. On a date and at a time to be notified later the RIGHT Inf. Brigade 42nd Division are attacking enemy trenches on K.34.a., c. and d. with the object of capturing and consolidating VALLADE TRENCH and GREEN TRENCH.

2. 42nd Divisional Artillery will co-operate as follows:-

   (a) <u>SMOKE BARRAGE</u> (4.5" Hows.).

   <u>Zero minus 5 to Zero plus 35.</u>

   D/211. - K.35.d.20.35. to K.28.c.90.50.

   D/210 & D/295. - K.34.b.30.60. to K.29.d.10.00.

   Rate of Fire. - A salvo followed by Battery fire 10 seconds.

   (b). <u>18-pdr. Barrage.</u>

   (1) <u>Zero to Zero plus 10.</u>

   Six 18-pdr. batteries barrage GREEN TRENCH & VALLADE TRENCH from K.34.d.45.15. to K.34.a.65.80.

   O.C., Right Group will allot the tasks to batteries of Right and Left Groups employing enfilade fire where possible.

   <u>AMMUNITION</u>. - H.E. for batteries whose fire is frontal.
   Shrapnel (50% Graze) for batteries whose fire is in enfilade.

   <u>RATE OF FIRE</u>. - "RAPID".

   Batteries will sweep sufficiently to cover the front allotted to them.

   (2) <u>Zero plus 10 to Zero plus 35.</u>

   Above barrage will lift to the line -

   K.35.c.00.45. to K.28.d.25.00.

   <u>AMMUNITION</u>. 50% Shrapnel (50% Graze).
   50% H.E.

   Rate of fire. - "NORMAL".

3. 21st Divisional Artillery are co-operating as follows:-

   (a) <u>Zero minus 5 to Zero plus 35.</u>

   Two 4.5" How. Batteries are putting down a Smoke Barrage from Q.4.b.85.90. to K.34.d.85.35.

   (b) <u>Zero minus 5 to Zero plus 35.</u>

   One 18-pdr. Battery is putting down a Smoke Barrage on the high ground in vicinity of Q.10.b.70.80.

Cont/d.

– 2 –

4. N.Z., Divisional Artillery are co-operating as follows:-

   Zero to Zero plus 35.

   2½ Batteries of 18-pdrs, are bombarding the Trenches in K.28.d. (No fire to be directed further South than the junction of LEGEND TRENCH & FLAG AVENUE at K.34.b.3.8.).

   AMMUNITION.- 50% Shrapnel - 50% H.E.

   Rate of fire.

   Zero to Zero plus 5 . "INTENSE"
   Zero plus 5 to Zero plus 35 - "NORMAL".

5. IV Corps H.A. are firing as follows:-

   Zero to Zero plus 35.

   (a) Three 6" Hows. on H.Q. at K.35.c.35.07. (H.E.).
   (b) Three 6" Hows. on MATTHEW COPSE. (H.E.).
   (c) Six 6" Hows. on K.35.c.55.80. to K.35.c.85.65. to K.35.c.55.35. (H.E.).
   (d) Four 8" Hows. on K.29.c.50.10. to K.29.c.95.10, to K.35.a.90.90. (H.E.).

   Zero minus 5 to Zero plus 35.

   (e) One Battery 6" Hows. firing GAS on SERRE (K.30.central).

6. 6" T.Ms. will fire as follows :-

   Zero to Zero plus 35.

   1 T.M. on K.35.c.65.59. - 30-75. ⎫
   1 T.M. on K.34.b.50-90.   ⎬
   1 T.M. on REDAN.   ⎬ 1 round per minute.
   1 T.M. on OBSERVATION WOOD.   ⎬
   1 T.M. on K.28.d.15.45. - 15.00. ⎬
   1 T.M. on K.28.c.80.40.   ⎭

7. The H.T.M. will fire on OBSERVATION WOOD from Zero to Zero plus 35.

8. Counter Batteries are requested to neutralize any hostile batteries that become active during and after the operation.

9. Right Group R.A. will re-adjust S.O.S.Lines to fall 250 yards beyond Infantry Line of Posts from Zero plus 35 onwards.

10. Acknowledge.

P. R. Mitchell
Major., R.A.
Issued at 12 midnight Brigade Major, 42nd Divisional Artillery.
By D.R. On 9/8/18.
Copies to :-

   No.1. 42nd Divn. 'G'   No.10. 31st D.A.
      2. R.A., IV Corps.   11. 125th Inf, Bde.
      3. IV Corps.H.A.   12. 126th Inf, Bde.
      4. C.B., S.O. IV Corps,   13. S.C.R.A., 42nd Divn.
      5. Right Group.R.A.   14. 19 Balloon Coy.
      6. Left Group R.A.   15. S.O.for Reconnaissance.
      7. D.T.M.O. 42nd Div.   16. War Diary.
      8. Corps,H.T.M.Bty.   17. File.
      9. N.Z., D.A.

SECRET.

App III

42nd Divisional Artillery - Location List.

Reference 1/40,000 - Sheet 57 D.   6 p.m. 18th August 1918.

Unit	Position	No. of Guns or Hows.	Approximate Front Covered	Wagon Lines.
42nd D.A., H.Q.	CHATEAU BUS LES ARTOIS			J.26.a.50.50.

(RIGHT GROUP R.A. (Lt. Col. D.J.MASON D.S.O. 210th Bde. R.F.A.)

H.Q.	K.32.a.4.4.			J.25.a.6.4.
'A' Battery.	Q.3.a.8.9.	6 G 'A'		J.26.c.50.60.
'B' Battery.	K.32.d.3.7.	6 G 'A'	R.1.a.00.00.	J.19.a.9.5.
'C' Battery.	Q.4.a.35.85.	6 G 'A'	to	J.25.a.4.2.
'D' Battery.	(K.32.c.70.25.	4 H 'A'	L.31.c.60.80.	J.25.a.7.1.
	(Q.3.a.40.90.	2 H 'A'		
1 - 18pdr. (A.R.)	K.32.a.0.4.			

(LEFT GROUP R.A. (Major. J.NALL D.S.O. 211th Brigade R.F.A.)

H.Q.	J.23.a.7.1.			
'A' Battery.	K.27.a.8.8.	6 G 'A'	L.31.c.60.80.	P.1.a.
'B' Battery.	K.20.d.6.4.	6 G 'A'	to	and
'C' Battery.	K.21.c.1.9.	6 G 'A'	L.26.a.20.20.	O.6.b.
'D' Battery.	K.20.d.95.05.	6 H 'A'		
1 - 18pdr.(A.T.)	K.26.c.00.20.			

O.Ps. manned by 42nd D.A.

CODE NAME	Right Group R.A. Location.	When manned.	CODE NAME	Left Group R.A. Location	When Manned.
AT	Q.2.b.5.5.	Day & Night.	LOOT.	K.30.c.85.65.	3 a.m. - 9 p.m.
	K.36.c.central.	Day	ROD.	K.30.d.	-- do --
	K.30.d.0.8.	Day & Night.	CAT	K.21.c.84.00.	24 hours.
			DOG.	K.21.b.5.7.	When necessary.
			RAM.	LA SIGNY FM.	Dawn to Dusk.

D.T.M.O. 42nd Division - BUS LES ARTOIS.

X/42 T.M.Bty.	(Q.3.a.85.67. 2 'S'	X/42 T.M.Bty.	(K.25.d.37.75. 1 'S'
	(Q.4.a.42.50. 1 'S'	Y/42 T.M.Bty.	(K.27.c.50.90. 1 'S'
	(Q.4.a.42.45. 1 'S'		(K.27.c.68.86. 1 'S'
	(Q.4.a.40.65. 1 'S'		(K.27.c.35.85. 1 'S'
	(K.25.d.33.60. 1 'S'		K.21.a.40.25. 1 'S'
	(K.25.d.38.66. 1 'S'		(K.26.d.50.90. 1 'S'.

A.R.P. 42nd Division - I.24.d.3.5.
42nd D.A.C. - LOUVENCOURT - I.35.a.80.30.

H.A. affiliated to 42nd D.A. - 54th Bde.R.G.A. H.Q. J.32.a.60.90.

D.Malcolm Lieut. R.H.A.
18th Aug.1918.   S.O. for Reconnaissance, 42nd Divisional Artillery.

SECRET.   6 p.m. 21st August 1918.

RIGHT SECTOR - IV CORPS.

Location of Artillery Units.

Unit.	No. of Guns.	Location.	Wagon Lines.
H.Qrs. 42nd Divnl.Arty. (Brig-Gen. F.W.H.WALSHE D.S.O.,R.A.)			
Front Covered. R.3.a. to L.20.c.(approx).			
H.A.Bde. in Liaison, 54th. Bde. H.Q. - J.32.a.90.90.			
Right Group.R.A.(210th Bde.R.F.A.) H.Q. K.32.a.4.0. (Lt.Col.D.J.MASON D.S.O.)			J.25.a.6.4.
Front covered. - R.3.a. to L.33.a.			
A/210th Battery R.F.A.	6	K.34.c.75.05.	J.25.c.50.60.
B/210th -do-	2	K.34.d.20.10.	J.19.a.9.5.
	3	K.34.c.30.10.	
C/210th -do-	6	Q.4.a.35.85.	J.25.a.4.2.
D/210th -do-	6	Q.4.c.55.60.	J.25.a.7.1.
Left Group R.A.(211th Bde. R.F.A.) H.Q. K.25.d.6.2. (Major. J.HALL D.S.O.)			
Front covered. - L.33.a. to L.28.c.			P.1.a.
A/211th Battery. R.F.A.	6	K.29.b.0.9.	and
B/211th - do -	3	K.28.b.2.2.	C.6.b.
C/211th - do -	6	K.28.b.2.0.	
D/211th - do -	6	K.29.a.5.0.	
42nd D.T.M.O. H.Q. - BUS LES ARTOIS. - 6" T.Ms.			
X/42 T.M.Battery.	2	Q.3.a.85.67. x	
	1	Q.4.a.42.50. x	
	1	Q.4.a.42.45. x	
	1	Q.4.a.40.65. x	
	1	K.25.d.33.60. x	
	1	K.25.d.38.66. x	
	1	K.25.d.37.75. x	
Y/42 T.M.Battery.	2	K.27.c.50.00. x	
	1	K.27.c.6.8. x	
	1	K.27.c.35.85. x	
	1	K.21.a.40.25. x	
42nd D.A.C.		LOUVENCOURT.	I.35.a.30.30.
42nd A.R.P.		I.24.d.3.5.	
	Advanced	COUNCELLIES.	

x Silent.

21st August 1918.   S.O. for Reconnaisance, 42nd Divisional Artillery.
                                                                Lieut. R.H.A.

app. V "C.F." File

42nd Divisional Artillery.
H.Q. B.M.

Right Group.
Left Group.

1. When the advance is resumed and our front line is established on the spurs in N.E. central and N.D. central, the 127th Infantry Brigade will drop back and 126th Infantry Brigade will take over the whole Divisional front.

2. When this takes place both Groups will act in conjunction with the 126th Infantry Bde. Commander, remaining distributed in depth and advancing by alternate Bdes. or Batteries.

3. In case the advance becomes a rapid pursuit, the 210th Bde. is detailed to move forward at once with the 126th Infantry Bde. Column, the O.C., 210th Bde. detailing one Battery to accompany closely the main body of the advanced guard. The O.C. the Battery of the A.G. will be in close touch with the Battalion Commander and will usually move forward by sections covering each other's advance. He will bring his guns into action when necessary on his own initiative without awaiting orders from the A.G. Commander. Guns will be run up to the crest when necessary and fired direct on M.G. nests or other suitable targets.
He will always act with the greatest boldness.
   In action horses will be kept near the guns but need not be always harnessed up.

4. Semi-covered positions close to a crest from which good observation can be obtained and the guns can be controlled by voice, megaphone, or semaphore, are to be taken up when possible.

5. Every possible opportunity will be taken by Artillery to open communication by visual. Messages will be sent daily by this means from D.A. to Groups and Groups to Batteries.

6. Acknowledge.

T.R. Mitchell
Major, R.A.,
Brigade Major, 42nd Div. Arty.

29/5/18.
Issued at 12.10 p.m.

Copy to 42nd Div. "Q".
       B.A. IV Corps.

App VI

42nd Divisional Artillery.
No. B.M. 121.

ARTILLERY NOTES FOR MOBILE WARFARE.

1. During the advance Officers' patrols will be detailed by the leading Artillery Brigade daily to accompany leading infantry and report on Artillery positions.

2. Intercommunication on the move and in action is both important and difficult. Visual and mounted orderlies must now largely replace telephones, but lines will be laid (and recovered) when feasible.

3. B.Cs. should ride at the head of the Brigade on the march in column so as to be ready to join Brigade Commanders quickly.

4. Positions of readiness often save more time than getting into action too soon, when the situation is obscure.

5. Ground Scouts should always be used when moving in the open. On rough ground Nos. 1 should also ride ahead of the guns.

6. Employ Look-out men in action always and patrols on the move when at all exposed.

7. Finally Save the Horses. Graze every spare five minutes off-saddle whenever possible, if not, loosen girths and leave heads loose to graze. Water at every opportunity. Make detachments walk and don't carry a pound of unnecessary weight on vehicles.

Brig. General, R.A.
Commanding 42nd Div'l Artillery.

3/9/18.

Issued down to Officers.

Vol 20

CONFIDENTIAL

WAR DIARY

OF

H.Q. R.A., 42nd Divn.

From 1/9/18. To. 30/9/18

VOL. XIX

Sheet 1. September 1918. **WAR DIARY** or **INTELLIGENCE SUMMARY.**

Army Form C. 2118.

Reference map:
FRANCE 57C 1/40,000.

Place	Date	Hour	Summary of Events and Information	Remarks and references to Appendices
GREVILLERS	1st		42DA fired barrage in support of 21st and NZ Div	ja.
	2nd		42DA fired barrage to assist 42 Div in capture of VILLERS-AU-FLOS.	
	3rd		42DA advanced to positions E & SE of VILLERS-AU-FLOS and arrived in positions to position in O18c & O23b and in capture of BUS. In the afternoon to position to capture YTRES.	ja.
	4th		Bde first in support of operation to capture YTRES. Bde moved to NW of YTRES and W of BUS and fired creeping barrages to assist in capture of NEUVILLE-BOURJONVAL. RAHQ to RIEN COURT (N.46.b.)	ja.
RIENCOURT	5th		42DA fired barrage in support of operation to capture POWER TR, E of NEUVILLE-BOURJONVAL.	ja.
	5/6		NZDA retired 42 Div, 210 and 211 Bdes remaining in action under NZ Div	ja
	6th		211 Bde RFA withdrawn from action to rest at BEAULENCOURT.	ja
	7th		RAHQ at RIENCOURT at rest	ja
	11th		211 Bde RFA moved into action under NZ Div	ja
	12th		LIEUT J.D. MALCOLM MC & LIEUT J ALMOND attd RA HQ from B/211 RFA.	ja
	13th		210 and 211 Bdes withdrew to wagon lines at YTRES	ja
	18th		Orders received for 42DA to be prepared to move to 1st Army Area. Location Statement	Appx I ja.
	19th		Orders received for 42DA to be ready to move to BULLS COURT tonight. Later these orders were cancelled.	ja.

Sheet II. September 1918. **WAR DIARY** *or* **INTELLIGENCE SUMMARY.** Army Form C. 2118.

Reference map FRANCE 57C ⅟₂₀,₀₀₀

Place	Date	Hour	Summary of Events and Information	Remarks and references to Appendices
RIENCOURT	20		LIEUT H.W.L. KEARNS A/211 acted RAHQ learns to take up appointment as SCRA 46th DA.	fa.
	21		CAPT E. NUTTALL acted to RAHQ from SAA. left 42 DAC.	fa.
VELU	22	10am	CRA arrives command of Arty covering left Sector, N.Z.Div having taken over from 37th Div on the 21st. RAHQ to VELU (I36d8.1).	fa.
	24		Preliminary Instructions issued re forthcoming Operations	App II
	25"		Location Statement	App III
	25/26	8pm	4th Bty 3rd N.Z.F.A. Bde reverted to command of Right Div III Corps.	fa.
	26		Additional Arty moved into position in left Sector	fa.
	26/27		Orders issued re Operation on 27th inst.	App IV
	27"	5.20am	Additional Arty moved into position in left Sector (21D and 211 Bdes R.F.A.)	fa.
			Arty covering N.Z.Div fired barrage for attack on HINDENBURG LINE	
	28"	2.30am	Orders issued for advance of 42nd Div on 28th. Arty fired barrage as laid down in App V.	App V fa.

Sheet III.

September 1918. WAR DIARY or INTELLIGENCE SUMMARY.

Army Form C. 2118.
Reference map.
FRANCE 57c ⅟₄₀,₀₀₀

Place	Date	Hour	Summary of Events and Information	Remarks and references to Appendices
VELU	28/9		NZ Div passed through 42nd Div and command of Arty covering left Sector passed to NZDA. 210 and 211 Bdes RFA remained in action under NZDA	
	29"		LIEUT J.D. MALCOLM returns from leave in UK	

Almond Lieut RFA

Appendix 1

42nd Divisional Artillery - Location Statement.

H.Q., R.A.   -   M.4.d.5.5.

210th Brigade R.F.A. -   P.34.d.9.9.)
) At rest.
211th Brigade R.F.A. -   P.1.d.1.8.)

42nd D.A.C.

H.Q.   )
No.1 Section.   )   -   Q.14.c. and d.
No.2 Section.   )

S.A.A. Section.   -   M.31.d.2.2. on salvage.

42nd D.T.M.O.   -   Q.15.a.7.2.
X/42 T.M. Bty.   -   Q.15.a.7.2.
Y/42 T.M. Bty.   -   Q.15.a.7.2.

15/3/18.   Major., R.F.A.
                    for Brigade Major., 42nd Divisional Artillery.

SECRET.   42nd D.A., No. B.M. 1/44.

Reference 42nd D.A. Instructions No. 1 (Preliminary).

Para. 11.   Delete Line 4 and substitute the following :-

    "RIGHT GROUP at Q.10.Central."

                                            P.R. Mitchell
                                            Major., R.A.
28/9/18.   Brigade Major., 42nd Divisional Artillery.

Copies to all recipients of 42nd D.A. Instructions No. 1 (Pre).

SECRET.

AMENDMENT NO:1 to
42nd D.A.Instructions No.1 (Preliminary)
───

Para.2. Line 3.   For K.32.c.d. and b.   READ
                     L.32.c,d, and b.

Please acknowledge.

P.R. Mitchell
Major., R.A.
24/9/18.   Brigade Major., 42nd Divisional Artillery.

Copies to All recipients of 42nd D.A.Instructions No.1.

SECRET.

app. II

WD

Copy No. 25

42nd D.A. Instruction No. 1. (Preliminary)

1. ALLOTMENT & GROUPING OF FIELD ARTILLERY.

The allotment and grouping of the Field Artillery to cover 42nd Division in the forthcoming operation will be as follows:-

RIGHT GROUP. (Lt. Col. VASEY D.S.O. Cmdg. 210th Bde. R.F.A.)

210th Bde R.F.A.)
211th Bde R.F.A.) Covering RIGHT Infantry Brigade.
123rd Bde R.F.A.)

LEFT GROUP. (Lt. Col. CROFTON D.S.O. Cmdg. 317th Bde R.F.A.)

124th Bde R.F.A.)
317th Bde R.F.A.) Covering LEFT Infantry Brigade.
1st Bde. N.Z.F.A.)

2. BRIGADE AREAS.

Positions have been selected from which the final objective (Sunken Road along HIGHLAND RIDGE in K.7.b., R.8.a., R.2.c., R.8.a., K.32.c, d. and b.) can be covered, viz, -

317th Bde.R.F.A. in Q.3.c.
124th Bde.R.F.A. in K.33.a, & c.
123rd Bde.R.F.A. in Q.2.c. (2 Bties), Q.10.d. (2 Bties).
210th Bde.R.F.A. in Q.9.c.
211th Bde.R.F.A. in Q.9.c.
1st Bde.N.Z.F.A. in Q.3.a, & c.

The above areas are approximate only.
Battery positions are being accurately resected by a Corps Topographer who will live at the H.Qrs. of 317th Bde.R.F.A.
As soon as he has finished the positions for the LEFT Group he will commence on those for the RIGHT Group.
O.C., Right Group will get in touch with 317th Bde. in this matter and arrange for the work to be continuous.
123rd Bde.R.F.A. will move forward 2 Batteries, after the second objective has been taken and during the operation, to positions South of TRESCAULT.

3. FORWARD MOVE OF BRIGADES.

(a) Certain Batteries, to be detailed later, will be prepared to move forward after the capture of the final objective to cover the line of exploitation which will be along WELSH RIDGE.

(b) When the final objective has been definitely consolidated all Brigades will move forward by batteries to positions disposed in depth from 3,000 yards to 5,000 yards from the new front line.

4. CREEPING BARRAGE.

Details as to the Infantry Jumping Off Line, the various objectives and timings, and rates of Fire have not yet been definitely settled.

Cont/d.

4 Contd.

The following details as to the nature of the Barrage are given :-

(a) Each Brigade will superimpose one 18 pdr. Battery on the other two.
(b) Each 4.5" How. Battery will be distributed along its Brigade front, 100 yards in front of the 18 pdrs.
(c) 6" Hows. will "Creep" 200 yards in advance of 4.5" Hows.

Super Heavy Hows.(12" & 15") 800 yards in front of /8 ...

These latter are dwelling on the best available targets until the 18 pdr. Barrage approaches to 800 yards.
(d) R.F.A. Brigade Commanders will arrange to thicken up the Barrage where it passes over points likely to give trouble.
(e) A round of SMOKE will be fired from alternate 18 pdr. guns as an indication to the Infantry, at the first round of the initial barrage, and on arrival at, and departure from, each intermediate protective Barrage, and final protective Barrage.
(f) Ammunition (exclusive of the few rounds of Smoke) must depend on the proportion of various natures available, as large a proportion as possible of 18 pdr. H.E. will be fired.

The bulk of this H.E. should be kept for the longer ranges and where the Angle of Sight is difficult to assess. Such Time Shrapnel as has to be used being kept for the shorter ranges and for those portions of the barrage where the Angle of Sight is fairly accurately known.

5. AMMUNITION.

Ammunition for the operation will be stacked as follows:-

18 pdrs.- At Battery Positions - 600 rounds per gun.
          At A.R.P.   - 250   "   "   "

4.5"Hows- At Battery Positions - (450 rds H.E. per gun.
                                  (50 rds GAS   "   "

          At A.R.P.   - (150 rds H.E. per gun.
                                  (50 rds GAS   "   "

6. PREPARATION OF POSITIONS.

Preparation of positions will be proceeded with at once.
Platforms will be prepared and positions got ready to receive guns and ammunition.
Camouflage must be erected for all guns that are being moved up into position on X/Y Night.
Greatest possible care will be taken not to give away positions and not to give away the fact that an offensive is in view.

7. MOVING FORWARD INTO POSITION.

Approximately 50% of the Artillery will be placed in position on X/Y Night, the remainder moving into position on Y/Z Night.

Those Batteries that will be moved in on X/Y Night are :-

The whole of the   Bdes.R.F.A. and any other Batteries and Sections whose new positions are well concealed.

Cont/d.

7. Contd.

Group Commanders will report as early as possible which Batteries they consider could be moved in with advantage on X/Y Night.

8. F.O.Os. and F.I.Os.

Each Brigade will detail one F.O.O. to proceed forward behind the Barrage and to send back information (negative or positive) at stated times at regular intervals.

Every facility will be given by Brigades to these F.O.Os. and Brigades will see that they are amply provided with wire, means for visual signalling and an adequate party to accompany them.

Brigade Commanders will consider this matter of F.O.Os. of first importance and no effort will be spared to get back quick and accurate information.

Arrangements for visual will be arranged beforehand and Brigades will make a careful study of the ground with a to selecting good positions for transmitting stations on the line of advance in German territory.

F.O.Os. will also act in Liaison with Infantry Battalion and Company Commanders.

In addition to F.O.Os. one F.I.O. (Forward Intelligence Officer) will be sent out from each Group.

This officer will be specially selected and given all possible help in the matter of communications – pigeons, lamps, telephone &c.

One Brigade Signalling Officer will go forward with a party of 10 or 15 Linesmen and Signallers laying a wire close behind the F.I.O. This line will be laid on Group H.Q. on a route to be chosen beforehand and explained to F.I.O. and F.O.Os. for their future use.

The Brigade Signalling Officer's party will establish posts for repairing the line at each 500 yards.

9. COMMUNICATIONS.

All Brigade and Battery mobilization wire will be carefully overhauled and made up to establishment.

Group Commanders will at once get out estimates of what wire they will require over and above that already in possession.

O.C., R.A. Signals will get in touch with Group Commanders and arrange to supply whatever is necessary in the way of cable.

10. TRENCH MORTARS.

D.T.M.Os. 37th and 42nd Divisions will arrange to put 24 T.Ms. in positions close to the present Front Line to be used for the preliminary bombardment on Y/Z Night.

Those T.Ms. that are not well concealed will be kept "silent" until that night, the remainder will bombard trenches and cut wire in front of present Front Line continuously, having due regard to the fact that they must retain a sufficient supply of ammunition at the mortar positions for Y/Z Night.

Special attention will be paid by Trench Mortars from now until 'Z' Day to the wire and trenches in Q.5.a. & d., and Q.11.b.

D.T.M.Os. 37th and 42nd Divisions will consult together as to the division of tasks.

Cont/d.

- 4 -

11. **GROUP R.A. H.QRS.**

Group R.A. H.Qrs. will be established alongside Infantry Brigade H.Qrs., i.e, -

RIGHT Group at PLACE MORTEMARE in Q.6.d.

LEFT Group at TRESCAULT TRENCH in Q.3.b.

If adequate arrangements cannot be made with Infantry Brigadiers concerned this office will be notified at once.
125th Inf. Bde. will be RIGHT Inf. Bde. and 127th Inf. Bde. will be LEFT Inf. Bde. Present H.Qrs. are -
 125th Inf. Bde. ... I.30.a.9.8.
 127th Inf. Bde. ... P.6.a.4.9.
Arrangements will be put in hand at once to effect the necessary communications by O.C., R.A. Signals.

12. **HOW. BTY. 3rd BDE. N.Z.F.A.**
The 4th Bty, 3rd Bde. N.Z.F.A. will not be available to shoot on 42nd Division Front during the operation.
Orders regarding the return of this Battery to its Brigade will be issued later.

13. **ACKNOWLEDGE.**

              R.R.Mitchell
              Major., R.A.

Issued at 6 AM
On,......... By..... DR   Brigade Major., 42nd Divisional Artillery.

Copies to :-

Copy No. 1.	42nd DIVN 'G'	No. 13.	3rd D.A.
2.	R.A., IV Corps.	14.	D.T.M.O., 37th Divn.
3.	IV Corps R.A.	15.	D.T.M.O., 42nd Divn.
4.	42nd Divn 'Q'	16.	42nd D.A.C.
5.	210th Bde. R.F.A.	17.	37th D.A.C.
6.	211th Bde. R.F.A.	18.	125th Inf. Bde.
7.	123rd Bde. R.F.A.	19.	126th Inf. Bde.
8.	124th Bde. R.F.A.	20.	127th Inf. Bde.
9.	317th Bde. R.F.A.	21.	S.C.R.A., 42nd Divn.
10. 1st Bde. N.Z.F.A.		22.	S.O. for Reconnaissance.
11. 3rd Bde. N.Z.F.A.		23.	O.C., R.A. Signals.
12. 5th D.A.		24.	H.A. Liaison Officer.
		25.	War Diary.
		26.	File.

SECRET.   APP. III

42nd Divisional Artillery – Location Statement.

                              Position.   Wagon Lines.

H.Q. 42nd D.A.   VELU (I.32.d.9.1.).

210th Bde.R.F.A.,H.Q.)
  A/210.R.F.A.   )
  B/210.R.F.A.   ) P.27.c. (VALLULART WOOD) – At rest.
  C/210.R.F.A.   )
  D/210.R.F.A.   )

211th Bde.R.F.A.,H.Q. – O.3.d.2.4.
  A/211.R.F.A.)
  B/211.R.F.A.)
  C/211.R.F.A.) – B.1.b. and d.   – At rest.
  D/211th.T.F.A.)

183rd Bde.R.F.A.,H.Q. – Q.13.Central.
  A/183.R.F.A.   – Q.13.c.3.3.   P.9.c.3.3.
  B/183.R.F.A.   – Q.14.c.1.7.   P.20.c.7.8.
  C/183.R.F.A.   –(Q.19.c.0.9. (2)   P.19.b.9.9.
                        (Q.8.c.3.0. (3)
  D/183.R.F.A.   – Q.13.c.3.9.
  4th Bty.N.Z.F.A.   Q.20.c.7.9.   P.19.b.9.9.
                                               O.6.d.7.5. (leaves 42nd
                                               D.A. at 8 P.M. 25/9/18.

184th Bde.R.F.A.,H.Q. – P.8.c.5.4.   J.20.d.30.10.
  A/184.R.F.A.   – P.12.c.05.10.   Q.5.d.60.30.
  B/184.R.F.A.   – P.18.d.92.15.   P.9.d.40.20.
  C/184.R.F.A.   – P.11.b.80.00.   P.9.a.80.20.
  D/184.R.F.A.   – P.11.b.60.00.   P.13.a.40.70.

317th Bde.R.F.A.,H.Q. – Q.2.c.7.5.
  A/317.R.F.A.   – P.6.d.50.15.   P.10.a.0.9.
  B/317.R.F.A.   –(Q.1.c.25.50. (2)   P.9.c.3.4.
                        (Q.8.c.3.1.   (3)
  C/317.R.F.A.   – Q.1.c.1.7.   P.9.b.4.9.
  D/317.R.F.A.   – Q.1.a.0.3.   P.9.c.5.5.

42nd D.A.C.,H.Q. – P.14.b.   37th D.A.C.,H.Q. – I.35.d.0.5.
  No.1 Sect.   – P.14.b.   No.2 Sect.   – I.13.c.5.2.
  2   "   – P.14.b.   1   "   – I.34.b.9.9.
  S.A.A. "   – J.26.d.1.1.

13rd H.A.G. – No.2 Sect. – I.23.b.9.0.

42nd M.T.M.O. – P.19.d.08.50.
  X/42 Battery – Q.4.a.7.1. (2)
  Y/42   "   – Q.4.d.3.7. (6)

37th D.T.M.O. – J.32.a.5.6. (REAR)
                P.6.d.25.80. (ADV)
  X/37 Battery – Q.10.d.4.3. (1)
                 Q.11.a.0.3. (2)
                 K.35.a.0.3. (3)
  Y/37   "   Q.10.b.9.3. (1)
                 K.35.a.0.3. (2)

A.R.P. – VELU (J.31.d.2.2.) and RUYAULCOURT (P.15.Central)

                                       J.Almond
                                       Lieut.R.F.A.
25/9/18.   S.O. for Reconnaissance, 42nd Divnl.Arty.

SECRET.   Copy No...149...

42nd Divisional Artillery Order No. 38.

Reference maps 57.C. N.E. & S.E. 1/20,000 and Barrage
Map attached.
----

1. In conjunction with operations by the First Army, the
   Third Army is resuming the advance.
   The 5th Division will be on the right of the 42nd
   Division and the 3rd Division on the left.

2. The attack on the 42nd Division Front is being carried
   out by the 125th Inf. Bde on the Right and by the 127th
   Inf Bde on the left.
   The objectives of the IV Corps and the Divisional and
   Brigade Boundaries are shown on the attached map.
   In conjunction with the attack, the IV Corps is to
   capture BEAUCAMP Ridge and HIGHLAND Ridge and is to clear
   the HINDENBURG FRONT SYSTEM as far as the COUILLET VALLEY.
   If the advance of the VI Corps on MARCOING is successful
   the IV Corps is to advance to WELSH Ridge to cover the
   flank of the VI Corps.

3. The Infantry advance will be covered by a creeping
   barrage arranged in depth.
   The Artillery available for this barrage is 6 Brigades
   R.F.A., grouped as shown in 42nd D.A. Instruction No.1.
   (Preliminary) dated 24/9/18., and two batteries of 6" Hows:

4. The details of the creeping barrage on the 42nd Division
   Front are shown on the attached barrage map.
   In this connection the following points will be noted:-

(a). Lanes A, B, & C are allotted to the Right Group R.F.A.
     Lanes D, E, & F to the Left Group R.F.A.

(b). The Right half of the barrage commences on the initial
line at ZERO plus 152 while the Left half commences at ZERO
plus 180.
     The timings are therefore not identical across the
whole of the Divisional Front and the two halves must be
regarded, from an Artillery point of view, as two distinct
barrages <u>until</u> ZERO plus 320 after which hour the timings
of the lifts are identical and the two halves proceed
Eastwards as one continuous barrage.

(c). The rate of advance of the barrage is 100 yards
every four minutes except in the <u>Left</u> half from ZERO plus
270 to ZERO plus 320 when the rate becomes 100 yards every
<u>six</u> minutes.

(d). The various objectives and intermediate objectives
are shown on the map together with the lines on which the
barrage dwells to form protective barrages.

(e). One round of Smoke will be fired from every alternate
18-pdr gun at the first and last round on the initial
barrage line and also for the first and last round of each
Protective barrage line where the barrage dwells for
eight minutes and upwards.

(f). Each 4.5" How: Battery will be distributed along the
front covered by each Brigade R.F.A. but will keep 150
yds in advance of the 18-pdrs.
     The timings shown, therefore, are for the 18-pdrs
also.

- 2 -

(g). All 4.5" Hows. will fire GAS (GG) for the first 5 minutes on the Final Protective Barrage.

(h). Ammunition. (exclusive of the rounds of Smoke and Gas mentioned above)

18-pdrs. - H.E.(106 fuze), H.E. delay at short ranges, and Shrapnel (50 % graze), according to supply.-
As large a proportion of H.E. as possible will be used. Shrapnel being reserved for the shorter ranges (under 5,500 yards) and where the angle of sight can be easily assessed.

4.5" Hows. - H.E.(106 fuze) and delay action against buildings.

(i) RATE OF FIRE. First six minutes "INTENSE"
next twenty minutes "RAPID"
after that "NORMAL"
except for the first four minutes after moving on from each 'dwell' of eight minutes or over, when fire will be "RAPID" for four minutes.

On all Protective Barrages of over 8 minutes duration - "SLOW".

(j). The section of the super-imposed batteries of the Left Group will be kept continually walking along each trench of the HINDENBURG FRONT LINE.

5. ACTION OF HEAVY ARTILLERY.- One 8" How: Battery will "creep" 400 yards ahead of the 18-pdr barrage, along the Trench system in Q.12.a.& b., R.7.a,b, &c. and R.8.b., keeping N. of the 42nd Divisional Southern Boundary.
One 8" How: Battery will similarly "creep" along the HINDENBURG FRONT LINE.
During the advance the B.G., C.H.A. is arranging to bombard the HINDENBURG FRONT SYSTEM on the IV Corps Front with one battery 12" Hows and two 15" Hows.
In addition one 60-pdr Battery, shooting from near HERMIES will enfilade the HINDENBURG FRONT LINE, keeping ahead of the 18-pdr Barrage.

6. BATTERIES OF OPPORTUNITY.- The super-imposed battery in each Brigade R.F.A. will be prepared to engage targets reported from the ground or from the air.
They will have a direct telephone line to their Brigade Wireless dug-out.

7. 6" TRENCH MORTARS. - As soon as the Right Infantry Bde commence their attack, but not before, i.e., at ZERO plus 152, all 6" Trench Mortars will open fire as rapidly as possible on selected points opposite the whole Divisional Front.
At ZERO plus 164 those Trench Mortars that are firing opposite the Right Infantry Brigade Front will switch their fire on to points on the Left Infantry Brigade Front and continue firing until all ammunition is expended.
All 6" Trench Mortar Fire will cease at ZERO plus 190 whether ammunition is expended or not.

8. ASSISTANCE TO VI CORPS.- Prior to the advance of the 42nd Division the Left Group R.A. (3 Bdes) will assist the advance of the VI Corps by putting down a combined bombardment and smoke screen on the HINDENBURH FRONT SYSTEM where it passes over the high ground in K.35 and K.36 and L.31.c.

- 3 -

Time. - From daybreak to ZERO plus 140.

AMMUNITION ALLOTMENT. - 2,000 rounds A.Smoke.
1,000 rounds A.
300 rounds BX.
50 rounds BCG.

8. ASSISTANCE TO 5TH DIVISION. - Right Group R.A. will, prior to ZERO plus 152, assist the 5th Division by thickening up their barrage for a short period.
Detailed orders will be issued later.

9. Orders re Communications, F.O.Os, F.L.Os and forward moves of Brigades R.F.A. after the capture of the final objective are embodied in 42nd D.A.Instructions No.1.(Preliminary) dated 24th Sept 1918.

X 11. "Z" day and ZERO hour will be notified later.

12. Groups R.F.A. and D.T.M.Os 37th and 42nd Divisions will synchronise watches with the Infantry Brigades they support.

13. ACKNOWLEDGE.

P.R. Mitchell
Major R.A.,
Brigade Major 42nd Div'l Artillery.

25/9/1918.

Issued at ....
By ....

Copy No. 1 42nd Div "G".
2. R.A. IV Corps.
3. IV Corps R.A.
4. 42nd Div 'Q'.
5 to 9. 210th Bde R.F.A.
10 to 14. 211th Bde R.F.A.
15 to 19. 123rd Bde R.F.A.
20 to 24. 125th Bde R.F.A.
25 to 29. 312th Bde R.F.A.
30 to 34. 1st Bde R.A.F.A.
35. S.T.M.O. IV Corps.
36. 5th Div Arty.
37. 3rd Div Arty.

No. 38. D.T.M.O. 37th Div.
39. D.T.M.O. 42nd Div.
40. 42nd D.A.H.
41. 37th D.A.C.
42. 125th Inf Bde.
43. 126th Inf Bde.
44. 127th Inf Bde.
45. S.O.R.A. 42nd Div.
46. O.y. for Reconnaissance
47. O.C.R.A.Signals.
48. R.A.Liaison Officer.
49. War Diary.
50. File.

X Zero Hour:- 5.20 A.M. on Sept 27th 1918

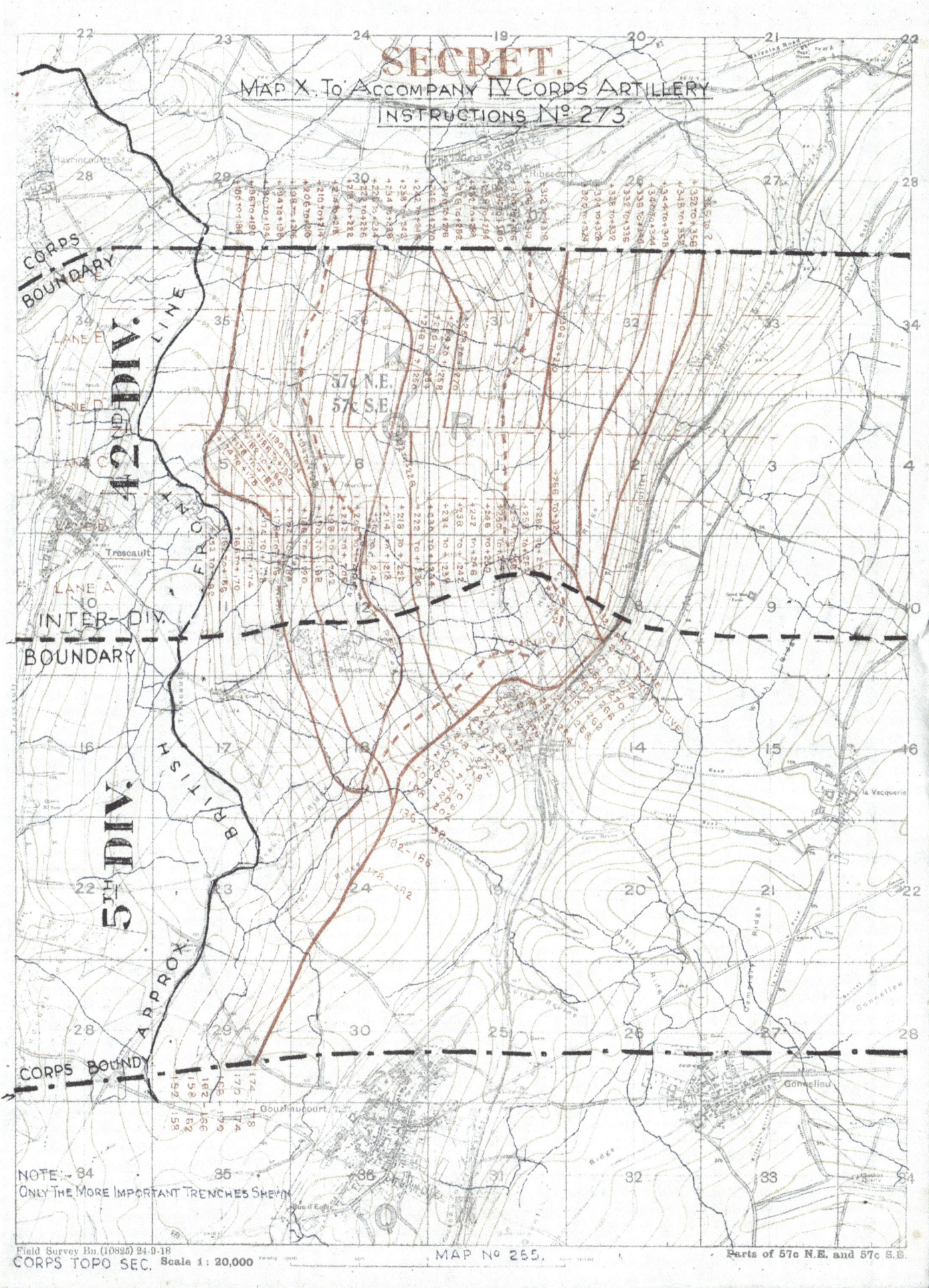

42nd D.A., NO.S.M.1/47.

Right Group .R.A.
Left Group .R.A.
──────────────

1. The advance of 42nd Division is being resumed at 1.30 A.M. (ZERO HOUR) Sept. 28th under a "Creeping" Barrage, vide barrage tracing attached.

2. Barrage will advance 100 yards every 3 minutes dwelling on Protective Barrage Lines as indicated on the tracing.

   RIGHT Group will fire the Right half of the barrage, LEFT Group the left half.

3. 4.5" Hows. will advance 150 yards ahead of the 18pdr. barrage.

4. AMMUNITION as available.

5. Rate of fire :-

   1st 3 minutes ... ... "INTENSE"

   After that "RAPID" or "NORMAL" at discretion of Group Commanders.

   On Protective Lines ... ... "SLOW"

6. HEAVY ARTILLERY.

   6" Hows. are creeping in the barrage, 400 yards ahead of the 18pdrs. and walking down the following trenches :-

   VILLAGE TRENCH, PLOUGH TRENCH, MISTERY TRENCH, PLUSH TRENCH, and the HINDENBURG FRONT LINE (RIDGE TRENCH & SUPPORT and WOOD TRENCH & SUPPORT.).

7. ACKNOWLEDGE.

27/9/18.   Brigade Major., 42nd Divisional Artillery.

Copies to :- 42nd Divn."G".   Right Inf. Bde.
             IV Corps R.A.   Left Inf. Bde.
             IV Corps H.A.   War Diary.
             5th D.A.   File.
             63nd D.A.

Zero hour: 2.30 AM Sept 28th

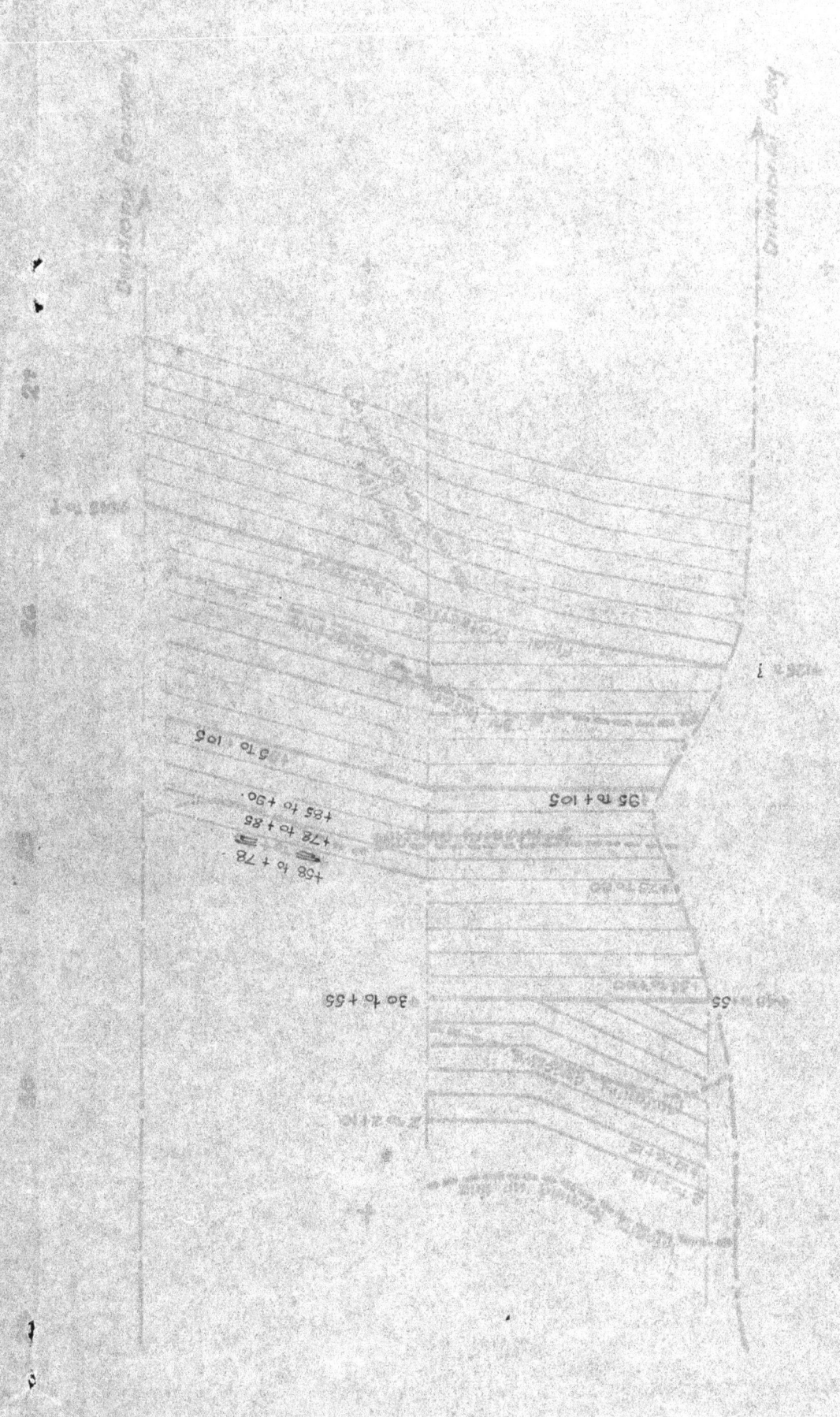

Vol 21

Confidential

War Diary

of

H.Q., R.A., 42nd Division

To 31/10/18

Vol. XX

From 1/10/18

Sheet 1.

WAR DIARY
or
INTELLIGENCE SUMMARY.
(Erase heading not required.)

Army Form C. 2118.

October 1918

Reference maps: 57C 1/40,000
FRANCE 57B 1/40,000

Place	Date	Hour	Summary of Events and Information	Remarks and references to Appendices
VELU	1st		42 D.A. in action under N.Z. Div	
			H.Q.R.A. 42 Div at VELU WOOD (I36d81 – 57c) – Arment	fa
	8		H.Q.R.A. to TRESCAULT (Q10 cent – 57c) with 42 Div	fa
TRESCAULT	9		H.Q.R.A. to ESNES (H34d2.4 – 57B) with 42 Div	fa
ESNES	12		H.Q.R.A. to BEAUVOIS-EN-CAMBRESIS (I9c9.4 – 57B) with 42 Div	fa
BEAUVOIS	13	1830	CRA 42 Div assumes command of Artillery covering LEFT SECTOR IV Corps,	fa
			42 Div (less Arty) having relieved N2 Div (less Arty) on night 12/13	
	14		Orders issued re "COUNTER PREPARATION"	App. A fa
	16		Disposition Report	App. B fa
	17		Arty covering Left Sector re-grouped as follows	
			Rt Group :– 1st and 3rd Bdes NZFA under Lt-Col STANDISH – CMG. DSO.	
			Left Group :– 210 and 211 Bdes RFA under Lt-Col MASON. DSO	
			MAJOR P.R. MITCHELL to IV Corps As SORA (acting).	
			CAPT. F.E. MORGAN acts BMRA 42 Div.	
			CAPT. E. NUTTALL acts SCRA 42 Div.	
	19		Orders issued for Arty support on resuming advance on 20th inst.	App. C fa

Sheet II   October 1918   **WAR DIARY** or **INTELLIGENCE SUMMARY.**   Army Form C. 2118.

Reference map FRANCE 57/3 1/40,000
51 A 1/20,000

(Erase heading not required.)

Place	Date	Hour	Summary of Events and Information	Remarks and references to Appendices
BEAUVOIS	19		Disposition Report	App D JA
	20		Arty fired creeping barrage in support of Infantry advance	JA
	20/21		Arty moved EAST of RIVER SELLE	JA
	21		Arty covering 42 Div re-grouped	App E JA
	22		Order issued for Arty Support when advance is resumed on 23rd inst	App F JA
	23rd		Arty fired creeping barrage in support of Infantry Advance	JA
		0905	42 Div Inf having reached BLUE LINE, NZ Div Inf passed through them & continued the advance. He commenced of the Arty covering left Sector passing to C.R.A. NZ Div.	
			& BRIG-GEN. F.W.H. WALSHE DSO to ENGLAND on leave	JA
	24		RAHQ remains at BEAUVOIS-EN-CAMBRESIS — Arrest	JA
			LT-COL D. MASON DSO from 210 Bde RFA to RAHQ as a/CRA.	
	25/31		Brigades & DAC of 42 DA functioning under N.Z division	En
	31		Capt F.F. MORGAN acting BMRA 42 Div. Lt J. ALMOND a/S.O. for Reconnaissance and Capt E.W. GILL R.E. officer i/c R.A. Signals sick to hospital	En

Mulholl. Capt. RFA for
a/BM.R.A. 42 Division.

SECRET.   app B

42nd Divisional Artillery — Location Statement.

1800 hours – 16/10/18.

R.F.A. Group 42nd Division. – H.Q. J.3.c.8.7.

(Lt.Col. CROFTON, D.S.O., Cmdg. 317th Bde.R.F.A.)

Approximate Front covered – E.19.c.5.8. to D.12.d.5.5.

Unit.	Position.	Wagon Lines.
317th Bde.R.F.A. H.Q.	J.3.c.8.7.	)
A. Battery.	J.3.a.9.1.	)
B. "	J.3.a.75.20.	) J.13.a. & b.
C. "	J.3.c.9.9.	)
D. "	J.3.c.8.6.	)
210th Bde.R.F.A. H.Q.	J.3.a.8.0.	)
A. Battery.	D.27.d.75.82.	)
B. "	D.27.d.52.52.	) D.28.d.
C. "	D.27.d.5.8.	)
D. "	D.27.d.2.4.	)
211th Bde.R.F.A.	D.28.c.5.2.	)
A. Battery.	D.22.c.9.2.	)
B. "	D.21.d.4.4.	) D.28.a. & c.
C. "	D.22.c.1.3.	)
D. "	D.22.d.1.2.	)
42nd D.T.M.O.	– – – –	I.9.d.3.3.
A.R.P. 42nd Division.	– – –	J.7.c.1.4.
42nd D.A.C. H.Q.	– – –	I.11.Central.
Nos.1 & 2 Sections.)	– –	I.11.a.
S.A.A. Section.)		
53rd D.A.C. (No.2. Section.	–	I.13.Central.

R.A. affiliated to 42nd D.A. – 90th Bde.R.F.A. H.Q. J.3.c.8.7.

15/10/18.   Lieut., R.F.A.
              for S.O. for Reconnaissance, 42nd Div. Arty.

42nd D.A., No. B.M. 2/1.

App A

R.F.A. Group.
42nd Division.

COUNTER-PREPARATION.

1. In every case of heavy bombardment of our Front Line by the enemy, F.O.Os. will at once report to their Batteries and Brigade H.Qrs. giving the general direction and nature of the fire and whence it is judged to be coming.

2. If it is apparently the beginning of an enemy attack, Brigade Commanders will at once put down Counter-Preparation i.e., Searching and Sweeping on all likely places of assembly for the enemy Infantry at a slow rate. These places will be settled beforehand in conjunction with Infantry Brigade and Battalion Commanders and will continue as long as the hostile bombardment goes on or until an S.O.S. signal goes up.

3. This action will at once be reported to Group H.Qrs. and to the Infantry and by Group H.Qrs. to the D.A.,H.Q.

T. Pitchie

Brigadier-General., R.A.
C. R. A., 42nd Division.

14/10/18.
Copies to: 42nd Division "J", 125th, 126th & 127th Inf. Bdes.

SECRET.   app.c

Amendment No. 1 to 42nd D.A. Order No. 31.
----

1. Para. 2 - Second sub para. for 210 minutes read 195 mins

2. Para. 4 add.-

"One 18-pdr. Battery in each Brigade will be superimposed on the Brigade Front. After daybreak this Battery will be a "Battery of opportunity" to take on targets reported by F.O.Os. and to answer LL or GF calls. For this purpose a direct line will be laid from this Battery to the Brigade Wireless Station.

"In addition the whole of the 1st Bde. N.Z.F.A. will be prepared to answer LL and GF calls during the creeping barrage".

3. Para. 5 (c). - From Z plus 40 to Z plus 45 this Battery will fire only on railway bounding the Triangle on N. side.

Para. 5. - Delete last sub para. and substitute

"From Z plus 45 to first protective barrage inclusive, 1st Bde. N.Z.F.A. will be superimposed on Right Group Front. From Z plus 300 to final protective barrage inclusive 1st Bde. N.Z.F.A. will be superimposed on Left Group Front, but will remain under Command of the Right Group.

4. Para. 6 - First sub para. - Lines for flank guns are not shown on map. Right flank gun will follow the inter-Divisional boundary. Line for Left flank gun as follows:-

E.13.c.3.7. to N.8.c.7.4.

Note. This line marks the advance of the Left flank of the 42nd Division Infantry attack.

5. Para. 7, last sub para. add:-

"If wind is between N.E. and S.E. no gas will be fired on bombardment area No. 1.

/Para. 8.

— 2 —

6. <u>Para. 9, page 4</u> - Delete lines 7 and 8 and substitute:-

"Hows. of 1st Bde. N.Z.F.A. will fire at "RAPID" rate from Z to Z plus 40, quickening to "INTENSE" from Z plus 40 to Z plus 45."

7. <u>Para. 10. 18-pdrs.</u> Add:-

"All 18-pdrs. taking part in creeping barrage will fire one round Smoke in every 6 rounds after daylight."

8. <u>Para. 12.</u> For "first daylight" read "05.00 hours".

Add to Para. 12 - "These Sections will be specially on the look out for enemy tanks."

9. Barrage Map should be amended so that the Left Group creeping barrage on the Sunken Road in E.3.b. and d. is extended northwards to cover the line of fortified shell holes shown on the map as a red dotted line.

10. Acknowledge.

L.E.Morgan

Capt. R.A.,
a/Brigade Major, 42nd Div. Arty.

19/10/18.

Copies to all recipients of 42nd D.A. Order No. 38.

SECRET.

Copy No. .....

42nd D.A. ORDER No. 39.

1. The Third and Fourth Armies are resuming the advance.

   42nd Division will attack with the 5th Division on the right and 62nd Division of VI Corps on the left.

2. The attack on the 42nd Division front is being carried out in two stages.

   During the first stage the 126th Infantry Brigade advances under a creeping barrage to the 1st Infantry objective, shown on the attached map. After a pause on this line of 210 minutes, the 127th Infantry Brigade leap-frogs over 126th Infantry Brigade and continues the advance to the final objective, under cover of various barrages and bombardments shown on the map.

   The 5th Division is advancing approximately level with 42nd Division, and at Z plus 45 a Brigade of the 62nd Division is advancing through the Railway Triangle in E.7.c. along the Railway South of SOLESMES and mopping up the village.

3. The Artillery available to cover the advance of 42nd Division is six Brigades of Field Artillery and three Batteries of 6" Hows.

   The Field Artillery will be grouped as follows:-

RIGHT GROUP. (Lt.Col. F.B. SYKES, D.S.O.)

        223rd Bde. R.F.A.
        1st Bde. N.Z.F.A.
        3rd Bde. N.Z.F.A.

LEFT GROUP. (Lt.Col. M. CROFTON, D.S.O.)

        317th Bde. R.F.A.
        210th Bde. R.F.A.
        211th Bde. R.F.A.

   O.C., Left Group, will control both groups.

4. The details of the 18-pdr. creeping barrage are shown on attached map, together with the Infantry objective and protective barrages to cover them.

/2.

— 2 —

5. The action of 1st Bde. N.Z.F.A. will be as follows, the creeping barrage on the Right Group Front being provided temporarily by 2 Brigades only.

From Z to Z plus 45.
(a) 1 - 18pdr. battery will fire incendiary shell into the Railway Triangle in B.7.c. and along the S.W. embankment of the Triangle.

(b) 2 - 18pdr. Batteries will form a Smoke screen as shown on the attached map.

(c) 4 - 4.5" Hows. will fire BX into the Railway Triangle and on to the Railways bounding it.

Two 4.5" Hows. will fire on the Factory B.13.a.6.7. from Z. to Z. plus 30, and from Z. plus 30 to Z. plus 45 on the Railway Triangle.

From Z. plus 45 onwards the 1st Bd. N.Z.F.A. will revert to the control of O.C. Right Group and will be superimposed on the Group front for barrage purposes.

6. From Z to Z plus 90 one 18-pdr. of each Group will fire time incendiary shell on the line marked on the attached map. This fire is to be kept continuously 200 yards in front of the 18-pdr. creeping barrage.

From Z to Z plus 65 one 18-pdr. of Right Group will fire time incendiary shell on the cross roads B.14.c.7.7. These shell should be burst high at first so as to be visible to the advancing Infantry all the time. At Z plus 65 this gun will lengthen its range by 500 yards and continue firing until Z plus 90.

7. The action of 4.5" Hows. will be as follows:-

All Hows. of each group will engage the following targets on the Group front in succession in the order given. When the 18-pdr. barrage falls 200 yards short of any target the Hows. will jump to the next target. In cases where the line of any target is not parallel to the barrage, the jump to the next target will take place by Batteries in succession.

/Targets.

Targets for Right Group.

(a) Railway.
(b) N. and S. roads through E.19. central.
(c) Ravine in E.19.b. and E.20.a.
(d) Road E.14.c. to E.20.b.
(e) Bombardment Area   No. 1.
(f)   "   "   No. 2.
(g)   "   "   No. 3.
(h)   "   "   No. 3.
(i)   "   "   No. 4.
(j)   "   "   No. 5.

Targets for Left Group.

(a) Sunken Road E.13.a.8.4. to E.15.a.6.2.
(b) Railway.
(c) Quarry and Ravine E.13.d.
(d) Sunken road in E.13.b. and 14.a.
(e) Bombardment Area No. 6.
(f)   "   "   No. 7.
(g)   "   "   No. 8.
(h)   "   "   No. 9.
(i)   "   "   No. 10.

For first protective barrage all Hows. will fire on road in E.8.c. - E.14.b. & E.15.c.

For all other protective barrages Hows. fire 150 yards ahead of 18-pdrs.

During the pause between first and second stages of the attack all 4.5" Hows. will fire 4 minute bursts of C.G. Gas under Group arrangements on Bombardment Areas Nos. 1, 3, 4, 7 and 8. No Gas will be fired after Z plus 250 minutes.

8. Enfilade fire will be provided as follows:-

One 18-pdr. Battery of 62nd D.A. will enfilade Ravine in E.13.d. - 19.b. and 20.a. at an INTENSE rate from Z to Z plus 30.

Single gun of 1st Brigade N.Z.F.A. will enfilade railway in E.13.c. and 19.a. at INTENSE rate from Z to Z plus 10.

9. Rates of Fire will be as follows:-

18-pdrs.   -   Z to Z plus 3 - "INTENSE".
               Z plus 3 onwards - "NORMAL", except where
barrage falls on railways, ravines or sunken roads, when rate
/will

will be "RAPID".

On protective barrages rates will be "SLOW" for the first half of the period, then "VERY SLOW".

4.5" Hows. – "INTENSE" on first target, then "NORMAL" throughout, except for first 5 minutes on Bombardment Areas 7 and 8, when it will be "INTENSE".

Hows. of 1st Brigade, N.Z.F.A. will fire at "INTENSE" rate from Z to Z plus 45.

18-pdr. Smoke. – 1 salvo from all guns, then "SLOW".

18-pdr. Incendiary. – "NORMAL" throughout.

6" Trench Mortars. – "INTENSE" throughout.

10. Ammunition.

18-pdrs. – 50% A, 50% AX for barrages.

AX (Fuze 106) will be used for long ranges and whenever angle of sight is liable to error.

100% Shrapnel will be used for the first three lifts.

AS and AEW will be fired as specified above.

4.5" Hows. – BX in barrages and BOG as specified above.

11. 6" Trench Mortars will fire as follows:-

1 gun on Railway from Quarry in E.13.d. inclusive for 200 yards North from Z to Z plus 25.

8 guns on Railway E.13.b.6.0. to E.7.c.2.7. from Z to Z plus 45.

1 gun on Factory E.13.a. from Z to Z plus 25.

12. Close support of Infantry. One Section will be detailed by each Group to go forward at first daylight for close support of Infantry Battalions. The Commander of each Section will have an extra Officer told off to help him and will get all information he can from Battalion and Company Commanders, but will not necessarily stay with them. He will place himself where he can best see the subsequent Infantry advance and bring his guns into action in semi covered or open positions to fire

/direct.

- 5 -

direct if necessary. It is hoped that these guns will prove of great value in knocking out M.Gs. or enemy's forward guns.

Groups will send forward officers to reconnoitre for positions for all Brigades in the MAROU Valley, or that behind the R.14. Ridge.

All guns will be prepared to move forward as soon as the final objective is reached. Not more than one Brigade per Group to be out of action (on the move) at any one time.

13. **Information.** Each Group will send forward one F.I.O. accompanied by a Brigade Signal Officer, who will go out with a party of linesmen and endeavour to keep the line going at all costs.

14. **F.C.O.** In addition to the F.I.O. one F.C.O. per Brigade R.F.A. should be sent out. His duty will be to observe and direct fire and also to send in important intelligence.

15. **The action of Heavy Artillery** is being order by B.G., G.H.A., IV Corps and will include bombardments similar to those ordered for 4.5" Hows.

16. The attack will take place on October 20th.

ZERO HOUR will be 0200 hours. (TWO A.M. 20/10/18)

Watches will be synchronised by Group and F.T.M.O. at 126th Infantry Brigade H.Q. at 18.00 hours on October 19th.

17. ACKNOWLEDGE.

/s/ J E Morgan

Captain., R.A.
A/Brigade Major., 42nd Divisional Artillery.

/ Distribution.

Issued at 11 A.M
on 19/10/18   by S.D.R

Copies to:-

Copy No.		
1	-	R.A., IV Corps.
2	-	42 "A".
3	-	42 "Q".
4	-	IV Corps H.A.
5	-	C.B.S.O., IV Corps.
6	-	210th Bde. R.F.A. (5 copies.)
7	-	211th Bde. R.F.A. (5 copies.)
8	-	317th Bde. R.F.A. (5 copies.)
9	-	223rd Bde. R.F.A. (5 copies.)
10	-	1st Bde. N.Z.F.A. (5 copies)
11	-	3rd Bde. N.Z.F.A. (5 copies).
12	-	D.T.M.O., 42nd Division.
13	-	90th Bde. R.G.A.
14	-	42nd D.A.C.
15	-	63rd D.A.C.
16	-	N.Z.D.A.C.
17	-	5th D.A.
18	-	32nd D.A.
19	-	59th Squadron, R.A.F.
20	-	S.O.R.A., 42nd Division.
21	-	S.O. for Reconnaissance, 42nd D.A.
22	-	Officer i/c R.A. Sigs.
23	-	War Diary.
24	-	File.

SECRET. 42nd D.A., No.B.M.13/4.

APP.'D'

R.A.,
 IV Corps.

Herewith locations of units of 42nd Divisional Artillery at ZERO HOUR.

W L

Unit		Location
317th Bde.R.F.A.	H.Q.	J.3.c.8.7.
A/Bty.	–	D.17.c.31.81.
B/Bty.	–	D.22.b.45.84.
C/Bty.	–	D.22.b.35.65.
D/Bty.	–	D.17.c.49.90.
210th Bde. R.F.A.	H.Q.	J.3.a.80.05.
A/Bty.	–	D.22.d.00.60.
B/Bty.	–	D.22.c.99.00
C/Bty.	–	D.22.c.98.97.
D/Bty.	–	D.22.a.90.42.
211th Bde.R.F.A.	H.Q.	D.28.c.5.2.
A/Bty.	–	D.22.c.93.28.
B/Bty.	–	D.28.b.01.83.
C/Bty.	–	D.22.c.97.00.
D/Bty.	–	D.22.c.92.58.
223rd Bde.R.F.A.	H.Q.	J.4.b.95.85.
A/Bty.	–	J.4.c.89.16.
B/Bty.	–	J.4.d.46.20.
C/Bty.	–	J.4.c.90.27.
D/Bty.	–	J.4.b.40.40.
1st Bde.N.Z.F.A.	H.Q.	J.4.b.45.65.
15th Bty.	–	J.5.b.34.80.
1st Bty.	–	J.5.b.98.52.
3rd Bby.	–	J.5.b.95.67.
7th Bty.	–	D.29.d.5.5.
3rd Bde.N.Z.F.A.	H.Q.	D.29.d.1.1.
4th Bty.	–	J.5.b.34.96.
13th Bty.	–	D.29.d.40.54.
12th Bty.	–	D.29.d.46.13.
11th Bty.	–	J.5.b.77.83.

J14 a 5.5
J8 a 8.3
J3 cent –
J8 a 8.3

42nd Division T.Ms.	N.Z. Division. T.Ms.
1 – D.18.a.75.30.	1 – D.18.a.60.20.
1 – D.18.a.70.38.	1 – D.18.a.55.20.
1 – D.18.a.68.40.	1 – D.18.a.50.20.
1 – D.18.a.65.45.	1 – D.18.a.50.25.
1 – D.18.a.60.50.	1 – D.19.a.55.25.

Morgan Capt
for Brigadier-General., R.A.
C. R. A., 42nd Division.

19/10/18.

SECRET.
42nd D.A., No.B.M.1/115.

210th Bde.R.F.A.   1st Bde.N.Z.F.A.
211th Bde.R.F.A.   3rd Bde.N.Z.F.A.
317th Bde.R.F.A.   2nd Army Bde.N.Z.F.A.
42nd D.T.M.O.   42nd D.A.C.

Consequent on arrival of 2nd Army Brigade N.Z.F.A. and transfer of 317th Brigade R.F.A. to 5th Division, Field Artillery covering 42nd Division will be grouped as follows :-

    RIGHT GROUP. (Lt.Col.R.S.McQUARRIE D.S.O.,M.C.)

        3rd Brigade N.Z.F.A.
        1st Brigade N.Z.F.A.

    LEFT GROUP.(Lt.Col.N.S.FALLA C.M.G.,D.S.O.)

        2nd Army Brigade N.Z.F.A.
        210th Brigade R.F.A.
        211th Brigade R.F.A.

above to take effect from 1800 hours today.

The O.C.,Left Group will control both Groups and will make his H.Qrs. with H.Qrs. of Infantry Brigade in the Line.

                                    Captain,,R.A.,
                              A/Brigade Major., R.A.
31st Oct. 1918.   42nd Division.

Copies to :-   R.A.,IV Corps.
               42nd Division 'G'
               125th Inf. Bde.
               126th Inf.Bde.
               127th Inf.Bde.
               42nd Division Signals.
               59th Squadron R.A.F.
               HA. IV Corps.
               90. Bde. RGA.

SECRET.   Copy No. 28

App. F.

42nd Divisional Artillery Order No. 59.

Reference Maps - Sheets 51A S.E. & 57B N.E. 1/20,000

1.   The Third Army is continuing the advance on Oct. 23rd.
     Zero hour will be notified later.

2.   The 42nd Division is attacking with 5th Division on the right and 3rd Division of VI Corps on the Left.

     When the 42nd Division has reached the BLUE LINE the N.Z. Division will pass through & then and continue the advance.

3.   The advance of 42nd Division will take place under a Creeping Barrage. Details of this barrage and objectives are shown on the attached map.
     The Barrage will dwell for 6 minutes on the Initial Line and then roll forward at a uniform rate of 100 yds in 6 minutes.

     The Artillery covering the 42nd Division will be controlled by C.R.A., 42nd Division up to the time when fire ceases on the first Protective Barrage covering the BLUE LINE. Command of the Artillery will then pass to C.R.A., N.Z. Division.

4.   One 18pdr. Battery of each Brigade will be superimposed on the other two and will be available to answer LL and GF Calls during the Creeping Barrage.

5.   4.5" Hows. will precede the 18pdr. Barrage by 150 yards.

6.   6" T.Ms. will open at ZERO on Cross Roads W.28.c.0.8. and on roads radiating from it. They will keep 200 yds ahead of 18pdr. Barrage. When 18pdr Barrage falls 200 yards from Cross Roads, T.Ms. will lift on to the Railway Junction W.28.a.9.3. When the 18pdr. Barrage falls within 200 yards of this Junction T.Ms. will cease fire and prepare to advance.

/2.

-- 2 --

7. Rates of Fire.

    18pdr. - "INTENSE" for initial line (S minutes) then "NORMAL" quickening to "RAPID" when crossing roads, railways or buildings. On arrival at line of Protective Barrage for BLUE LINE rate will be "NORMAL" for 2 minutes then "SLOW" for 8 minutes, then as ordered by C.R.A., N.Z. Division.

    4.5"How. - As for 18pdrs.

    6" T.Ms. - As ordered by D.T.M.O.

8. Ammunition. - As available.

    2 rounds per gun of AS will be fired by each gun during the 2 minutes "NORMAL" on arrival at the BLUE Protective Barrage Line.

    See also Para. 9.

9. Thermit. One gun on each flank of the Divisional Front will fire ATH only during the Creeping Barrage along the Divisional Boundary keeping 200 yds ahead of the barrage.

    One gun will fire ATH continuously on Cross Roads E.4.b.4.5. until the barrage falls within 200 yds when it will lift on to Railway Crossing W.29.c.4.6.

    All Thermit guns will fire at NORMAL Rate and will revert to the control of Battery Commanders as soon as the Barrage on the front on which they are shooting has reached the BLUE Protective Barrage Line. *Thermit will be burst high so that the Infantry can see it.*

10. Heavy Artillery. Three 6" Hows. Batteries will fire on the Divisional Front giving depth to the Barrage and keeping not less than 500 yds in front of 18pdr. Barrage.

11. O.C., Group will arrange to send forward one F.I.O. and party. This F.I.O. will report on the situation every half hour from ZERO.

    Each Brigade will send forward one F.O.O. Every effort must be made to keep lines through by pooling resources of Brigades and Batteries. An efficient system of Lamp Signalling must be organised as an alternative means of communication.

/12.

— 3 —

12. Two sections of 18pdrs. will go forward at daybreak in close support of the Infantry. The Officers in charge of these sections must ascertain the position of the Infantry whenever possible by actual observation and not rely entirely on "outside" information.

13. Watches will be synchronised at H.Q., 125th Inf. Bde. at 1000 hours Oct. 22nd 1918.

14. ACKNOWLEDGE.

F. Morgan
Captain., R.A.
A/Brigade Major., R.A.,
42nd Division.

Issued at 1630 hours

on 22/10/18 by DR

Copies to :-

Copy No.	
1.	R.A., IV Corps.
2.	42nd Division 'G'
3.	42nd Division 'Q'
4.	IV Corps H.A.
5.	C.B., S.O., IV Corps.
6.	210th Bde.R.F.A.
7.	211th Bde.R.F.A.
8.	1st Bde.N.Z.F.A.
10.	3rd Bde.N.Z.F.A.
11.	2nd Army Bde.N.Z.F.A.
12.	D.T.M.O., 42nd Division.
13.	125th Inf.Bde.
14.	126th Inf.Bde.
15.	127th Inf.Bde.
16.	90th Bde.R.G.A.
17.	42nd D.A.C.
18.	N.Z. D.A.C.
19.	5th D.A.
20.	3rd D.A.
21.	59th Squadron R.A.F.
22.	S.C.,R.A., 42nd Division.
23.	S.O. for Reconnaissance, 42nd D.A.
24.	Officer i/c R.A. Signals.
25.	War Diary.
27.	File.
28.	N.Z.,D.A.

NOTE. - Barrage Maps are being amended and will be issued later to all concerned.

SECRET.

Amendment No.1. to 42nd D.A. Order No.39.

1. Para.1. - Delete 2nd Line and substitute :-
   "ZERO HOUR will be 02.00 hours (2.A.M.) Oct.23rd 1918.

2. Para.6. - Delete ZERO and substitute ZERO plus 80.

3. ACKNOWLEDGE.

                                                             Captain., R.A.

28nd Oct. 1918.   A/Brigade Major., 42nd Divnl. Artillery.

Copies to all recipients of 42nd D.A., Order No.39.

4R22

CONFIDENTIAL

WAR DIARY

OF

42nd D.A.H.Q.

FROM NOV. 1st 1918 To NOV. 30th 1918

VOL. XXI

Sheet I.

WAR DIARY
or
INTELLIGENCE SUMMARY.
(Erase heading not required.)

November 1918   Ref. maps 57B 1/40,000   Army Form C. 2118.
FRANCE 51 1/40,000

Place	Date	Hour	Summary of Events and Information	Remarks and references to Appendices
BEAUVOIS	1		R.A.H.Q. at rest at BEAUVOIS-EN-CAMBRESIS	ja
	5		R.A.H.Q. to POTELLE CHATEAU and took over from N.Z. D.A.H.Q.	
			Command of following Arty.	
			1st N.Z.F.A. Bde. ⎫	
			2nd N.Z. Army Bde F.A. ⎬ Supporting/ relieving Infantry Bde.	
			3rd N.Z.F.A. Bde. ⎭	
			210 Bde R.F.A. ⎫ with Support Infantry Bde.	
			211 Bde R.F.A. ⎬	
			14 Army Bde R.H.A. ⎭ in reserve	
			14 Heavy Bty R.G.A.} in action in S.E. part of MORMAL FOREST	
			244 Siege Bty R.G.A.}	
			MAJOR R. MILES D.S.O. R.N.Z.A. acting B.M.R.A. 42nd Divn	ja
			LIEUT. R.S. PARK R.N.Z.A. acting S.O. for Reconnaissance 42DA.	ja
POTELLE	8th		R.A.H.Q. to LA HAUTE RUE	
			210 Bde R.F.A. 211 Bde R.F.A. and 14 Army Bde R.H.A. relieve	
			1st 2nd and 3rd Bdes N.Z.F.A.	ja

Sheet II. November 1918

Army Form C. 2118.

WAR DIARY
or
INTELLIGENCE SUMMARY.
(Erase heading not required.)

Place	Date	Hour	Summary of Events and Information	Remarks and references to Appendices
LA HAUTE RUE	9		RA HQ to HAUTMONT	ja
HAUTMONT	11	1100	Hostilities concluded	ja
	12		LIEUT. J. ALMOND S.O. for Reconnaissance rejoins from hospital	ja
	13		MAJOR. R. MILES. DSO. RNZA and LIEUT. R.S. PARK. RNZA. Leave to rejoin N.Z.D.A.	ja
	14		CAPT. F.E. MORGAN 2/BMRA rejoins from hospital	ja
	17		BRIG-GEN. F.W.H. WALSHE. DSO. and LIEUT. J. ALMOND proceed on leave to U.K.	ja
	19		CAPT. E.W. GILL RE. rejoins from hospital	ja
	23		CAPT. E. NUTTALL 2/SCRA. proceeds on leave to PARIS	ja
	29		DISPOSITION REPORT	ja
	30		CAPT. E. NUTTALL 2/SCRA rejoins from leave in PARIS. RA HQ. remains at HAUTMONT	ja

J. Almond Lieut RGA
for 2/BMRA 42nd Div.

No 23

Confidential

War Diary of HQ, RA, 4th Division

From 1/12/1918 To 31/12/1918

Vol. XXII

WAR DIARY or INTELLIGENCE SUMMARY.
(Erase heading not required.)

Army Form C. 2118.

DECEMBER 1918

Ref map.
VALENCIENNES 1/100,000
NAMUR 1/100,000

Place	Date	Hour	Summary of Events and Information	Remarks and references to Appendices
HAUTMONT	1		R.A.H.Q. at HAUTMONT. (12)	ja.
	3		BRIG-GEN. F.W.H. WALSHE D.S.O. rejoined from leave in U.K. LIEUT. J. ALMOND rejoined from leave in U.K.	ja.
	4		BRIG-GEN. F.W.H. WALSHE D.S.O assumed command of 42nd Div.	ja.
	13.		BRIG-GEN. F.W.H. WALSHE attached to 42 D.H.Q	ja.
	14.		LT-COL. F.G. CROMPTON 211 Bde. assumes temporary command of 42 D.A. and is attached to 42 D.H.Q.	ja.
			H.Q.R.A. move from HAUTMONT to JEUMONT. (8)	ja.
JEUMONT	15.		H.Q.R.A. move from JEUMONT to THUIN. (3)	ja.
THUIN	16		H.Q.R.A. remains at THUIN	ja.
	18		H.Q.R.A. move from THUIN to MONTIGNIES-SUR-SAMBRE (9)	ja.
MONTIGNIES	19		BRIG-GEN WALSHE rejoin from 42 D.H.Q. LT-COL. F.G. CROMPTON relinquishes command of 42 D.A. and rejoin 211 Bde. CAPT E.W. BILL R.E. rejoin 42 Div. Sig. Coy.	ja.
	20/31		R.A.H.Q. remains at MONTIGNIES-SUR-SAMBRE. During Dec. units carried out military, Recreational and Ceremonial training.	ja.

G.J. Almond Lieut RA
for A.B.M.R.A. 42 Div

CONFIDENTIAL.

WAR DIARY.

OF

Head Quarters, 42nd Div. Artillery.

From 1st January 1919.

To 31st January 1919.

VOLUME XXIII

Army Form C. 2118.

WAR DIARY
or
INTELLIGENCE SUMMARY.
(Erase heading not required.)

JANUARY 1919

Ref. map. NAMUR 8 1/100,000

Place	Date	Hour	Summary of Events and Information	Remarks and references to Appendices
MONTIGNIES S/SAMBRE	1		R.A.H.Q. at MONTIGNIES-SUR-SAMBRE.	A.
	12		CAPT. F.E. MORGAN proceeds on leave to U.K.	A.
	"		CAPT. F. KNOWLES, M.C. attached from B/211 a/CRTYRA.	A.
	19		CAPT. F. KNOWLES, M.C. rejoins B/211	A.
	31		R.A.H.Q. remains at MONTIGNIES-SUR-SAMBRE.	A.
			During the whole of Jany, units carried out military recreational and educational training.	

Jasmond Wied. R.A.
for a/BrigRA. 42nd Div.

Vol 25

CONFIDENTIAL.

WAR DIARY.

OF

HEADQUARTERS, 42nd DIV. ARTILLERY.

From 1st February 1919.   TO 28th February 1919.

VOLUME XXV

VOLUME XXV
Ref. map. 1/100,000
NAMUR 8

Army Form C. 2118.

FEBRUARY 1919 WAR DIARY
or
INTELLIGENCE SUMMARY.
(Erase heading not required.)

Instructions regarding War Diaries and Intelligence
Summaries are contained in F. S. Regs., Part II.
and the Staff Manual respectively. Title pages
will be prepared in manuscript.

Place	Date	Hour	Summary of Events and Information	Remarks and references to Appendices
MONTIGNIES	1st		R.A.H.Q at MONTIGNIES SUR SAMBRE	ga.
	15th		CAPT. F.E. MORGAN rejoined from leave in U.K.	ga.
	28th		R.A.H.Q. remains at MONTIGNIES SUR SAMBRE	ga.
			Location Statements of 42nd Div. Arty. during FEBRUARY APP "A"	ga.

J. Almond. Lieut. RA.
for BMRA 42nd Div.

Vol 26

CONFIDENTIAL.

War Diary

of

Head Quarters, 42nd Div.Arty.

From 1st March 1919

To 31st March 1919.

Volume XXVI.

Army Form C. 2118.

Volume XXVI
Ref map. 1/100,000
NAMUR-8

WAR DIARY
or
INTELLIGENCE SUMMARY.
(Erase heading not required.)

MARCH 1919

Instructions regarding War Diaries and Intelligence Summaries are contained in F.S. Regs., Part II. and the Staff Manual respectively. Title pages will be prepared in manuscript.

Place	Date	Hour	Summary of Events and Information	Remarks and references to Appendices
MONTIGNIES SUR SAMBRE	1		R.A.H.Q. at MONTIGNIES-SUR-SAMBRE.	
	5		Capt. F.E. MORGAN proceeded U.K. to report to War Office	
	31		R.A.H.Q. remain at MONTIGNIES-SUR-SAMBRE.	

Almond Lieut. R.A.
for B.M.R.A. 42nd Div.